Steelworkers in America

The Nonunion Era

1·P.
10⁰⁰

6⁹⁰

Steelworkers in America

The Nonunion Era

DAVID BRODY

HARPER TORCHBOOKS
Harper & Row, Publishers
New York, Hagerstown, San Francisco, London

This book was originally published by Harvard University Press in 1960. It is here
reprinted by arrangement.

For SUSAN

Contents

Preface

American steel manufacture came to maturity at the opening of the twentieth century. The magnitude, technology, and structure of the industry were by then clearly defined. So too was the place of the several hundred thousand steelworkers in its mills. Their history in the years that followed is the subject of this book.

This is a labor history. The approach, however, is somewhat out of the ordinary. The steelworkers themselves have been the focus, not one or another of the institutions or events of which they were a part. My aim has been to study the process by which their working lives in America's steel mills were shaped in the nonunion era of the industry.

The book proceeds on two lines. It seeks, first, the causes of the shaping circumstances. Why, for example, did the developing industry impose a twelve-hour day and a subsistence wage? At a later stage, treatment of labor measurably improved and welfare programs rapidly developed. What new conditions forced the progress? Trade unions had flourished in the early years of the industry. What accounted for their virtual disappearance by 1910? What were the sources within organized labor for the continuing interest in the steelworkers and for the futile efforts to reorganize them? I have considered similarly the other operative elements: the life of the mill towns, the immigrant background of the unskilled, the role of the "English-speaking" group, the recurrence of unemployment, the technology of steelmaking, and the aims of management.

My second objective was to explain the effect of these factors on the laboring ranks. My central idea was that the varied elements, acting together, created in the mills a situation of labor stability. This was seriously disrupted only once in the nonunion period — during the steel strike of 1919. The great conflict, involving over 300,000 men, did not arise from ordinary industrial conditions. It resulted rather from the injection of a new factor: the steelworkers'

experience in the First World War. Industrial strife became inevitable in steel, as elsewhere, when the postwar reaction frustrated
the heightened expectations of the newly organized steelworkers.
The twenties restored the peaceable labor system to the industry.

The character of the book was dictated by my approach. This
necessitated an organization at once topical and chronological. It
barred the comparative method employed in some labor studies.
Considerable selectivity also was required in handling the mass of
material in each area. I have not tried, for example, to provide a
detailed account of all the important strikes. Nor have I given much
space to the internal history of the remnant steelworkers' union.
Only the facts relevant for my purposes have found a place here.
The Southern segment of the industry, finally, was not treated because labor there fitted into a different pattern.

The book ends in 1929. Thereafter, the great depression and the
New Deal initiated another set of forces — requiring another investigation — that would transform the millworker into a new man.

This study is a revision of a dissertation written at Harvard University under the direction of Professor Oscar Handlin. My debt
to Professor Handlin is very great for his unfailing encouragement,
for his critical reading of the manuscript at various stages and, most
of all, for his influence on my thinking. I have benefited also from
the acute comments of Professor John T. Dunlop. Mr. A. J. Lichten-
berg read the manuscript from a layman's viewpoint and offered
several very useful suggestions. Librarians at a number of institutions have been helpful. I am especially grateful to Mr. Robert
Lovett of the Baker Library at the Harvard School of Business
Administration for leading me to the American Steel and Wire
Company Collection. A Harvard Graduate School of Arts and Sci-
ences fellowship made possible the vital year of uninterrupted work
at the beginning of my research. I owe debts of another sort to my
wife. She knows why the book is dedicated to her.

D. B.

Cambridge, Massachusetts
February 1960

Steelworkers in America

Chapter I

The Psychology and Method
of Steelmaking

British steelmasters, visiting the United States in 1901, marveled at the progress of the iron and steel industry. Thirty years earlier, the American steel trade had been of minor consequence. Annual pig iron production had not reached one-sixth of the English output. The mills had been backward and inefficient. Now the inspecting Britons were unsettled by the mechanical perfection of American operations. From the unloading of ore to the final pass in the finishing rolls, the massive mills functioned with the efficiency of single geared machines. Twice as much pig iron was produced yearly as in Great Britain. American firms exported over a million tons of steel in 1900, recently taking orders in England itself — an unprecedented event.

The touring manufacturers pondered the success of their competitors. What accounted for the swift rise of the American industry? The Englishmen surveyed the abundant natural resources, the expanding home market, and the extensive transport system. But repeatedly their minds returned to the special character of their hosts. J. Stephen Jeans summed up the impression. "The American manufacturer is not so conservative in his methods and ideas." His decisions, regardless of "trouble, cost or interference with preconceived ideas and vested interests," rested on one chief consideration: whether they would "make for increased economy."[1] The preoccu-

[1] J. Stephen Jeans, ed., *American Industrial Conditions and Competition,* Reports of Commissioners appointed by the British Iron Trade Association (London, 1902), p. 255, and *passim* for comments.

pation with economy seemed, indeed, at the root of the steelmaking achievement.

Andrew Carnegie was the preëminent example of the American type. "Carnegie never wanted to know the profits," a partner once remarked. "He always wanted to know the cost." Carnegie had very early seen the possibilities of economy. "What do you really figure we put rails at cost," he asked the superintendent of his newly constructed Edgar Thomson Works. "Cant [sic] we shade 50 dollars. If so where is there such a business." Every effort went into the reduction of production costs. By December 1878, the total charges amounted to only $36.52 a ton of steel at the Thomson Works. Twenty years later, the company was making rails for $12.00 a ton.[2]

That impulse for economy shaped American steel manufacture. It inspired the inventiveness that mechanized the productive operations. It formed the calculating and objective mentality of the industry. It selected and hardened the managerial ranks. Its technological and psychological consequences, finally, defined the treatment of the steelworkers. Long hours, low wages, bleak conditions, anti-unionism, flowed alike from the economizing drive that made the American steel industry the wonder of the manufacturing world.

The visit of British steel men in 1901 was opportunely timed. By then the Carnegie spirit ruled, and its consequences were largely completed.

The industry's economizing temper was bred in the unrestrained competition preceding the merger movement. Steelmaking then "was a merciless game . . . in the hands of strong men," the veteran Joseph G. Butler recalled. "The profits were for those who pursued business relentlessly." Before 1890 the demand for steel, chiefly railroad construction, was notoriously unstable. The industry was either "panic-stricken" or "strained to utmost capacity." The re-

[2] Charles M. Schwab, quoted in *They Told Barron,* eds. Arthur Pound and Samuel T. Moore (New York, 1930), p. 85; Carnegie quoted in J. H. Bridge, *The Inside History of the Carnegie Steel Company* (New York, 1903), pp. 95–96.

curring imbalance between supply and demand embittered competition. Overextended companies slashed prices in the fight for existing orders in depressed years. From the boom of 1880 to the collapsed market of 1885 the price of steel rails fell from $85.00 to $27.00 a ton.[3] Only efficient producers could then survive.

Sharpened competition forced economy on the steelmakers. John W. Gates, for example, informed the superintendent of his Rankin wire works of a price collapse in 1890. "As a consequence it behooves us to be very careful in the matter of cost and I desire to impress upon your mind the importance of reducing your cost to the lowest possible figure."[4] This was the normal response to the precipitous market.

The lesson, however, was only reluctantly absorbed. For one thing, most early steel producers had also manufactured wrought iron, which, for technological reasons, was not susceptible to cheapening improvements. There was no economizing tradition in the iron trade. More important, economy was not in itself attractive. It demanded the continued reinvestment of earnings and unremitting concentration on operations. Without the competitive spur, the ordinary manufacturer would have contented himself with his established methods. The Colorado Fuel and Iron Company, for instance, seemed in a secure situation. Its plant at Pueblo supplied the Western rail market. Favored by nearby resources and strategic location, the company foresaw steady, substantial earnings. Its surplus went into an additional blast furnace instead of economizing work. Then in 1888 a railroad war broke out, freight rates fell, and Eastern railmakers were able to invade the territory. The Colorado firm could not meet Eastern prices and barely avoided bankruptcy.[5] Most concerns did not have its opportunity for complacency.

[3] Joseph G. Butler, *Recollections of Men and Events* (New York, 1927), p. 151; *Iron Age,* November 30, 1882, p. 14, February 10, 1887, p. 17, cited hereafter as *IA.*

[4] John W. Gates to William Govier, April 23, 1890, Braddock Wire Company, American Steel and Wire Company Collection, Baker Library, Harvard University.

[5] *Commercial and Financial Chronicle,* April 29, 1882, p. 489, March 24, 1888, p. 386, March 19, 1891, p. 427.

After 1887, however, the competitive situation in basic steel began to relent. Rails steadied and, more significant, the demand was becoming "general." Nine-tenths of the steel output went into rails in 1882, less than half in 1890. Surely, reasoned the *Iron Age,* "the whole country cannot at once drop into a state of collapse." Thus reassured, the industry eased its efforts for cost reduction. Profits were diverted into dividends and extensions. Prosperity was dissolving bitter rivalry and rendering unnecessary the burdensome drive for economy.

Had all steel manufacturers relaxed, the economizing spirit would have passed. Even hard times would not threaten the inefficient producers if price competition was avoided and the shrunken market fairly divided. That was, indeed, the objective of numerous efforts to establish pools and agreements.[6] A few firms, however, remained imbued with the competitive temper. Jones and Laughlins, Cambria, and Carnegie willingly joined the pools, but they were not softened by fat profits. Many prospering mills "have thought it unnecessary to economize," observed a Carnegie partner. "That has never been our history. When we have gone out of a pool, we have always been in good shape to follow the business."[7] So they were in 1893.

The ensuing business collapse put an end to the complacency of the steel manufacturers. A period of unmatched rivalry was inaugurated. When prosperity returned at the end of the decade, the rule of economy would be permanently impressed on the American steel industry.

Carnegie saw in 1893 the opening that led to domination of the market. He directed the Board to leave the rail pool. "I do not think any one can stand in our way. . . . I get no sweet dividend out of second fiddle business, and I do know that the way to make even money *is to lead."* Surveying his cost sheets, Carnegie concluded,

[6] For effective pools at this period, see U.S. Commissioner of Corporations, *Report on the Steel Industry* (3 vols., Washington, 1911–1913), I, 69–71.

[7] Charles Schwab, Carnegie Steel Company, Executive Board Minutes, October 22, 1900, *United States* v. *United States Steel Corporation, 223* F. 55 (1912), *Government Exhibits,* VI, 1898.

"we needn't hesitate, take orders and run full, there's a margin." [8]
The company went out to fill its order books. In New York, for
instance, it contracted to furnish the Elevated Railroad with 50,000
tons of structural steel "at the lowest figure ever made." Competitors found themselves consistently undersold.

The future rested with the Carnegie Company. Other low-cost
producers had economized at the expense of growth. Carnegie managed to accomplish both, mainly by the shrewd purchase of plants
in difficulty. The Homestead and Duquesne mills were thus acquired in 1882 and 1890. Quickly made profitable, the earnings of
the new properties soon liquidated the bond issues. Between 1888
and 1894 Carnegie's steel capacity climbed from 332,111 to 1,115,466
tons, one-fourth of the national output. He could monopolize a
depressed market.

The year 1893 was disastrous in the iron and steel trade. Most
plants shut down, and many firms failed. Illinois Steel lost $350,000;
Pennsylvania Steel went into receivership. None of Carnegie's rivals
was in a position to make up the lost ground. That was part of his
plan. "Now, in my opinion," Carnegie told his managers, "is the
time to cause them to delay spending money to compete with us." [9]

Meanwhile, he embarked on a program to perfect economical
steel manufacture. Despite the grumbling of partners that they never
saw the profits (three millions in 1893, four millions in 1894), the
works were rebuilt and transport facilities acquired. In 1896 Carnegie leased the vast Rockefeller holdings in the Mesabi ore fields
for the exceedingly low royalty of twenty-five cents a ton. Years before, he had established a cheap coke supply by buying into the H.
C. Frick Company. He was in the envious position of getting his
coke at cost while the Frick firm, in whose profits he shared, was
selling to his competitors at high market prices. By 1897, the economizing work was completed. "This company," one journal commented,

[8] Carnegie to H. C. Frick, February 13, 1894, Carnegie Papers, Library of
Congress.
[9] Carnegie Minutes, October 6, 1893, *U.S.* v. *U.S.S., Government Exhibits,*
III, 978.

. . . is so situated as to be absolutely in control of the market, and make the prices of steel what it will. . . . The situation is not altogether a comfortable one, and many are looking anxiously for the result.[10]

Their worst fears were soon realized.

A respite had come in 1895. Then late in 1896 the rehabilitated pools, after holding for a time, crumbled before the declining market. The ensuing contest was the bitterest in the industry's history; it tested — and proved — the validity of the economizing view. Notified of the collapse of the rail pool, Carnegie chairman Henry Frick announced: "We will at once name a lower price and take all the business we can." The Carnegie Company drove rails from $28.00 to an average of $18.00 a ton, selling large amounts at $16.00, and going to the phenomenal figure of $14.00 to capture some orders. To the astonishment of competitors, those prices were profitable for the company. It cleared $7,000,000 in 1897. Elated, Carnegie congratulated his managers: "It is a splendid year's business . . . and proves once more that there is nothing like meeting the market, taking the business, and running full." [11]

Other producers found the results less pleasing. Despite the increased demand brought out by the low prices (from five to nine million tons in two years), few companies were operating profitably. As Elbert H. Gary of Illinois Steel observed, Carnegie's low costs could not be matched. The price war, however, had stimulated tonnage far beyond his capacity. Carnegie therefore concluded an agreement with the Illinois, Colorado, and Cambria companies. He would limit himself to his natural Eastern market. "No effective competition is possible," he informed the Board. "The East is a clear field for us at $15.00 or $16.00 per ton for Rails." Bethlehem quit the steel trade, selling its rolling mills largely to Carnegie.[12] But

[10] *Engineering and Mining Journal*, quoted in *Steel Report*, I, 78.

[11] Carnegie Minutes, February 9, 1897, December 21, 1897, and Report of H. P. Bope, Assistant General Sales Agent, January 3, 1899, *U.S.* v. *U.S.S.*, *Government Exhibits*, III, 1071, 1096, 1176–1179.

[12] Gary, in *U.S.* v. *U.S.S.*, *Testimony*, XIV, 5300; Carnegie Company Minutes, April 5, 1898, November 22, 1898, January 10, 1899, February 7, 1899, October 16, 1899, *Government Exhibits*, III, 1112, 1163, 1181, 1195, 1285.

rising prices in 1899 saved the other Eastern producers. Carnegie's campaign thus fell short of its mark.

His example, however, was stamped on the minds of the steelmasters. No longer was it possible, President John W. Gates told the stockholders of Illinois Steel, "to do business on the basis of large profits for comparatively small tonnage. . . . We must meet competition and reduce the cost of production to the minimum." Economizing efforts were quickly evident at the company's plants. Charles Schwab observed that "the South Works never showed such activity as now." Economy became the rule at Illinois Steel.[13]

Carnegie's fourteen-dollar rails — priced below their manufacturing cost — had a similar effect on the managers of the Lackawanna Company of Scranton. "That was an object lesson, that rail fight," recalled President Walter Scranton, "that made us look around to get a new location." A giant Lackawanna plant was soon rising near Buffalo, strategically situated both for resources and markets.[14]

In less striking ways, all steel producers revealed the new concern for economy. Within a few years every American steel mill achieved a rough equivalence of efficiency, and every company acquired adequate supplies of ore and coking coal. The cruel market had taught its lesson.

Competition provided the stimulus. But economizing efforts succeeded only because of the openness of steel manufacture to technological improvement. At every point in the steelmaking process, engineers were able to mechanize operations.

Wrought iron offers an instructive comparison. Before the introduction of the Bessemer converter, the iron industry had become firmly established; its output in 1866 was a million tons. Steel immediately proved superior for rails, then armor plate and structural material. But wrought iron was admittedly better suited for plate, sheet, and bar. Yet increasingly steel displaced iron. Even in the

---

[13] Illinois Steel Company, *Annual Report* (1898); Carnegie Minutes, December 20, 1898, *U.S. v. U.S.S., Government Exhibits*, III, 1168; *Engineering and Mining Journal*, August 27, 1898, p. 242, cited hereafter as *EMJ*.

[14] *U.S. v. U.S.S., Testimony*, VIII, 3200.

making of pipe, for which wrought iron's malleability and non-corrosiveness were ideal, steel gradually became dominant.

The 1890's saw the widespread dismantling of iron mills. The largest producer, Jones and Laughlins, had operated 110 puddling furnaces. In 1884 the firm built a five-ton converter, then two more in 1890, and began reducing its iron production. It closed down thirty-three furnaces in February 1892 because iron was being "crowded out." Its employees were advised to seek work elsewhere. Soon after, the Carnegie Company began shutting its eighty-four furnaces. The basic steel companies, all iron manufacturers in 1890, employed hardly a puddler among them in 1900.[15]

The fatal weakness of wrought iron manufacture was its resistance to mechanization. The procedures were entirely manual. The puddler agitated small batches of molten pig iron and cinder until the purified metal crystallized into balls — "coming to nature," it was called. The succeeding squeezing and rolling operations were likewise manual. Until puddling could be mechanized, no other important changes were possible.

Ironmasters had the same stimulus from the market for economy as the steel men. The two groups were, indeed, largely identical. Competition from steel lent further urgency. And experimental efforts were not lacking. The Phoenix Iron Company, for instance, in 1882 had partly perfected a mechanical puddler. The Otis Steel Company developed a revolving device. Numerous other inventions sustained the hopes of iron companies. In the end, the experimentation failed, and, after the shift to steel became general, subsided.[16]

[15] American Iron and Steel Association, *Statistical Report* (1890), pp. 44, 50; John Fritz, "The Progress of the Manufacture of Iron and Steel," American Society of Mechanical Engineers, *Transactions,* XVIII (1897), 39–69; *EMJ,* March 5, 1892, p. 282; *Iron Trade Review,* October 15, 1914, p. 699, cited hereafter as *ITR.* The course of the Republic Iron and Steel Company, a merger of twenty-seven iron mills with a capacity of over a million tons, indicated the extent to which puddling seemed incompatible with prosperity. The company, shortly after being formed in 1899, began abandoning the iron mills, erecting in their stead a large steel plant at Youngstown. At a cost of $25,000,000 Republic became by 1914 almost exclusively a steel producer.

[16] *IA,* August 19, 1882, p. 24; *EMJ,* June 9, 1892, p. 89, April 18, 1903, p. 604; Institute of Mining Engineers, *Transactions,* XXXVI (1905), 205–207,

Steel production surpassed that of iron in 1892. By 1913, 23,000,000 tons of steel were rolled, while iron output was only 1,676,257 tons, half of the 1890 level.

Compared to puddling, steel manufacture offered unlimited opportunities for improvement. The basic methods of smelting, refining, and rolling had come from Europe. But Americans mechanized the processes beyond the expectation of the inventors. A remarkable inventiveness developed, pressing forward steel technology at an exceedingly rapid pace. By 1900, engineers had solved the major problems of mechanization: the handling of materials, integration of production stages, and continuous rolling of steel.

Numerous devices were perfected to move the materials at the blast furnaces. A superintendent in 1910 described the changes in his department from the laborious manual methods of 1895. A huge car-dumper gripped the freight cars and turned them over, discharging the ore and limestone. At Jones and Laughlin Steel Company (the name was changed from Jones and Laughlins in 1902) the car bottom dropped, an equally effective unloading method. Electric trolleys rolled the weighed ingredients to a skip hoist that carried them to the furnace top and dumped them inside automatically. The pig casting machine and Jones mixer did away with the hot work around the sand beds. Ladle cars, an improvement that had appeared as early as 1882 at the Isabella Furnace Company, caught and carried away the molten slag. Blast furnace operation in 1910 was almost completely mechanized.[17]

Similar progress occurred in the refining processes. Electric traveling cranes simply solved the problems in feeding the Bessemer converter. But the open-hearth furnace, whose mouth was on the side, required a more complex arrangement. Boxes of pig iron were

---

806. On the sustained efforts of James P. Roe in later years, see *IA,* August 2, 1906, pp. 289–290, May 1, 1913, p. 1069; Mining Engineers, *Transactions,* XXXIII (1902), 551–561, and *Transactions,* XXXVI (1905), 204–215, 807–815.

[17] For Carnegie's early interest in mechanical buckets ("which reduce the cost to about 6 cents") on ore boats and other economies in bringing Mesabi ore to his plants, see Carnegie to John Shaw, December 9, 1895, and James Andrews to Carnegie, December 23, 1895, Carnegie Papers.

rolled on rail cars to the furnace platform. Here the arm of the Wellman charger lifted the boxes, thrust them into the furnaces, overturned and then replaced them on the car. When the Carnegie Company adopted the Wellman machine in 1897, the president reported that the cost "was notably better in Open Hearth No. 1 . . . a reduction of 27 cents."[18] An English visitor in 1904 could not recall an American open-hearth plant without a charger among the thirty or more he inspected.[19]

Mechanical handling permitted the enlargement of operating equipment. Blast furnaces in 1890 rarely topped 80 feet in height. Nine furnaces being built in 1901 averaged 100 feet, and Lackawanna planned one of 110 feet. Periodically, new construction was announced larger than anything in existence. Lackawanna erected a slab mill at its Buffalo works unsurpassed in capacity, an object of awe for practical steel men. The Gary mill, when completed in 1914, was even more massive. Thus was the size of optimum efficiency approached.

The second direction of improvement was to integrate production stages. Steel manufacturers early recognized the savings in connecting smelting and Bessemer operation. Started at Bethlehem and North Chicago, the practice of conveying liquid iron in ladles directly to the converters soon became general. The Jones mixer, capable of holding large quantities of molten pig iron, perfected the procedure by largely eliminating the need to cast and later remelt excess iron. To gain the advantages of integration, Carnegie, on acquiring the Carrie Furnaces, built a bridge across the Monongahela River to deliver molten iron to the Homestead plant. Republic did likewise when it erected furnaces across the Mahoning River for its Youngstown mill.[20]

[18] Carnegie Minutes, May 11, 1897, *U.S. v. U.S.S., Government Exhibits,* III, 1083.

[19] Frank Popplewell, *Some Modern Conditions and Recent Developments in Iron and Steel Production in America* (Manchester, 1906), p. 95.

[20] *IA,* December 21, 1882, p. 26, August 11, 1882, p. 26, April 6, 1905, p. 1154; *EMJ,* August 13, 1898, pp. 187–189. Robert N. Grosse, "The Determinants of the Size of Iron and Steel Firms in the United States, 1820–80," unpublished Ph.D. thesis, Harvard, 1948, pp. 178–179, 190, 197, gives early history of steel and iron firms acquiring blast furnaces.

Integration with rolling mills developed more slowly. Although Bessemer converters were usually located in the same plant, the ingots were not conveyed directly to the rolling department. Integration would save heat and handling, but the main stimulus came from improvements in converters and rolling mills. The capacity of both was rising rapidly. The lag in between of "facilities for getting the ingots out of the road," said Captain William Jones in 1881, "is the sticking point just now." Casting ingots on cars completely eliminated the bottleneck. When Carnegie bought the Duquesne Works, where the practice had been inaugurated in 1889, he introduced the casting cars at his other plants, and others during the competitive period hastily followed.[21] Overhead electric cranes and a mechanical plunger to strip the ingot from the mold perfected the rapid handling of steel from converter to rolling mill. Production was integrated from blast furnaces to rolling mills.

The rolling mills were the third area of advance. Here the objective was continuous, mechanical operation. In 1857 John Fritz invented the three-high roller — the first, basic step — by which metal could be given a second pass while returning to the front of the rolls. The demand for steel rails intensified experimentation. R. W. Hunt finally overcame the main obstacle in 1884 when he perfected an automatic rising and falling table for the three-high roll. Captain Jones then set out to incorporate in a mill for the Carnegie Company all the recent developments. "Instructions were given him," related Hunt, "to build the best rail mill he knew how, regardless of cost."[22] Finished in 1888, the Edgar Thomson mill became the prototype for the industry.

From the heating furnace a small electric car ran forward and tilted, depositing the ingot upon live-rolls leading to the three-high blooming mill. Provided with tables and side racks, the rolls pressed the ingot down to nine by seven inches in five passes. Automatically sheared and reheated, the lengths traveled on driven rolls to two roughing mills for ten passes and on to the finishing rail mill.

[21] Jones quoted in Bridge, p. 109, also, pp. 175–176.
[22] R. W. Hunt, "The Evolution of American Rolling Mills," American Society of Mechanical Engineers, *Transactions,* XIII (1892), 45–69; John Fritz, *Autobiography* (New York, 1912), ch. 15.

The rails were then stamped, cut, cooled, and run down into waiting cars. English visitors were greatly impressed.

> To stand on the floor of such a mill and to witness the con-
> version, in the space of half an hour, of a red-hot steel ingot
> weighing several tons into finished, stamped steel rails 90 feet
> long . . . is to gain new ideas of the possibilities of mechanism
> — of the subservience of matter to mind.[23]

The smaller products offered more formidable problems, but
when finally mastered, the rolling operations would be more truly
continuous. Wire rods led the way. In 1881 Charles H. Morgan
attached the Bedson back-and-forth roughing mill to the Belgian
looping mill, creating the first continuous rod rolling system.
Another Morgan mill quickly superseded the back-and-forth
method. Morgan lined in tandem a series of rolls carefully geared
to take up the elongation after each pass. The metal, led by guides,
emerged in finished form without interruption. Refinements
quickly followed. A mill designed by William Garrett used standard billets, eliminating the need to roll smaller rod billets first.
This advance capped the effort to perfect rod manufacture.

"Continuity of operation has been the touchstone throughout,"
said Morgan. "Operations which heretofore hindered and delayed
have now disappeared . . . until it is a familiar sight to see a
billet, one end still in the furnace — its length in all the reducing
passes of the mill, and the other end coiled on the reel, a finished
wire rod." "The development has been so rapid," concluded the
inventor F. H. Daniels, "as to astonish even the most sanguine of
our rod rollers."[24]

[23] Popplewell, pp. 103–105.
[24] C. H. Morgan, "Some Landmarks in the History of the Rolling Mill,"
American Society of Mechanical Engineers, *Transactions,* XXII (1901), 31–
64; F. H. Daniels, "Wire Rod Rolling Mills and Their Development,"
American Society of Mechanical Engineers, *Transactions,* XIV (1893), 583–
618. See also, Cost Data, August 14, 1891, Washburn and Moen Mfg. Company, American Steel and Wire Collection.

Of all the light forms, only sheet and tin plate resisted improvement. Before 1890 Wales had supplied tin plate to the United States. The McKinley tariff opened the field to Americans, and by 1900 they were producing 425,000 tons. Importing Welsh workers and methods, manufacturers immediately saw the need for "changes which will cheapen the production." They introduced heavier equipment, traveling cranes, and electric power. Machines were devised to mechanize the annealing, pickling, and polishing processes. "As soon as the manufacturing of tin plate was commenced," boasted an expert in 1899, "American enterprise and inventiveness took up the matter of introducing improvements" and carried the mills "far ahead of those in England or Wales."[25] Nevertheless, the central problem of manual, disconnected rolling methods remained unsolved.

The challenge itself sharpened the inventive effort. The first ambitious attempts to produce plate directly from molten metal ended in failure. Progress clearly would have to come along lines already established. At Monessen, Pennsylvania, stands of rolls were connected in tandem so that a sheet going through the first was fed automatically into the others. When the American Tin Plate Company acquired the plant in 1899, it applied the system elsewhere. At the Monongahela Works the output increased from 5,750 to 6,500 pounds a turn. This modest success, however, was very far from the final result envisaged by American steel men.

The Tin Plate Company determined, at whatever cost, to perfect sheet and tin plate manufacture. Charles W. Bray, the chief engineer, developed a number of ingenious devices. In its final form, the Bray arrangement mechanically heated the sheet bar, fed it through six stands of roughing rolls, and carried it to the intermediate set of three stands in tandem. The company estimated that the eight Bray mills at the Monongahela Works in 1903 produced the equal of fourteen ordinary mills. But the system was not continuous. At no point was the metal in two or more stands at the

---

[25] W. C. Cronemeyer, U.S. Bureau of Census, *Twelfth Census* (1900), X, 119. On early tin plate history, see *ibid.*, pp. 111–119.

same time, and the sheets had to be finished in standard manual mills.[26]

Here progress halted. Gradually, expectation turned to pessimism. The *Iron Age* reflected the general view of 1912 that "a striking innovation in these methods has become very unlikely." [27] The Bray process, incomplete and costly, did not spread. Along with crucible steel and wrought iron, sheet and tin plate manufacture remained technologically backward. The failures here only heightened the inventive achievements elsewhere in the industry.

The mechanical advances would have been largely wasted without comparable improvements in the qualities of steel. Playing for high stakes, American steel men spared no effort to make a good "soft" steel. The early successes came about through the experiments of D. C. Dudley and H. M. Howe to reduce the carbon content of pig iron during the Bessemer process. It was, however, impossible to exercise adequate control in the Bessemer converters. The use of open-hearth furnaces overcame this difficulty. The culmination came in 1906 when the American Rolling Mill Company successfully made a "pure" iron — one, that is, with all the qualities of wrought iron. The way was open for the thorough displacement of the expensive puddling system.[28]

Innovations, once made, were eagerly adopted throughout the industry. American manufacturers had no commitment to standard methods and proved equipment. The steelmakers, it seemed to conservative foreign observers, were seized by a destructive passion. A Bessemer manager told the Englishman Enoch James in 1901 that his plant, supervised by the same engineer, had been rebuilt from its foundations four times. The Scranton Steel Company, for instance, started its two four-ton Bessemer converters in May 1883. By December 1885 alterations had nearly tripled the ingot output.

[26] Hunt, Mechanical Engineers, *Transactions*, XIII, 67–68; *Iron and Steel Trade Journal*, March 24, 1900, p. 274; *IA*, September 22, 1904, p. 29, January 5, 1905, p. 1214; *EMJ*, January 17, 1903, p. 125.

[27] *IA*, August 8, 1912, p. 311.

[28] *EMJ*, September 2, 1893, p. 234, January 3, 1903, p. 40; *ITR*, May 14, 1914, p. 871; American Rolling Mill Company, *The First Twenty Years* (Middletown, Ohio, 1922), ch. 9.

Six months later the company replaced the straining converters.[29] Equipment, often barely worn, was scrapped as soon as improved models appeared.

Companies occasionally attempted to monopolize important inventions. Carnegie, for instance, brought suit against the Cambria Company for copying his metal mixer. The United States Circuit Court validated the Carnegie patent in 1898; but infringements continued. Popplewell observed a mixer in nearly every large works he visited in 1904. The Carnegie Company attempted to control the Uehling pig casting machine, but met with a similar lack of success.[30] These disputes were not typical. Ordinarily, improvements flowed into general use easily and rapidly.

Specialization speeded the process. Once a man had demonstrated his inventive talent, he was rarely satisfied to remain a company employee. Julian Kennedy, for example, worked at Carnegie's Braddock plant until his experiments in blast furnace operation made his reputation. In 1891 he became a consulting engineer in Pittsburgh. Machine and foundry companies, led by men like Kennedy, developed into the innovating center for steel manufacture. Applying their experience and patents indiscriminately, Mackintosh, Hemphill and Company, Mesta Machine Company, and other firms built equipment for the entire industry. The one clear effort by the American Tin Plate and Sheet Steel companies in 1900 to monopolize the makers of their machinery was thwarted.[31] Any manufacturer with the means had equal access to the latest advances.

[29] *IA*, March 10, 1887, p. 19; Jeans, p. 518. Charles Schwab, *Andrew Carnegie, His Method With His Men* (Pittsburgh, November 25, 1919), pp. 9–11, tells the perhaps apocryphal story of having just remodeled a mill, only to see ways for further improvement. Carnegie told him to tear it down and do it again.

[30] Carnegie to J. A. Leishman, November 12, 1895, Carnegie Papers; Bridge, pp. 79–80. In 1914, 69 metal mixers were in operation, and 112 pig casters. U.S. Bureau of Census, *Census of Manufactures* (1914), II, 216, 237.

[31] *U.S. v. U.S.S.*, *Testimony*, V, 1928–1957, 1794–1803; U.S. Industrial Commission, *Reports* (Washington, 1899–1901), I, 852, 875, 888–890, cited hereafter as *Industrial Commission*. Kennedy patented numerous appliances, which

The merger movement also served to generalize technological progress. Almost the entire plant capacity for pipe, wire, hoops, sheet, and tin plate entered combinations at the turn of the century. These then were organized into the United States Steel Corporation, along with the Carnegie, National, and Federal Steel companies. Led by Carnegie men, the Steel Corporation immediately launched a modernization program. The value of its manufacturing properties, excluding the Gary Works, increased by $133,000,000 — 60 per cent — in one decade. The American Tin Plate Company, for instance, abandoned twenty-one mills between 1899 and 1907, and enlarged and improved many others. The half of the industry incorporated into the steel trust thus rapidly achieved a uniformly efficient level. The independent basic producers, stimulated by Carnegie's competition, did likewise. Finally, the many small finishing firms which entered the field after 1901, ordinarily without the resources to keep up with improvements, simply built the latest equipment into their new mills as part of the initial investment.

Technological requirements largely shaped the structure of the industry. The integration of every process from the blast furnace to the loading platform was necessary so that "everything worked with perfect regularity." The optimum size and arrangement for the basic mill appeared settled. "Two thousand or 2,500 tons a day would be about the point where the minimum cost in manufacturing could be reached," estimated Willis King of Jones and Laughlin. The thirty or so steel plants owned by the ten independents and the Steel Corporation were of at least that capacity and fully integrated. The finishing mills, on the other hand, generally remained small, since each machine operated independently. "A man can start in with six hot mills [in a tin plate plant] and make his product as cheaply as if he had sixty, proportionately," observed Julian Kennedy. While a steelmaking plant required a minimum investment of $20,000,000, a competitive finishing plant could be built for under $500,000. A host of companies of small capital and

---

were then available, at a price, to the entire industry. See, for example, *EMJ*, February 28, 1903, p. 340, March 7, 1903, p. 379.

tonnage were soon turning out sheet, tin plate, wire, hoop, and pipe.[32]

On the margins of the industry many obsolete blast furnaces, puddling and rolling mills continued to exist precariously. But to a remarkable extent the industry made its technological advance as a unit. The accomplishment was shortly undeniable. "The results aimed at," acknowledged the German expert Dr. J. Puppe, "have been fully achieved and must command the admiration of all practical iron manufacturers." [33] American steelmaking practice was unsurpassed.

The impulse for economy, responding to unrestrained competition, fostered the inventive efforts. Technological success in turn invigorated the economizing drive. Mutually stimulating, these parallel forces profoundly influenced the psychology of the steelmasters. Concerned always with costs and improvements, they could not permit "preconceived ideas and vested interests" to obstruct their exertions. In short, they became men of calculation and inquiry. The mind of the industry was eminently rational.

When Sir Lowthian Bell visited the United States in 1890, he was appalled at the "recklessly rapid rate of driving" blast furnaces that reduced the "interiors to a wreck about every three years." The Pittsburgh furnaces, Sir Lowthian admitted, were smelting six times as much iron as those at the Clarence Works in England. But his furnaces consequently were "performing their duty as well as they did . . . 17½ years ago." This argument amused Americans. "What do we care about the lining?" asked Superintendent Charles S. Price of Cambria. "We think that a lining is good for so much iron and the sooner it makes it the better." [34] Low costs, not

<hr>

[32] King, *Industrial Commission,* XIII, 505; Kennedy, U.S. House, Committee on the Investigation of the United States Steel Corporation, *Hearings,* 62 Cong., 2nd Sess. (1911–12), VII, 5128, cited hereafter as *Stanley Hearings.*

[33] Dr. J. Puppe, "American Rolling Mill Practice," *IA,* May 15, 1913, pp. 1172–1179.

[34] Bell, in British Iron and Steel Institute, *The Iron and Steel Institute in America in 1890* (London, n.d.), pp. 170, 172, 183; Price quoted in Herbert N. Casson, *The Romance of Steel* (New York, 1907), p. 362.

machines, were what Americans worshiped; and calculation showed that it was cheaper to drive a furnace than to prolong its life. Similar reckoning, devoid of sentiment or preconception, dictated the scrapping of still usable equipment, the high level of investment and, indeed, every decision.

The prerequisite for rational operation was exact information. Detailed records were not usually kept where costs were constant and methods settled, for instance, in wrought iron manufacture. Nor were such data widely used in the early years of the steel industry. Even in 1885 the Iron and Steel Association failed to gather information for a federal tariff study partly because many manufacturers "do not keep their records with sufficient minuteness. . . . Others do not care to take the trouble to compile the details."[35] Those cost data were the very source of success for steelmasters who were intent on economy.

When he entered the steel trade in 1875, Carnegie adopted cost accounting methods. The general manager of the company, William B. Shinn, had been a railroad auditor. He introduced a voucher system used by railroads and Standard Oil. The detailed costs and production figures were recorded daily and each month the compiled data were presented to the Board of Managers for consideration. The report for August 1897 was characteristic.

> Duquesne Steel Works. These Works produced during the month 36,355 tons of Ingots; 20,816 tons of Billets and 9,274 tons of Rails. Cost of manufacture from Pig Iron to Billets was the lowest ever obtained, being $3.55 from Pig to Billets, or 23 cents per ton less than the lowest cost ever obtained at these Works. It is now believed by the Superintendent at these Works that with his new Blowing arrangements completed and some other changes of minor character, which he is now making, that he can ultimately reduce this cost to about $3.25. . . . The practice at the Duquesne Works for the past month was the best we have ever had.[36]

[35] U.S. Commissioner of Labor, *Cost of Production: Iron, Steel, Coal* (Washington, 1891), p. 6.
[36] September 14, 1897, *U.S. v. U.S.S., Government Exhibits*, III, 1090, and 1083–1097, for a number of such reports of 1897. On Shinn and Carnegie's

The cost sheets, broken down and analyzed, were searched assiduously for slackness and points for improvement.

Charles Schwab described the procedure: "We made a careful . . . statement of each manufacture, with the cost as compared with each department, and the reasons . . . ; had the manager of that department make such explanations as were necessary. . . . Greater economies are effected by strict supervision over all departments than in any other direction." Julian Kennedy recalled his years as a Carnegie manager: "A careful record was kept of the costs. You are expected always to get it 10 cents cheaper the next year or the next month." From New York or Europe Carnegie would spot an increase in coke consumption. "This is, at least, five per cent more than it should be, and perhaps more. It should be investigated, beginning at the beginning. . . . We should do better than that." [37] The demand for excellence never slackened.

The Steel Corporation adapted the Carnegie system to its more complex organization. First, the statistics of the subsidiaries were standardized. By July 1901 a uniform system was in effect for blast furnace and open-hearth departments. The Executive Committee next established a bureau of comparative costs to determine "why costs are good and bad." Every Corporation plant sent monthly detailed forms to the New York office. The bureau compiled from these reports two sets of comparative cost sheets, a technical one for plant managers and another for higher officials. The technical sheets included practice statistics and detailed costs. Over 8,000 items were recorded in the blast furnace forms. A committee of furnace superintendents met each month, studied the figures, and recommended changes. According to President Schwab, such analysis saved over $4,000,000 in blast furnace operation alone during the first year.[38]

---

early interest in cost accounting, see Bridge, pp. 85–86; Andrew Carnegie, *Autobiography* (Boston, 1924), p. 202; *EMJ*, May 7, 1892, p. 495.

[37] Carnegie to J. A. Leishman, January 15, 1896, Carnegie Papers; Schwab, in *Industrial Commission*, XIII, 452; Kennedy, in *Stanley Hearings*, VII, 5115.

[38] *U.S. v. U.S.S., Testimony*, XIII, 4975, XIV, 5546–5550; *Statement of the Case*, pp. 187–188; *Defendants' Exhibits*, VIII, 619, prints the first simple

Decision based on exact data became habitual. When Carnegie was debating withdrawal from a beam pool, for instance, Schwab calculated the greater profitability of running full at a tenth of a cent less per pound than at three-quarters speed at the regular price. The Steel Corporation in 1908 began systematically to gather information on its competitors as a basis for its competitive policies.[39] That form of rational action was evident at every turn.

The economizing calculation, for example, was one determinant in the formation of the United States Steel Corporation. Technological advance seemed to be reaching its limits. "We cannot get Costs down any more," Frick had reported in 1898. Further economies, Schwab argued, were attainable only through organization and distribution. His eloquence strengthened J. P. Morgan's decision to undertake the unification of half the industry into one company.[40]

Appointed president of U.S. Steel, Schwab set to work putting his preachings into practice. He eliminated wasteful duplication. Ore and coal mining, coke manufacture, and lake transportation were systematized under a single management. No longer would ore pile up on one dock, while boats at the next waited weeks for a full load or departed half empty. "Now, owning all the fleet, . . . it doesn't make any difference what ore is ready." Plant specialization promised further economies. The Youngstown and South works both made rails. "One of the first things we did was to run one of these two works entirely on rails and the other on commodities best suited, thereby saving in freights, shipments and deliveries." The expectations for economy "have been fully real-

---

comparative cost sheet for the blast furnaces, July 2, 1901; U.S. Steel, Executive Committee Minutes, September 9, 1902, *Stanley Hearings*, VI, 3804.

[39] Carnegie Minutes, February 4, 1896, *Government Exhibits*, III, 1006; U.S. Steel, General Sales Managers' Minutes, November 20, December 16, 1908, *Stanley Hearings*, VI, 3966.

[40] Frick, in Carnegie Company Minutes, September 20, 1898, *U.S. v. U.S.S.*, *Government Exhibits*, III, 1138; *Testimony*, XIV, 5489; B. J. Hendrick, *The Life of Andrew Carnegie* (2 vols., New York, 1932), II, 129–131.

ized," Schwab reported after the first year, and much was yet to be accomplished.[41]

Careful cost analysis also determined commercial policies. The head of a firm, said T. J. Bray of Republic, "should have constantly before him complete cost data" when making sales decisions. Here, as elsewhere, Carnegie is the best example. "The surest way to continued leadership," he lectured his managers, was "to adopt policy of selling a few finished articles which require large tonnage." Bridges were "not so good because every order different." In addition, Carnegie sought quantity orders. His company agreed to a five-year contract for steel slabs at a very low figure because of "the advantage of cheaper production on the rest of the material from that train [of rolls]." [42] Large standard forms and capacity operation, according to the cost sheets, maximized economical production.

U.S. Steel, extending Carnegie's sales aims, became the country's quantity producer of standard lines of steel. A subsidiary sales manager reported in 1905:

> Our "back-log" tonnage, and the ability to turn out enormous production, have been better than to get top prices by taking more undesirable work. . . . Even in bad times we should be able to run our works fairly full.

A car company contract was favorable because "they would order in large lengths and do their own cutting, and would take such quantities as to make desirable rollings." Long-term contracts also permitted better scheduling in transportation and production. The Steel Corporation insisted on making deliveries at its con-

[41] *Industrial Commission,* XIII, 451; U.S. Steel, Executive Committee Minutes, April 12, 1901, *U.S. v. U.S.S., Testimony,* XIII, 4975; U.S. Steel, *Report to the Stockholders* (1902).

[42] Bray, in *ITR,* May 28, 1914, p. 597; Carnegie Company Minutes, January 31, 1899, February 21, 1899, October 11, 1900, *Government Exhibits,* III, 1193, 1215, VI, 1896; Carnegie to J. A. Leishman, September 18, 1895, and to F. T. F. Lovejoy, December 9, 1895, Carnegie Papers.

venience from plants of its designation.[43] Premium sales, rush orders, and special products it left to the independents. Finally, U.S. Steel determined to be self-contained through the finished product. By 1907 this last step was achieved to provide the economies of standardization, scheduling, and full operation.

The cost calculation thus shaped decisions at every point in the steelmaking enterprise. The spur of economy made the mental cast of the industry surpassingly objective and rational.

Ultimately, success or failure rested on the men who managed the furnaces and mills. They had to be a special breed. An executive, observed a prominent steelmaster, "must constantly endeavor to do a little better, accomplish a little more, save a trifle here, improve a detail there." The superintendent who repairs "on the same lines as last time, without seeing his way to improve, to strengthen, and to make more effective his furnace; we have no use for that class of men." [44] Kennedy remarked, "The pressure is always on you to make all the economies you can." Carnegie's president, J. A. Leishman, urged the recording of reasons for votes at board meetings in order to "form a correct judgement of the ability of our managers."[45] For they were the critical element in the quest for economy.

The youthfulness of American superintendents was frequently noted by English visitors. One took the Pressed Steel Car Company, employing ten thousand men, as an example: the president was thirty-eight; his assistant, thirty-six; the secretary, thirty-six; and the chief engineer was thirty-two years old. W. E. Corey and A. C. Dinkey were general superintendents of the Carnegie Company in their twenties, and Schwab became president when he was barely

[43] Carnegie Company Directors' Minutes, March 16, 1903, October 30, 1905, *Government Exhibits*, II, 487, 502, 506. See interchange of letters between C. W. Bryan of the American Bridge Company and the Union Pacific Railroad, in which insistence on control of manufacture schedule and desire for large orders is clearly illustrated. *Government Exhibits*, XIII, Nos. 428–432.

[44] Jeans, p. 500.

[45] J. A. Leishman to Carnegie, December 23, 1895, Carnegie Papers.

thirty. College men increasingly filled the managerial ranks as steel manufacture grew complex and technical, but the accent on youth remained. Of twenty-one blast furnace plants visited by Axel Sahlin in 1901, eighteen were managed by young university men. "When a college graduate, who shows that he has the right stuff in him, reaches the age of 25 or 30 years, he is ready for a position of trust," one manufacturer told Sahlin. Older, experienced men made excellent specialists, "but for managers and executives we select young men with brains and education." Lacking "time to wear themselves into a groove," they were unfettered in their efforts for improvement.[46]

They had, moreover, the vigor and enthusiasm required for peak operations. As a youthful superintendent of the Minnequa rail mill in Colorado, Tom Girdler worked practically all his waking hours. British steel men, visiting the Duquesne Works at night, found the managers still on duty, and this appeared to be the usual practice at other plants. The energy of Americans, conjectured the Englishmen, was partly the secret of their success.

But youth alone would not guarantee top performance. Steelmasters shrewdly devised incentives for their managerial forces. Charles Schwab, for instance, would not select one manager over all departments. "I put one good man at each of them and then rivalled one against the other, and in that way got better results." Rivalry was widespread. Trade journals immediately published production records, setting the mark for others to beat. The competition between the Edgar Thomson and South works became famous. In November 1891 the Thomson mill set out to beat the best twenty-four-hour mark of the South Works — 1,700 tons. By the day's end 2,074 tons was the new record, soon itself to be surpassed. A huge steel broom at the Thomson Works hung above the blast furnace that had swept away the pig iron record. When the Steel Corporation was formed, President Schwab intended to "put one works as a rival against another works, as to practices, wastes, supplies, everything that goes into cost." The comparative cost sheets ranked

[46] Jeans, pp. 500–501.

units by cost per ton; the ambition of every manager was to reach the top.[47]

Handsome reward was the chief spur to special achievement. Carnegie dangled partnerships before his managers. They invested nothing. Shares were set aside, paid for out of accruing profit, and then awarded. The first four were chosen in 1884, and in time every responsible official became a partner. The system worked exceedingly well. It kept the managers at their peak, and guaranteed that the best men would come forward.

Carnegie had an uncanny ability for picking likely men out of the ranks; thirty of thirty-three superintendents rose from laboring jobs, some to become the leaders of the industry. He wrote Frick in 1896:

> There is one man I should like to see given one-sixth [of one per cent] — Mr. Corey. He is worth it. . . . Perhaps there are one or two others who deserve sixths. Every year should be marked by the promotion of one or more of our young men. . . . We can not have too many of the right sort interested in the profits.[48]

Then emerging from obscurity, W. E. Corey went on to become president of U.S. Steel. Carnegie often laid his success to the partnership policy and his "Young Geniuses." His company was renowned for its superb management.

The Carnegie incentive system seemed impractical for the corporate structure of U.S. Steel. Instead, Schwab proposed bonuses to reward performance. (The Carnegie Company had given its lesser officials bonuses.) A uniform policy, however, was not adopted until dissatisfaction arose among the executives. Under the U.S. Steel profit-sharing plan, an increasing percentage of earnings over

---

[47] Schwab, in *Industrial Commission*, XIII, 456; Bridge, pp. 107–110; *EMJ*, January 2, 1892, p. 33; *U.S.* v. *U.S.S., Testimony*, XIII, 4976, XIV, 5550.

[48] Quoted in Hendrick, II, 42. See also Andrew Carnegie, "The Human Side of Business," *Miscellaneous Writings* (2 vols., New York, 1933), I, 9–10. Carnegie once said a fitting epitaph for him would be: "Here lies a man who knew how to get other men to work for him."

$75,000,000 was set aside for distribution according to merit. Also, at the suggestion of the insurance magnate G. W. Perkins, a portion was held back for five years, and then shared by the executives still in the service of the Steel Corporation. Although the plan incorporated Carnegie's aims, the effect was considerably diluted.

The efficacy of bonuses was demonstrated by Schwab when he acquired Bethlehem Steel. His monetary incentives infused life into the moribund company. Schwab did not dismiss the staff, believing, as Carnegie had said, that "unsuspecting powers lie latent in willing men around us," needing only "appreciation and development to produce surprising results." They did produce surprising results; by 1915 Bethlehem was second only to the Steel Corporation. The bonus plan set a "cash premium on personal efficiency and endeavor." Bonuses were paid monthly, the men reaping their rewards directly and precisely. As Bethlehem prospered, bonuses mounted very high. Schwab's plan, like his mentor's, created a magnificent managerial organization. He became as famous for his "Boys" as Carnegie had been for his "Young Geniuses." Bonus systems, in many guises, spread through the industry.[49] Excellence was generously repaid.

Security, however, was not one of the rewards. The British habit of retaining aging employees, observed an English visitor in 1901, was far distant from the American practice "of getting rid of any man, however exalted his position, when there is the least evidence that his efficiency and his power of endurance are waning." Carnegie's limited association contained an "iron clad" clause that a partner could be ejected from the firm by a three-fourths vote and his share repurchased at book value. The clause was frequently invoked. When a partner was "sent to Europe," Pittsburghers joked, it meant he was being forced out.[50] Long contracts were few, and

[49] Arundel Cotter, *The Story of Bethlehem Steel* (New York, 1916), pp. 13–14, 20–22; New York *Times,* February 17, 1916. On other bonus systems, see, for example, *IA,* March 22, 1911, pp. 716–718, March 4, 1915, p. 518.

[50] Carnegie owned over half, usually about 58 per cent of the stock. Men who left their position in the firm were required to sell their shares back at book value. This did not always work out well. When Carnegie forced Frick out, Frick sued, claiming the actual value of the company was much

managerial changes frequent. There was little evidence that successful men dragged "relatives up with them irrespective of actual merit and proved capacity, as in Great Britain." Sentiment had no place in the steel business.

The managerial policy worked with marvelous effectiveness. In the hands of the untiring men who superintended the steel mills the industry became the wonder of the manufacturing world.

By the opening of the twentieth century the modern character of American steel manufacture had been formed. Mechanization was nearly completed. Rational calculation prevailed. And the managerial force assured peak performance. At every point, the impulse for economy had been paramount. So it was in fixing the place of labor in the steelmaking system.

---

greater than the book value, as it was, and Carnegie had to give in. See *Government Exhibits,* III, 1334–1340; Hendrick, II, chs. 3 and 4; George Harvey, *Henry Clay Frick* (New York, 1928), chs. 16–18.

Chapter II

Economy and Labor

A quarter of a million workingmen labored in the steel mills of America. Their lives were ruled by the circumstances of modern metal manufacture. Employers, however, were unconcerned with the steelworker as a man. "As humanitarians, we might regret" harmful overwork, observed the metallurgist H. M. Howe. "As managers . . . we would not be justified in diminishing our employers' profits." [1]

Labor was subject to the unsentimental and rational standard of the industry; for labor was primarily an item of cost. Operations were unchanged at the Edgar Thomson furnaces, recorded a Carnegie official, "labor being about three cents per ton higher by reason of having to stock larger quantities of ore than used." Reckoning thus, steelmakers based their decisions on the figures in the cost sheets. The Washburn and Moen wire works, reported the assistant manager, "can now figure up the costs of drawing by job rates in various ways, and see which is the cheapest." Later, the division heads were instructed to keep independent Time Books to improve "the Analysis of Pay Roll by Cost Department." [2] Economy governed here as elsewhere in the steelmaking calculation.

Labor savings were, in fact, the nub of the American accomplish-

[1] *Journal of the British Iron and Steel Institute* (1890), p. 113.

[2] Carnegie Company Minutes, June 15, 1897, *U.S. v. U.S.S., Government Exhibits,* III, 1088; C. S. Hall, Memorandum, April 13, 1889, F. H. Daniels to E. J. Watson, September 18, 1891, Washburn and Moen, American Steel and Wire Collection.

ment. The steelmasters, enterprising as they were, lagged behind Europe in utilizing waste gases and streamlining products. They did attain economies of fuel, transportation, and distribution. But their preëminent success came in the area of labor costs. That part of total manufacturing charges shrank almost one-third — from 22.5 to 16.5 per cent — in the twenty years after 1890. The proportional reduction of labor cost was the principal achievement of the economizing drive.

Every effort was directed toward lowering the labor cost per ton of steel. Cost per ton, however, had only bookkeeping meaning. The individual workman was the actual unit, and the variables in labor cost were his productivity and earnings over the same period. The goal of economy, as it related to labor, was to multiply the worker's output in relation to his income. Complex enough in its details, the steelmasters' labor policy reduced to that simple objective.

Its full attainment accounted for the superiority of the American steel industry. For the workingman the benefits were more dubious.

Of the two labor cost variables productivity took precedence. The exertions here were unceasing. A Carnegie executive, for instance, reported in 1897 "a marked reduction in the number of men employed." The Homestead Works "can now be run full with about 2,900 men," a decrease in the labor force of almost a quarter since 1892. Frick appointed an official to improve the utilization of workers, until there remained "not a superfluous wage-earner in the shops." The pace of work continually intensified. Gang foremen were, with reason, called "pushers." "The 'bosses' drive the men to an extent that the employers would never dream of attempting in this country," reported a returned English traveler, "getting the maximum work out of them, and the men do not seem to have the inclination or the power to resist the pressure." Work loads, however, could not be pushed up indefinitely. A Washburn and Moen official reported that "job hands, in many cases, seem to have reached their limit, so that a reduction in rates necessarily means a reduction in wages, which has not always been the case heretofore."[3] Human endurance had its bounds.

Here technology opened vast opportunities. The industry's continuing inventiveness had its chief effect on labor productivity. Either by eliminating men or by raising the pace of production, technological innovation vastly increased the output variable in the labor cost calculation. Mechanization of the handling of materials, integration of the production stages, and continuous rolling methods, all multiplied worker productivity.

The large gangs of laborers in the ore yards and on the floors of blast furnace and Bessemer departments soon disappeared. At the docks of one large plant, for example, 770 men had been required to shovel the iron ore from the boats. Then the holds were redesigned to make them accessible to new scooping machinery. Thereafter, fifteen times as much ore was unloaded per employee.[4] The completion of its "grab" system in 1906 permitted the South Works to discharge 650 men.[5] At land-locked plants, the shovelers were displaced by car dumpers and trestle systems.

Similar gains were made inside the mills. In one blast furnace department in 1887, 82 men had labored to charge the materials to produce 350 tons of pig iron a day. Larger barrows and an improved hoisting mechanism in 1902 almost doubled productivity. Several years later, electric trolleys and inclined skip hoists were introduced to carry the ingredients to the furnace top and automatically dump them inside. With mechanical operation thus per-

[3] Carnegie Company Minutes, June 15, 1897, *U.S.* v. *U.S.S., Government Exhibits,* III, 1089; Bridge, *Carnegie Company,* p. 296; James Kitson, "Iron and Steel Industries of America," *Contemporary Review,* LIX (May 1891), 629–630; C. S. Hall, Memorandum, April 12, 1889, Washburn and Moen, American Steel and Wire Collection.

[4] U.S. Bureau of Labor, *Report on Conditions of Employment in the Iron and Steel Industry* (4 vols., Washington, 1911–13), III, 341. Unless otherwise indicated in the footnotes, the statistical and descriptive information in this chapter comes from this exhaustive federal investigation, cited hereafter as *Labor Conditions.*

[5] Chicago *Daily Socialist,* October 29, 1906.

fected, 104 men were able to charge raw material for 5,293 tons, a twelve-fold increase per man since 1887.

The Wellman charger had an equivalent effect in the open-hearth furnaces. Under the old method, workmen fed the furnaces manually with a long flattened bar called a peel. Crews labored furiously for several hours to charge a single small furnace. Operating the ingenious Wellman device, one man could cover from four to six seventy-five-ton furnaces, charging each in less than an hour. A superintendent estimated that the Wellman machine multiplied the productivity of his charging force thirty-five times. Electric traveling cranes similarly displaced the labor gangs feeding the Bessemer converters.

When operations became integrated, the laborious casting and remelting work was avoided. Ladles carrying molten metal directly to the converters in one plant quadrupled the output of each employee. The Jones mixer and the pig casting machine ended the need, even with excess metal, for the manual sand casting method. Between Bessemer converters and rolling mills, the practice of casting ingots on cars also saved much heavy labor. Thus far, technological advances increased productivity mainly by displacing men, and only secondarily by raising the rate of operations. Beyond the converters, the reverse became true.

The mechanical devices in the rolling mills did, of course, eliminate many workmen. When Republic installed continuous furnaces at a guide mill, for instance, it was able to discharge two-thirds of the heaters. The McCallip repeater, reported a rod mill expert, conducted the lead end of the rod automatically from groove to groove, "thereby dispensing with about one-half of the catchers." Where mechanization was perfected, the steel was rolled entirely without direct human contact. Visiting Englishmen saw the operation of Pennsylvania rail mills conducted "practically by the agency of unseen hands." There was "no labour at all at the rolls." [6]

The real value of the rolling improvements, however, was that,

[6] Daniels, Mechanical Engineers, *Transactions*, XIV, 606; *British Iron and Steel Institute in America in 1890*, p. 285.

by excluding physical effort, the production rate could be greatly quickened. "Direct human labor to fatigue and hinder . . . had to stand aside," said the rod mill engineer C. H. Morgan.[7] A standard rail mill undergoing modernization, for instance, raised its daily production from 1,000 to 2,380 tons. (Its labor force meanwhile declined only by one-tenth.) Integration with Bessemer converters was mainly important because it permitted full advantage to be taken of the expanded capacity of the primary mills. Integration at the Edgar Thomson rail mill provided enough additional hot metal to double the output; every fifteen seconds an ingot was ready for the rolls.

The most spectacular increases came in the finishing mills. The first automatic rod mill in 1882 advanced the output to 70,000 pounds in ten hours. The perfected Garrett mill ten years later could roll 349,000 pounds. "This has been brought about," observed the engineer F. H. Daniels, "by being constantly on the alert to increase the output every time the possibility . . . presented itself." The productivity of rolling mill workers was immensely increased.

At some points mechanization failed. Men, not machines, continued to roll tin plate and puddle wrought iron. Labor output consequently did not change significantly here over the years.

These backward areas only made more impressive the general progress of the industry. Under the drive for economy, manual operations nearly disappeared from the American steel mills. The measure of the steelmasters' success was in the swiftly mounting productivity of labor.

The consequences of mechanization were as significant for the individual workman as for his employer's cost sheets. The steelmaking tasks were radically altered. Steelworkers had been the manipulators of raw materials and molten metal. They became the tenders of machines.

Earlier, rolling mills had required highly skilled men to catch and pass hot steel through the rolls. At every point rollers, roughers,

[7] Morgan, Mechanical Engineers, *Transactions,* XXII, 58.

and heaters had manually handled the metal. They were men of long experience and at a premium in America. Each new device that mechanized a difficult procedure undermined their favored position. Increasingly, mill workers became semiskilled operatives adept at routine mechanical duties which were not comparable to the virtuosity of hand-rolling steel. An Englishman, observing the modern mills, commented: "The various operations are so much simplified that an experienced man is not required. . . . The workmen in America do not act upon their own judgment, but carry out the instructions given to them."[8] The work, said the inventor Charles Morgan, was now "largely *supervisory* and *directory,* rather than *executory.*" The head roller, whose knowledge and experience remained essential, gradually took on the functions of supervisor. The mass of rolling men slipped into the ranks of the semiskilled.

The process was reversed in blast furnaces and converters, but ended in the same result. The few skilled men, the blowers and melters, were unaffected by technological improvement. The hordes of common laborers were rapidly supplanted. Electric cranes, cars, skip hoists, and charging machines required operators with some training. "While machinery may decrease the number of men, it demands a higher grade of workman," observed H. H. Campbell of Pennsylvania Steel.[9] The middling group of workmen thus grew at every stage of the manufacturing process. They constituted 28 per cent of the labor force of a typical modern plant.[10] Semiskilled work characteristically resulted from mechanization.

Its second effect was on the arduousness of steelmaking labor. Before machinery replaced men, only increased exertion raised output. Managers therefore often drove their workmen unrelentingly. The piece-rate system, the competitive spirit, and the pressure for production were all designed to speed up work. A British expert

<hr />

[8] Jeans, *American Industrial Conditions,* p. 561.
[9] Quoted in Charles Reitell, *Machinery and Its Benefits to Labor in the Crude Iron and Steel Industries* (Menasha, Wisconsin, 1917), p. 6, also, p. 32.
[10] *Labor Conditions,* III, 80. See ch. 9 for changes, 1900–1910.

noted that the high output at a Bessemer plant "was attained by great facilities for bringing up and getting away materials, and keeping everything at high pressure. The men, I dare say, are paid well, but it was hot weather when I was there, and they were certainly selling their lives." [11]

Many such remarks were made during the visit of the British Iron and Steel Institute in 1890. At that time mechanization was only partly perfected. An improvement at one point increased the speed for the entire mill. When, for example, a continuous furnace was installed at a Republic nine-inch hand mill, production immediately jumped 30 per cent. The work of every man except the heater was stepped up to that extent. The most recent innovation set the pace for the straining men.

The completion of mechanization ended the imbalance. Workmen no longer labored alongside machines; nor was output pushed farther. At one plate mill, for instance, output per man tripled in the ten years up to 1904, when technological changes came to an end. Thereafter, productivity remained relatively constant. Machinery thus became the measure of output; it fixed the upper limit to operations.

Toilsome labor was relieved in another way. To feed furnaces, converters, and rolling mills was heavy work, performed often under intense heat. Before the introduction of the pig iron caster, workmen had to hammer the red-hot iron into manageable pieces. "An exceedingly hard and laborious job," a plant superintendent characterized it. "They were working constantly in a cloud of moist vapor of high temperature, which of itself was . . . debilitating." The job of hand charging with a peel an open-hearth furnace, thought one steelworker, "was working aside of hell ahead of time." Top fillers, who dumped materials into blast furnaces, were equally badly situated. At one plant they labored in temperatures up to 128 degrees. When the wind was from the wrong direction, poisonous fumes enveloped them. An employer concluded, "Gorilla men are what we need." [12]

[11] Quoted in *ibid.*, p. 337.
[12] Quoted in *ibid.*, p. 299; and in Reitell, pp. 16, 24.

Machinery eliminated the worst of the onerous tasks. Yet, even at the most advanced plants much heavy work remained, and handling the controls of machines could also be tense and fatiguing. But the burden on the steelworker had greatly eased. English steel men in 1901 recognized the change. Enoch James noted that American wage earners "are generally supposed to be working much harder than they do in this country, but this is not my own view." Americans "have to be attentive in guiding operations, and quick in manipulating levers and similarly easy work," but they "do not work so hard as the men in England." American steelmasters, hardheaded businessmen as they were, did not overlook this fact in determining their labor policies.

Thus far, the effect of economy on labor, profound although it was, actually was the by-product of decisions essentially technological in nature. Reduced labor costs — the chief objective — were achieved by attention to machines, not labor. Even the transformation of the steelmaking tasks was an entirely secondary result of mechanization. There were, however, critical decisions that directly touched labor. Wages and hours were vitally important in the determination of labor cost, and as susceptible to the logic of economy as any other element of production expense. The steelmasters' rule of impersonal, rational calculation applied equally to the fixing of the schedules and earnings of their employees.

When testifying before a Congressional investigating committee in 1912, Percival Roberts, a director of U.S. Steel, was asked to explain the excessive hours prevailing in the steel industry. "Who shall say [what] is the proper limit?" said Roberts. "There is no doubt that the minimum number . . . is the pleasantest; but, in the economies of this world, how shall we determine what that limit may be?" The answer lay in "the laws of nature." [13] Despite the committee's skepticism, Roberts spoke accurately enough. He meant that the decisions were not arbitrary. The goal of maximum productivity per worker gave to employers definite criteria for settling the hours of labor.

[13] *Stanley Hearings*, V, 3264–3265.

A general work schedule had developed before the technological revolution. Puddling mills operated on approximate shifts of ten hours, the time required to work six heats of metal. This arrangement governed rolling mills, finishing plants, and even steel mills in the early days. The twelve-hour system prevailed only in blast furnace plants, which necessarily ran continuously.[14] As integrated operation attached steel plants to the uninterrupted production of blast furnaces, manufacturers were faced with the choice of a two- or three-turn day.

Technological improvement at first made the short shift preferable. "In increasing the output," commented Captain W. R. Jones of the Carnegie Company in 1881, "I soon discovered it was entirely out of the question to expect human flesh and blood to labor incessantly for twelve hours, and therefore it was decided to put on three turns." The change "proved to be of immense advantage. . . . The men can work harder constantly for eight hours, having sixteen for rest."[15] Incomplete mechanization intensified work, and consequently shortened hours.

The Homestead 119-inch plate mill, for instance, operated on two shifts of ten and eleven hours until 1886. Then the slabbing mill was improved to roll more and larger slabs for plate. The plate mill remained unchanged, so its hands went on eight-hour schedules. "Previous to that time we did not work so hard," testified one workman. There was time to eat and rest. But now "we stop only the time it takes to oil the engines, . . . working more steady and harder right along to produce this tonnage."[16]

Carnegie introduced the short shift in other departments, and experimented with it even at the Braddock blast furnaces. Cambria,

---

[14] U.S. Commissioner of Labor, *Annual Report* (1886), pp. 372–386; Ohio Bureau of Labor Statistics, *Annual Report* (1882), pp. 106–107. Even in blast furnaces, twelve hours were not universal. The furnace men at the Union Iron and Steel Company plant in Chicago were on eight hours until 1882. Illinois Bureau of Labor Statistics, *Annual Report* (1882), pp. 261–264.

[15] Quoted in Bridge, p. 110.

[16] U.S. House, Committee on the Judiciary, *Investigation of the Homestead Troubles,* 52 Cong., 2nd Sess. (1892–1893) Report No. 2447, p. 187. Cited hereafter as *Homestead Investigation.*

Jones and Laughlins, Joliet, and other plants likewise reduced the workday. An Englishman in 1890 commented that the Homestead Bessemer department had three turns "as usual." The eight-hour day did not, however, win universal acceptance.

The logic for shorter hours weakened with advancing mechanization; men no longer kept pace with machines. When the Edgar Thomson Works was being fully modernized, the managers reconsidered the working hours. The plant went on the twelve-hour day in December 1887, followed by other Carnegie mills within a few years. The movement became general. In a short time, complained the *National Labor Tribune,* most steel plants "have fallen away." When the South Works in 1902 and the Joliet Works in 1904 put their remaining departments on twelve hours, the short turn practically ended in primary steel manufacture.[17] The extensive federal investigation in May 1910 found twelve hours standard in the steel mills.

Finishing plants, without the necessity for continuous operation, also lengthened the workday. Rod mills, fully automatic by 1910, operated customarily on twelve-hour shifts. So did half the bar mills. (Continuous rolling had been perfected here, but many plants clung to the old methods.) In tube manufacture, only partly mechanized, one-third of the men worked twelve hours, the rest ten hours a day. Where innovation failed, the schedule did not increase. Wrought iron mills remained, as they had for half a century, on ten-hour shifts. Eight hours prevailed in sheet and tin plate mills.

The connection between hours and mechanization was explicitly recognized. The general superintendent of the U.S. Steel bar and hoop department thus explained a schedule change. Certain men had worked eight hours "on account of the positions being particularly laborious. Since then we have installed machinery and

[17] *National Labor Tribune,* July 24, 1886, April 14, 1888; John A. Fitch, *The Steel Workers,* Vol. 3 of *Pittsburgh Survey,* ed. Paul U. Kellog (6 vols., New York, 1909–1914), pp. 112–115, 119, 167; U.S. Commissioner of Labor, *Annual Report* (1890), pp. 372–386 (1904), pp. 115, 121–122; Bernard J. Hogg, "The Homestead Strike of 1892," unpublished Ph.D. thesis, University of Chicago, 1943, p. 202, and *passim.*

taken the heavy part out of it, and these men are now working twelve hours per day."[18] Similarly, when a continuous furnace replaced the hand furnace at an eight-inch mill, the crew immediately went on the long day.

The reasoning worked in reverse as well. Even where mechanization went furthest, gaps remained. In Bessemer departments, for example, steel was still poured manually into molds. The labor was heavy, intensely hot, and constantly dangerous. Over half the pouring crews in 1910 worked eight hours. Again, automatic looping guides in Garrett mills functioned only on one side of the rolls. On the other, skilled men — called oval and diamond roll hands — worked without pause to catch the swiftly moving rods and put them into the next pass. One-third of these had an eight-hour day; the others were frequently spelled. Many straighteners in rail mills, pit cranemen in blooming mills, chargers in open-hearth furnaces, and top fillers in blast furnaces were similarly privileged. And, of course, short hours in puddling and tin plate manufacture were the result of "the hardest physical labor in the industry."

The objective of maximum productivity decided the adjustment of working hours, lessening them in the early stages of mechanization, increasing them in the later period. American steel technology had about reached its completion when the Bureau of Labor made the investigation of 1910. Then nearly three-quarters of the steelworkers (excluding sheet and tin plate mills) were on the twelve-hour schedule. The nonproductive workers, forming almost half the total force, were evenly split between ten- and twelve-hour labor.[19]

The work week also lengthened. As far back as steel men could remember, iron smelting had been seven-day labor. The standard

[18] Walter Jenks, quoted in Chicago *Daily Socialist,* March 4, 1910.

[19] For hours at individual mills, see, for example, *Stanley Hearings,* V, 3285–3289, for hours per day for U.S. Steel plants for 1912; U.S. Immigration Commission, *Reports* (Washington, 1911), VIII, 377–381, for detailed hours at Cambria in 1908, 641–642, hours for Steelton; U.S. Bureau of Labor, *Report on Strike at Bethlehem Steel Works* (Washington, 1910), for hours there.

could hardly have been improved upon, and employers never tried to impair it. Indeed, they made its application more complete. Keepers in Ohio blast furnaces in 1882 averaged 77 hours a week, laborers 64 hours; in 1910, for the entire country, keepers worked 83.9 hours and laborers 72.6 hours.[20]

When integration was perfected, the temptation grew to extend the seven-day schedule to Bessemer converters and rolling mills. Fortunately, the Jones mixer and the pig casting machine made possible the efficient disposal of "Sunday metal." Therefore, steel plants normally shut down Saturday afternoon and started up again on Sunday evening.

Boom times tended to spread seven-day operation. The return of prosperity in 1898 put many Pittsburgh mills on Sunday schedules, despite the protests of workmen against the unprecedented change. Carnegie officials in February 1905 announced that the Homestead Bessemer department would run continuously because of the very active market for billets and bars. Most Pittsburgh open-hearth workers labored alternate Sundays in 1907, when the producing capacity was inadequate for the rising demand for open-hearth steel.[21] Plant managers grew accustomed to operating on Sundays whenever they fell behind their orders. Manual mills, however, never ran more than six days a week, and usually with only one Saturday shift.

The business cycle, paradoxically, increased the hours of labor at its troughs as well as its peaks. The important shifts to twelve hours, it appears, came mainly during depression — in the middle 1880's and 1890's. U.S. Steel hoop mills went on the double turn during the 1904 recession. The Cambria Company, an isolated advocate of the short day, ended its remaining eight-hour labor in the depression of 1908, and so did Jones and Laughlin with its few eight-hour men, only to return them to three shifts in 1909.[22]

[20] Ohio Bureau of Labor Statistics, *Report* (1882), pp. 106–107; *Labor Conditions,* I, lviii, lxi, 42.

[21] *Industrial Commission,* VII, 391; *IA,* February 2, 1905, p. 403; Fitch, pp. 39, 172–175.

[22] Fitch, p. 169; Hogg, pp. 203–204; *EMJ,* September 30, 1893, p. 35; *IA,* December 15, 1904, p. 36.

Steel men lengthened the workday as a means to raise worker productivity in depressed periods, when further economies became necessary. The spread of Sunday labor during prosperous times, on the other hand, was a response to the cry for more steel. Sunday work, unlike twelve hours, was not primarily an economizing measure.

Overtime further raised the weekly schedule over the normal 72 hours. The weekend layoff provided valuable time to clean up, repair machinery, and prepare for the next week. Eighteen per cent of rail mill crews in May 1910 worked on Sundays. Only rolling men uniformly had the day off. Nonproductive workers naturally were even more widely affected — over 30 per cent — both through overtime and as part of their regular schedule. This pattern, the Bureau of Labor estimated, was more or less characteristic of other steelmaking departments.

According to the federal investigation, three-tenths of the entire labor force worked regularly seven days a week in May 1910, a normal — perhaps slightly above normal — period. In addition, a survey of the payrolls of nine steel plants showed that three-tenths of their workmen, surely not those on seven-day schedules, labored an extra seven hours a week overtime. The progress of the iron and steel industry could perhaps be comprehended in the fact that Illinois workmen in 1882 averaged seven hours a week less than workmen in 1910, not counting overtime.[23]

Overworked, steelworkers were also chronically idle. Hard times of varying severity hit the industry every three or four years. The panic of 1907, for instance, threw half the 40,000 blast furnace men out of work; and until the middle of 1909 not more than three-quarters were reëmployed. Business fluctuation was beyond the control of steel manufacturers; but they contributed their share to intensify labor instability. The logic of economy, lengthening hours, also exaggerated irregular employment.

Optimum efficiency forbade half-speed operation. Consequently, steel men often preferred to shut down until sufficient orders ac-

[23] Illinois Bureau of Labor Statistics, *Annual Report* (1882), p. 245. The number of holidays decreased, only July 4 and Christmas remaining by 1907.

cumulated, or to concentrate the work in a single unit. Jones and Laughlin employees in 1907 complained that one mill was operating at top speed, stopping only for a half-day on Sundays, while another mill in the plant stood idle. Mergers enlarged the possibilities. Owning a number of plants, a concern like American Tin Plate could close the less efficient and run the others full. Pittsburgh workmen, idle for some time, charged bitterly in 1900 that the Monessen and New Castle tin mills were meanwhile breaking records.[24]

A policy of full production made employment uncertain except at peak periods. According to the census of 1909, a fairly active year, the lowest employment figures were only three-quarters of the highest — the largest fluctuation in the major manufacturing industries. With production reaching a new height in 1910, 7.9 per cent of the labor force of a representative group of steel mills had jobs for less than thirty weeks; 21.9 per cent less than forty weeks; and under 40 per cent forty-eight weeks or more. The logic that worked men 84 hours a week thus repeatedly idled them.

The test of mechanization, of lengthened hours, and of irregular employment alike was the effect on the productivity of the individual steelworker. That was the critical factor in the economizing formula of the steelmasters. In the twenty years after 1890, the output per workman in blast furnaces nearly tripled, the output in steel plants doubled. It was an immense achievement.

All that remained was the determination of wages — the second variable in the calculus of labor costs — to maximize the benefits of the rise in productivity.

Charles Schwab was appearing before a Congressional committee in 1912. Representative A. O. Stanley presented figures that showed a 58 per cent increase in the output of Pennsylvania furnace workmen from 1902 to 1909. Why had their wages risen only 10 per

---

[24] A. W. Mitchell, "The Labor Relations of a Large Steel Company in the Pittsburgh District (Jones and Laughlin)," unpublished Ph.D. thesis, University of Pittsburgh, 1939, p. 15; Fitch, pp. 176–177; *Iron and Steel Trade Journal*, January 27, 1900, p. 82; *Industrial Commission*, XIII, 905.

cent? Could not earnings have increased much more without eliminating profits? Yes, Schwab agreed, but "it would be bad manufacturing, I can tell you." [25] He spoke for the entire industry: no connection existed between earnings and productivity.

This view was quite recent. In earlier years the income of production men, paid on a tonnage basis, had actually reflected their output.[26] This, however, was a condition of manual operations. Mechanization, vastly increasing productivity, inevitably divorced output from earnings. As Schwab pointed out, the growth of blast furnace output came, not from greater human exertion, but from huge capital expenditure that had to be made profitable. The increase in worker productivity, even as a result of lengthened hours, operated ultimately to reduce labor costs.

The determinants of earnings lay elsewhere. Chief among these were the related factors of trade conditions and labor supply. The response of wages was very sensitive. Peak years invariably developed labor shortages. With prices up, pay raises were no hardship. The advances of 1905–6, said the *Iron Age,* "came from the recognition by employers of the fact that demand has outrun supply." [27] Wage increases alone seemed to fill the emptying ranks in prosperous years.

The tide ran the other way during depressions. Then steel men easily convinced workmen to accept reductions. "When you shut down and they get hungry, they are anxious to make any terms," observed John Topping of Republic Steel.[28] President J. A. Leishman told Carnegie that a 15 per cent cut for some Duquesne men

[25] *Stanley Hearings,* II, 1359–1360.

[26] The sliding scale policy of the Amalgamated Association of Iron and Steel Workers assumed the permanence of the rate structure. Once equitably settled, rates would fluctuate only with prices. The sliding scale was satisfactory for puddling and tin plate mills, but not for steel, where mechanical improvements continually forced changes in the rate structure.

[27] *IA,* December 27, 1906, p. 1748. For an example of responsive rate changes in the 1890's, see the Pennsylvania Steel scale in *Report on Immigration,* VIII, 611.

[28] U.S. House, Committee on Ways and Means, *Tariff Hearings,* 62 Cong., 3rd Sess. (1913), p. 966.

could be arranged "without much trouble. THE TOTAL SAVING would amount to about $25,000 per year. . . . We should give notice to-morrow as we start the works up next week." One steel official reported in 1897: "The American Wire Company about two weeks ago laid before its wire drawers the ultimatum of a ten per cent reduction or an indefinite shut-down of its works. The men took the reduction and the works are running." [29] This was common practice in the depression of the 1890's.

Earnings were the first target for economy. During the hard year of 1888, a wire mill manager reported, job rates "have been care-fully revised and reduced, so that I estimate that a saving of above $15,000 net per year has been made." [30] Announcing drastic cuts in 1893, a Carnegie official explained:

> With this new [wage] scale in force the firm will be in a posi-tion to compete more successfully than ever before, and will probably have a material advantage over many of its competitors in cost sheets.

That year wages fell an average 25 per cent in iron and steel. When the Carnegie-Illinois war broke out, Powell Stackhouse of Cambria recalled, "We were looking everywhere to reduce our costs, and labor got its share of it. . . . We got them down low. We had to." [31] These were unusually severe times, but at every downturn wages immediately plummeted after prices.

Steel wages were markedly less stable than in American industry generally. The annual variation in hourly rates during the 1890's from the ten-year average was never more than 3 per cent. For iron and steel occupations, on the other hand, hourly rates during the depressed middle 1890's ranged from 10 to almost 30 per cent below their decade averages, and were correspondingly above the

[29] J. A. Leishman to Carnegie, January 3, 1896, Carnegie Papers; William Edenborn to John Lambert, February 19, 1897, Consolidated Steel and Wire Company, American Steel and Wire Collection.

[30] C. S. Hall, Memorandum, April 13, 1889, Washburn and Moen, Ameri-can Steel and Wire Collection.

[31] Carnegie official quoted in *IA*, December 28, 1893, p. 1184; Stackhouse, in *U.S. v. U.S.S., Testimony*, IV, 1708.

averages at the opening and end of the decade. Again, while hourly rates for the country as a whole remained virtually constant during the recession of 1904, in steel they fell nearly 20 per cent in some occupations.[32]

Over a span of years the fluctuations canceled themselves, and the effect on the wage trend was negligible. But it helped to shape the steel men's views on pay determination. The general belief was "that labor, in its rewards, is as sensitive to the great law of supply and demand as any necessary of life." The analogy had a powerful influence. Manufacturers might differ on whether to "buy labor in the cheapest market" or hire "the best men and pay the highest wages." The basic assumption was identical: the labor market, not productivity, determined wages. And the hard logic of economy could be applied without qualm to workmen's earnings, since labor was "a commodity like anything else." The market-place concept of labor was at the root of wage calculation.

The labor market favored the aims of the steelmakers — which were, simply, to hold steady wages in the period of rapidly rising labor productivity. Two pools of labor existed: one of the possessors of the vital ironmaking and steelmaking skills; the other of men offering only their muscle. The industry achieved its ends in both areas.

Within the bounds of the business cycle, the wage of the ordinary laborer proved relatively stable in the two decades before 1900. Ohio blast furnace workmen averaged 12.3 cents an hour in 1882, and 12.7 cents in the equivalent year of 1900.[33] The scale of the Cambria Steel Company (see Table 1), which is available for the early period, typified the wage movement for the unskilled in the industry. The long-term supply of unskilled men, ample for the needs of the industry, necessitated no significant change of the wage level.

[32] U.S. Bureau of Labor, *Bulletin*, No. 77 (July 1908), pp. 7, 93–96.

[33] Ohio Bureau of Labor Statistics, *Report* (1882), pp. 106–107, and (1900), p. 414. See also U.S. Senate, Committee on Finance, *Wholesale Prices, Wages and Transportation* [The Aldrich Report], 4 vols., 52 Cong., 2nd Sess. (1893) IV, 1570.

TABLE I. Daily wage scale of laborers at the Cambria Steel Company, 1880–1900.

Classification	1880	1885	1890	1895	1900
Laborer, first class, blast furnace (12 hrs.)	1.10	1.04	1.00	1.00	1.20
Cinder man, blast furnace (12 hrs.)	1.55	1.15	1.20	1.26	1.40
Laborer, Bessemer dept. (10 hrs.)	1.23	1.00	1.10	1.10	1.10
Laborer, open-hearth (10 hrs.)	1.23	1.00	1.20	1.00	1.20
Ash man, blooming mill (10 hrs.)	1.23	1.50	1.30	1.00	—

Source: *Report on Immigration,* VIII, 448–451.

After 1900, however, the pay scale was gradually forced upward. The average hourly rate for common labor in forty-nine steel plants increased from 13.7 cents in 1901 to 16.1 cents in 1910. This was a period of generally rising wage rates, calculated by Paul Douglas to average almost 20 per cent for all manufacturing industries. It was also a time of increasing living costs — according to Douglas, 20.8 per cent from 1901 to 1910.[34] The ten-year gain of 17.5 per cent for unskilled steel labor, a response to these outside pressures, was not an excessive charge in the cost sheets of the steel companies.

Meanwhile the market position of the skilled men was deteriorating under the impact of technological advance. In short supply in the early years, their bargaining position had then been very strong. East St. Louis rollers and heaters, for example, had earned forty-two dollars a week in 1884 — 467 per cent more than laborers. Such a wide differential was characteristic of the early period.[35] When the strategic importance of the skilled steelworkers

[34] *Labor Conditions,* III, 232, 252; Paul H. Douglas, *Real Wages in the United States* (Boston, 1930), pp. 41, 130.

[35] See, for example, Illinois Bureau of Labor Statsitics, *Report* (1886), p. 354; U.S. Commissioner of Labor, *Report* (1886), pp. 372–386.

weakened, however, employers seized the opportunity to cut down the "aristocracy of labor."

Skilled men, although paid on a tonnage basis, did not benefit from their rising productivity. When new equipment was installed in some Homestead mills in May 1893, the company cut the rollers from fifteen to seven cents a ton and others accordingly. The tonnage scale at Cambria, shown in Table 2, demonstrated the rate decline under the pressure of mechanization.

TABLE 2. Tonnage rate (per hundred tons) scale for skilled workers at the Cambria Steel Company, 1880–1900.

Classification	1880	1885	1890	1895	1900
Rail mill roller	6.10	4.23	4.61	3.18	3.00
Rail mill heater	33.00	22.87	27.00	22.41	22.41
Blooming mill heater	2.60	1.68	1.76	0.42	—
Bessemer vesselman	3.83	1.89	1.60	0.80	0.88

Source: *Report on Immigration*, VIII, 448–452.

The weakening position of the high-priced men eventually manifested itself in their income. The top ranks "have been systematically brought down to a level consistent with the pay of other workers," a Pittsburgh official told John A. Fitch. Schwab remarked in 1901 that he had "materially reduced" wages at Homestead since 1892, putting an end to the system "by which one man receives $100 a day and another $1." The higher figure was a gross exaggeration, but Schwab expressed accurately enough the intention of steelmakers to achieve "a better distribution of the wages."

The actual decline in the earnings of the topmost group became evident after 1900. At twenty-eight plants surveyed by the Bureau of Labor, the small percentage of men earning sixty cents an hour fell by one-fifth from 1900 to 1910. The bar mills, which required many skilled workers, experienced a reduction of one-quarter in the percentage of men over fifty cents an hour. The daily earnings of the highly skilled men at the Homestead plate mill similarly shrank by one-fifth from 1892 to 1907, despite the change from eight- to twelve-hour shifts.[36] The application of the policy was most evident during the major adjustments at the peaks and troughs of the business cycle. Pay cuts invariably hit hardest the high-priced men and, conversely, increases benefited them least. The lower reaches of the skilled ranks and the growing semiskilled group suffered less from the efforts to narrow wage differentials. The

TABLE 3. The distribution of hourly earnings at twenty-eight steel plants, 1900 and 1910.

Classified hourly earnings	1900		1910	
	Number	Per cent	Number	Per cent
Under 14 cents	649	5.5	226	2.0
14 and under 16 cents	5,436	46.3	304	2.7
16 and under 18 cents	1,543	13.1	4,163	37.1
18 and under 20 cents	749	6.4	1,587	14.1
20 and under 25 cents	1,289	11.0	2,095	18.7
25 and under 30 cents	740	6.3	1,010	9.0
30 and under 40 cents	599	5.1	1,039	9.3
40 and under 50 cents	278	2.4	328	2.9
50 and under 60 cents	137	1.2	230	2.0
60 and under 70 cents	91	0.8	119	1.1
70 and under 80 cents	84	0.7	54	0.5
80 and under 90 cents	69	0.6	36	0.3
90 cents and under $1	25	0.2	17	0.2
$1 and over	48	0.4	20	0.2

Source: *Labor Conditions*, III, 236.

daily earnings of tonnage workers at two representative plants rose only 7 per cent from 1900 to 1910, as compared to the average hourly increase of 17.5 per cent from 1901 to 1910 for common laborers.

[36] *Labor Conditions*, III, 237; Fitch, pp. 157, 164. Discounting effects of the business cycle, the earnings of skilled steelworkers apparently remained fairly stable between 1880 and 1900. There appear to be no satisfactory statistics on the earnings of tonnage steelworkers from 1880 to 1890, although the Aldrich Report includes some data on skilled ironworkers. Bureau of Labor, *Bulletin*, No. 77, pp. 93–96 indicates no significant change in the average hourly earnings of skilled men in selected plants from 1890 to 1900.

The Bureau of Labor survey of twenty-eight plants in 1910, shown in Table 3, indicated the shifting distribution of wages. The trend in steel was not typical of industry generally. In New Jersey, whose labor statistics were presented in comparable form, the upward movement increased the percentages distributed in the higher wage categories.[37]

Pay determination for skilled workers was undergoing a fundamental change. There had once been a genuine difference between hourly rates and tonnage rates as methods of wage fixing. The distinction became only formal in later years. Piecework retained a general incentive value. But mechanization had ended its function as the determinant of labor costs and as the means of raising output. Tonnage rates, like hourly rates, were cut in 1904 solely for the purpose of reducing earnings. No significant technological advances came at this point, nor was output raised noticeably as a result of the reduction.[38] Wages were to be grounded on the common labor rate, the U.S. Steel Finance Committee had decided in December 1903, "other labor to be based on same." [39] Earning levels would henceforth be figured on the base of the rate for unskilled labor.

There were several minor wage determinants. Rates differed by districts: lowest in the South, highest in Pittsburgh and Chicago. They varied also by company. The Steel Corporation carried the "equalizing" process furthest, paying unskilled labor the highest wages in the industry, skilled labor the lowest. Regularity was also considered. John W. Gates of Illinois Steel defended the sharp re-

[37] New Jersey Bureau of Statistics, *Report* (1901), p. 101, (1911), p. 122, in *Labor Conditions,* III, 234. The comparison is not as conclusive as indicated by the U.S. Bureau of Labor writer, since the New Jersey statistics were for weekly earnings, and were not broken down beyond $20.00 in 1901, or beyond $25.00 in 1911. However, the increase during the decade in the percentage of New Jersey males earning $20.00 or more weekly was considerably greater than for steelworkers earning forty cents or more an hour: 6 to 10 per cent for New Jersey males, 6.3 to 7.2 per cent for steelworkers.

[38] See analysis of 1904 reduction in *Labor Conditions,* III, 256–258.

[39] U.S. Steel, Finance Committee Minutes, December 1, 1903, *Stanley Hearings,* VI, 3890.

ductions of 1897 by the resulting "benefit of steady employment." [40]
Blast furnaces often paid lower rates because work there was more
regular than in steel departments. And companies could attract
skilled mechanics at substandard wages because of longer hours
and steadier jobs in the mills.[41] Steel men took into account every
circumstance that would minimize pay rates.

The wage pattern of 1910 embodied the economizing aims of the
industry. The bottom half of the labor force earned under eighteen
cents an hour, one-fifth less than sixteen cents an hour. The semiskilled quarter received between eighteen and twenty-five cents an
hour. The skilled men were above that; but few — less than 5 per
cent — made more than fifty cents. Workmen not directly involved
in production were similarly divided. The one-fifth who were
skilled workers in the mechanical trades earned between twenty-
five and fifty cents an hour, below the standard outside the industry.

The test of wages lay as much in regularity as rate. Employed
for the entire prosperous year of 1910, almost no steelworker would
have totaled under $400; one-sixth would have received under $500.
The actual earnings were substantially less. In plants active for at
least six months in 1910, one-tenth could have earned no more than
$400, one-fourth $500. The average annual wage for 1910 was $697,
$46 over the average for all manufacturing industry. This was an
increase of 27 per cent over 1890, but, because of rising living costs,
the real wage gain was only 3 per cent.[42]

The censuses of manufactures tallied the achievement of a labor
policy focused on the cost sheets. In the two decades after 1890,
the furnace worker's productivity tripled in exchange for an income rise of one-half; the steelworker's output doubled in exchange
for an increase of one-fifth. At bottom, the remarkable cost reduction of American steel manufacture rested on those figures.

[40] Illinois Steel Company, *Annual Report* (1897).

[41] Although once customary, overtime work in 1910 was rarely paid at a
higher rate, even in the mechanical trades where time-and-a-half was general
outside the industry.

[42] Douglas, pp. 271–274; *Labor Conditions*, III, 218, 222.

The accomplishment was possible only with a labor force powerless to oppose the decisions of the steel men. That requirement of economy shaped the attitude toward labor unions and in the end determined their fate in the industry.

Chapter III

The Breakdown of Craft Unionism

Trade unions had become firmly established in the early years of the iron and steel industry. The Sons of Vulcan, the Heaters' and Rollers' Union, and the Roll Hands' Union covered all the skilled metalmaking crafts in the mills. For amity and mutual support during strikes, the three unions joined together in 1876 to form the Amalgamated Association of Iron and Steel Workers. The consolidated organization prospered. At its apex in 1891 the Amalgamated Association counted over 24,000 members, according to its estimate roughly two-thirds of the eligible workmen.[1] It was among the leading unions in the American Federation of Labor.

The main strength of the Association rested in the iron mills west of the Alleghenies. Developing out of the circumstances of iron manufacture, the union suited very well the needs of the industry. It negotiated annually uniform scales for the Western mills; equalized hours, output, and working conditions; kept in check the independent-minded ironworkers; and guaranteed union mills a supply of the scarce puddlers and rollers. The Amalgamated Association acted as a stabilizing force on the chaotic iron industry. Hard blows were dealt on both sides, and in the summer of 1882

[1] Edward W. Bemis, "The Homestead Strike," *Journal of Political Economy,* II (June 1894), p. 370. For the early history, see Jesse S. Robinson, *Amalgamated Association of Iron, Steel and Tin Workers* (Baltimore, 1920), ch. 1; C. D. Wright, "Amalgamated Association," *Quarterly Journal of Economics,* VII (July 1893), 400–432; Fitch, *Steel Workers,* pp. 75–89 and App. I, which gives the documents on amalgamation; W. H. Martin, "A Brief History of the Amalgamated Association," *Amalgamated Journal,* August 30, 1906, pp. 1, 9.

a bitter general strike broke out. But employers and union officials knew and respected each other. Usually, amicableness reigned.

The Amalgamated Association spread with less vigor into the developing steel industry. On entering steel manufacture, iron firms as a rule accepted the extension of the union into their new departments. Steel mills offered more resistance, but the Amalgamated was moderately successful here also. In the Pittsburgh district both the Homestead and Jones and Laughlins works were organized, but not the Duquesne plant or the Edgar Thomson Works after 1885. Ohio and Illinois steel companies generally recognized the Association. East of the Alleghenies, where the union had not achieved permanent success in the iron mills, the steel plants were unorganized. The Cambria Works at Johnstown had been nonunion since the early 1870's. An Amalgamated lodge started in 1890 at Steelton, Pennsylvania, but collapsed the following July for lack of support from the National Lodge. The steel industry was possibly half unionized in 1892.

Technological advance placed the union in a difficult position. Its policies were posited on an industry whose methods were fixed, manual, and uniform. The Amalgamated sought honestly to accommodate to steel manufacture. "The Association never objects to improvement," said President William Weihe. If changes "do away with certain jobs they make no objection. They believe in the American idea that the genius of the country should not be retarded." The contract with Illinois Steel required members, in case of changes, "to assist in developing such improvement and abide by whatever modification such improvement may permit in the rates and number of men." Machinery at the Edgar Thomson Works in 1885 displaced 57 of 69 men on the heating furnaces, 51 of 63 men on the rail-mill train, and similar numbers elsewhere. The two lodges at the plant dissolved as a result, but the union did not complain.[2]

[2] Weihe quoted, Bemis, *Journal of Political Economy,* II, 375; Amalgamated Association of Iron and Steel Workers, *Proceedings* (1891), p. 3412; Robinson, p. 125; *National Labor Tribune,* February 7, March 14, 1885, cited hereafter as *NLT.*

After repeated failures, the Amalgamated Association discarded its established policy of attaining a standard scale "to get the cost of labor as nearly uniform as possible . . . so as not to . . . give any manufacturer an advantage." Instead of an industry-wide wage conference, as was held in the iron industry, each steel mill lodge negotiated separately for local rates. "The improved machinery requires the men directly interested in that plant to know best what can be done," explained the president.[3] The Association accepted the principle that increased output through mechanical advance necessitated rate adjustments. At Homestead, for example, the men took sizable cuts in the settlement of a victorious strike in 1889. The tonnage rate there was half that at the unimproved mills at Jones and Laughlins.

The union acquiesced in other ways. Customarily, rollers and heaters had hired and paid their crews. The union allowed the Homestead managers to take "the responsibility from the rollers," and the practice was dropped eventually at other steel plants. The Association left also the determination of hours to the employers, although this was less concession than indifference. The union took up the A.F.L. eight-hour campaign halfheartedly, considering it inadvisable "to go into conflict in order to obtain it." Finally, output limitation, designed to protect the ironworkers from overstrain, fell into disuse in the mechanized steel plants.[4]

Accommodation did not satisfy the steelmasters. Indeed, as the logic of economy sharpened, only total submission could have finally sufficed. For the maximization of labor savings required complete freedom from union interference.

Manufacturers felt increasingly constricted. In the course of its experience in the puddling mills, the Amalgamated Association had accumulated an extensive stock of rules to protect its members.

---

[3] U.S. Senate, *The Employment of Armed Bodies of Men for Private Purposes,* Report No. 1280, 52nd Cong., 2nd Sess. (1892–1893), pp. 201–202. Cited hereafter as *Senate Report 1280.*

[4] *Homestead Investigation,* pp. 113–114, 124; *NLT,* July 18, 1890, July 14, 1892; Pittsburgh *Post,* July 4, 1892; *Industrial Commission,* VII, 389, XIII, 504; Robinson, pp. 107–110.

The regulations were carried over into the steel plants. The Memorandum of Agreement for the Homestead Works, for instance, contained fifty-eight pages of "footnotes" defining and limiting the rules of work for Amalgamated men. In addition, strong lodges often abused their power. A prominent Carnegie official years later told the investigator John A. Fitch that the union had run the Homestead plant, and old workmen corroborated his recollection. Amalgamated conventions, in fact, were obliged to pass resolutions against the frequent strikes "for little frivolous purposes." [5]

The union was a serious obstacle to efficiency. H. C. Frick complained to Carnegie: "The mills have never been able to turn out the product they should, owing to being held back by the Amalgamated men." Carnegie saw the ending of the union as the "chance to reorganize the whole affair, and . . . exact good reasons for *employing every man*. Far too many men required by Amalgamated rules." [6] A conflict soon became unavoidable.

The decisive issue was wages. Despite the union's willingness to accept cuts, the central problem of fixing the new rate after an improvement remained unsolved. According to Carnegie, the company rule was "to give the men one-half the advantage of improved machinery, and one-half for itself," but that was for public consumption. The matter was never clear-cut, nor were the interests of union and company easily reconciled. Renewed with every technological advance, squabbling over rates was a constant irritant to relations.

The wage debate leading to the Homestead strike of 1892 demonstrated the complexities. The company demanded cuts for 325 skilled men. It argued:

> We had put in new improvements in some departments which increased the output and reduced the work, and we thought we

[5] Amalgamated Association, *Proceedings* (1889), p. 2786; Fitch, p. 103. This view is generally accepted. See, for example, John R. Commons, "Wage Earners of Pittsburgh," *Charities and the Commons,* March 6, 1909, p. 1064; Charles A. Gulick, *The Labor Policy of the United States Steel Corporation* (New York, 1924), p. 90.

[6] Frick to Carnegie, October 31, 1892, quoted in Harvey, *Frick,* p. 177; Carnegie quoted in Bridge, *Carnegie Company,* p. 206.

were entitled to some of the benefits. . . . We were paying more money than our competitors in the same class of work and we had also invested more money in the machinery to do that work than our competitors.

The criterion was whether improvements resulted in a higher day's pay. The company had, in fact, recently hired a former Amalgamated secretary "to inquire into wages paid in other mills." The reductions, Frick claimed, were calculated to put earnings on a par with, not below, those of steelworkers elsewhere.[7]

The Amalgamated Association, on the other hand, emphasized costs and profits rather than wages.

It is stated by the company with much force that it is not their desire to reduce their workmen below others. The cost of production to the Carnegie Company at Homestead is decidedly in favor of the company as compared with mills of that character.[8]

The men had taken substantial cuts three years earlier. The company exaggerated the gains by using May 1892 — an abnormal month — for the comparison. The increased output, moreover, was largely due to harder work; delays were fewer and operations faster. And the improved machinery was repaying the investment by replacing men. While the firm pressed for equal earnings, the union wanted as nearly a standard tonnage rate as was possible with continuing improvements.

Both sides had legitimate arguments. But it was a Carnegie partner who pronounced the fateful judgment: "The Amalgamated placed a tax on improvements, therefore the Amalgamated had to go."[9]

The crisis had approached after the Amalgamated victory at Homestead in 1889. Membership jumped by half in the next two years, and the balance in the treasury rose to $146,000. Conscious of its mounting strength, the union grew more belligerent. Relations

---

[7] *Homestead Investigation*, p. 127; *Senate Report 1280*, p. 153.

[8] Quoted in *Homestead Investigation*, p. 186.

[9] Quoted in Hogg, "Homestead Strike," p. 242.

became increasingly tense. John W. Gates, after running into trouble with the union at his Joliet plant, angrily urged another wiremaker to "keep the Amal. Association out of your mill as they are certainly a bad lot." [10] Manufacturers talked, without much enthusiasm, of an employers' association at the meeting with the British Iron and Steel Institute in America in 1890. Clearly, only the Carnegie Company had the resources and leadership to take on the union.

The Pittsburgh firm was seeking the showdown in 1892. Before leaving for Europe, Carnegie drafted a notice breaking with the Amalgamated Association because a "firm cannot run Union and Non-Union." He instructed the Homestead superintendent to *"roll a large lot of plates ahead,* which can be finished, should the works be stopped for a time." [11] Frick rejected this frontal strategy. He would force the issue more deviously. The company's contract proposals, although not extreme, were offered as an ultimatum. If the union did not accept by June 24, no further conferences would be held, and the works would run nonunion. A meeting on June 23, despite minor concessions on both sides, ended fruitlessly; and on July 1 the Homestead Works closed down.

The fence, newly built and topped with barbed wire, made clear the objective of the company. It had never before refused to bargain over a contract offer. "The people employed in Homestead thought that it was simply a proposition made by the firm that they knew we would not accept," observed a strike leader during the Senate inquiry. "They did it with the intention of forcing this trouble." The local newspaper noted, "it was not so much a question of disagreement as to wages, but a design upon labor organization." The company had trapped the union into the strike.

When the cause became hopeless, the strikers appealed to Whitelaw Reid, the Republican vice-presidential candidate. "Simply let the Carnegie Company recognize the Amalgamated Association by reopening the conference doors. . . . There is no disposition

[10] Gates to G. S. Douglas, July 10, 1890, St. Louis Wire Mill Company, American Steel and Wire Collection.

[11] Bridge, pp. 204–205, gives the entire notice.

on the part of the employees to stand upon a question of scale, or wages, or hours, or anything else." [12] The company's refusal was the final proof of its intentions.

The battle against the Pinkertons had played into Frick's hands, enabling him to put the issue on the high ground of principle. The strikers had kept the owners from lawful possession of the works. The violation of the rights of property, indeed, was the essence of unionism. After the battle Frick announced:

> The question at issue is a very grave one. It is whether the Carnegie Company or the Amalgamated Association shall have absolute control of our plant. . . . Under no circumstances will we have any further dealings with the Amalgamated Association as an organization. This is final.

Not even Reid's plea that the strike was damaging the Republican campaign could move Frick to relent. By the time the strike ended on November 17, the union had been rooted out of the Carnegie mills.[13]

The fruits of the conflict seemed well worth the expense. The company ascribed the successes of the next years largely to the strike. When steel war threatened in 1900, Carnegie wrote confidently, "we have a great advantage over others, running non-union." [14] The firm was determined not to lose the asset. It crushed an organizing effort in 1896. A more formidable movement began in May 1899, when three hundred Homestead men formed a lodge. President T. J. Shaffer tried without success to secure a conference. Frick cabled from London: "stop Works if necessary to

[12] H. O'Donnell to W. Reid, July 16, 1892, Bemis, *Journal of Political Economy,* II, 385.

[13] Frick, in Pittsburgh *Post,* July 8, 1892. On June 21–22, the scales had been signed for the Carnegie iron and finishing mills. These struck in sympathy and were declared nonunion at the end of the strike. At the unorganized Duquesne Works the men also came out, but returned in early August.

[14] Carnegie Company Minutes, July 31, 1900, *U.S.* v. *U.S.S., Government Exhibits,* VI, 1889.

hold present position." When the union attempt collapsed, the Carnegie Company was irrevocably lost.[15]

The tide turned swiftly against the Amalgamated Association. During the 1889 Homestead strike other steel firms had withheld signing a contract. A Jones and Laughlins official stated: "This company will make no terms with its men until there is a settlement at Homestead." It could not pay higher wages than its chief rival. This view hardened after the second strike, which was followed immediately by the great depression. The superintendent at the Joliet steel mill handed the men an ultimatum: unless they took a one-third slice, he would start up nonunion. The Association accepted. In general, wage cuts matched those at the Carnegie plants. The disability of the Association continued into prosperity. It was unable to hold back Sunday labor. "The steel mills are getting away from us," lamented President Shaffer. "It is becoming worse in the steel mills." [16]

With the union's weakness demonstrated, other steelmakers contemplated following Carnegie's example. During the Homestead strike, John Gates had assured the Carnegie Company of his willingness to postpone the fulfillment of its contract until after the struggle with the Amalgamated: "Fight them to a finish with hard gloves, and give them no quarter after you get them in a corner and we will take the rods in 1894 if necessary." [17] The grudge against the Amalgamated was not forgiven.

Efforts at dislodgement soon began in earnest. Jones and Laughlins refused to sign the scale in 1897; by 1900 not a steel plant of consequence in western Pennsylvania recognized the Association. The union continued somewhat longer in the steel mills of the

[15] Carnegie Company Minutes, June 27, 1899, August 15, 1899, *Government Exhibits*, III, 1257, 1264; *Industrial Commission*, VII, 385; Pittsburgh *Dispatch*, August 4, 1901.

[16] *Industrial Commission*, VII, 391-392; *EMJ*, July 15, 1893, p. 60, September 30, 1893, p. 376; *Iron and Steel Trade Journal*, December 8, 1900, p. 542; Hogg, pp. 34, 203.

[17] Gates to J. C. Fleming, August 9, 1892, St. Louis Wire Mill Company, American Steel and Wire Collection.

West, where relations had long been amicable. Nothing demonstrated more sharply the debility of the Amalgamated than the ease
with which these lodges were uprooted. Some disbanded voluntarily. In 1903 at Mingo Junction, Ohio, the last of the great steel
plants became nonunion. Even minor steel companies had little
difficulty in freeing themselves.

The precipitous decline of a firmly established and conservative
union, puzzling to observers, rested on a fatal weakness. The
Amalgamated Association was limited to skilled men; its strength
lay in its control of the supply of vital steelmaking skills. The
method of coercing recalcitrant employers was simple and effective:
"to withhold our skills from them until such time as they agree."
This strategy worked very well where skill was paramount. The
Association failed to hold a plant only when the "company could
get all the non-union men it wanted." In general, the Amalgamated held the loyalty of the skilled men, and was consequently
successful. During this period, significantly, Carnegie was known
for his friendly attitude toward the Amalgamated.

Mechanization undermined the base of the union's power. When
union men were irreplaceable, strikes were a waiting game. Using
improved machinery, however, employers could start up with new
men and a nucleus of loyal experienced hands. Thus, in 1901
Schwab observed that the relation of skills to union strength had
been greatly exaggerated. He could take a green hand — say an
intelligent farmworker — and make a melter of him in six or
eight weeks. Strike tactics therefore changed from quiescence to
importing strikebreakers.

The Carnegie management had astutely perceived the shifting
situation. During the 1889 strike the company sent one hundred
deputy sheriffs to take possession of the works. The strikers, no
less astute, disarmed them, and shipped them back to Pittsburgh
minus coats and caps. No violence accompanied this tentative
effort, and the company retreated. The following year, however,
Carnegie prevented the unionization of his newly acquired
Duquesne Works by utilizing inexperienced help. The lesson was

learned for 1892. The Duquesne success, together with the elimination of the Amalgamated from the Edgar Thomson Works in 1885, provided also the special advantage of a multi-plant operation which was only partly unionized; Carnegie could count on some production no matter what happened at Homestead.

Frick had previously contacted the Pinkerton agency, and on June 25 he requested three hundred guards. Frick planned to open the works to nonunion men on July 6. Determined to keep the plant down, the strikers organized on military lines, and took virtual control of the town. Forewarned by an elaborate alarm system, they were prepared when barges attempted to slip up to the plant under cover of darkness. The Pinkertons were met by a barrage of gunfire. The strikers won a Pyrrhic victory that led only to the arrival of the militia and the opening of the works.[18]

Homestead was in fact exceptional; for the eight lodges in the plant, despite a membership limited to 800 of the 3,800 workmen, were able to bring out almost the entire labor force. But for the battle, the union might well have won the strike. Laborers, however, would not usually follow the skilled men. Dislodgement at other steel mills therefore occurred peacefully and easily with the

---

[18] Carnegie's position on bringing in the Pinkertons is rather obscure. In a famous article in the *Forum* in 1886 he had argued against trying to replace strikers with nonunion men; a man's right to his job was supreme. During the strike, Carnegie hid himself away in Scotland and would only say that matters were out of his hands. Hendrick, his biographer, claims that Carnegie was against the move but felt obliged to support Frick, especially after the latter's near-assassination. Hendrick quotes as evidence this letter of Carnegie to George Lauder, a partner, July 17, 1892: "Matters at home *bad*. Still we must keep quiet and do all we can to support Frick and those at the seat of war." *Carnegie*, I, 404. But the letter in the Carnegie Papers in the Library of Congress reads: Matters at home *bad* — such a fiasco trying to send guards by Boat and leaving space between River and fences for the men to get opposite the landing and fire — Still we must keep quiet and do all we can to support Frick and those at the seat of war." Carnegie saw the wisdom of opening with new men in an improved plant like Homestead. He simply felt that Frick had bungled the job.

lessening dependence on Amalgamated men. By 1910 the Association listed but one small open-hearth plant under contract. The union had been driven from the basic steel industry.

The Amalgamated Association faced its decline in steel with a certain equanimity. With the perfection of continuous rolling, it was true, all the organized rod and wire mills had also been lost. And the union had fared poorly in its iron mills during the depression. The Association, nevertheless, continued to dominate the iron industry in the West. It had contracts also with the hoop mills outside the Pittsburgh district, and with several plants of the National Tube Company.

Mainly, its confidence rested on the rapid growth of the sheet and tin plate industries since 1890. Both required highly trained men — willing Amalgamated recruits. The union, in fact, had helped to build the supply by urging displaced rolling men into the related occupations in the sheet and tin mills. The Amalgamated Association's growth there coincided with its decline in the steel mills. By 1900 its scale covered three-quarters of the sheet mills and all but one of the tin mills in the country, and it had added "Tin Workers" to its title.

The union remained limited to the skilled crafts. Its commitment was demonstrated in 1899 when the tin house workers were organized, largely through Amalgamated efforts. Because theirs was not skilled work, the tinners were told to form a separate organization. The puddling and finishing branches of the industry promised a flourishing future without painful alteration of the union's craft basis. Only when it was too late did the Amalgamated leadership perceive that the expectation was false.

The mergers at the close of the century were grossly misjudged. The movement at first appeared to be a healthy development, driving out speculators and giving stability and uniformity to wages. More important, combinations favorable to the union greatly eased the tasks of negotiation and organization. Six of the plants entering the American Tin Plate Company had been unorganized. The company agreed after a token strike to recognize the union at five, excepting the Monessen, Pennsylvania, mill because of its special equipment. It accepted also the unionizing of the tin house workers. The Amalgamated Association understandably took a bright view of consolidations. "I have so much respect for them I never call them trusts," said the president in 1899. "We believe the men who work in rolling mills can control the situation." [19] As it turned out, he was overly optimistic.

For combination, if it bestowed benefits, contained also seeds of destruction. The American Sheet Steel Company, organized a year after the tin plate trust, was not friendly. The possibility of contracting with the Association for its seven nonunion mills "was not a matter for discussion and could not even be considered." [20] Now appeared the darker side of mergers that controlled both union and nonunion mills. While all the unorganized sheet plants ran full in the first six months of 1901, nine union mills were idle. The Amalgamated Association lost several mills in the half-year because "the trust, by refraining from operating these mills, forced our people into agreeing to leave the Association." Only unionization of every plant could nullify the threat. That immediately became the goal of the union. The constitution was amended to enable the union to focus its full strength against hostile combinations.

> Should one mill in a combine or trust have a difficulty, all mills in said combine or trust shall cease work until such grievance is settled.

When the United States Steel Corporation merged the earlier trusts, the Amalgamated Association saw that it had no time to waste. Once firmly established, the Corporation would be impregnable.[21] Resolving to press its demands, the union presented scales for every mill in the American Tin Plate, Sheet Steel, and Steel Hoop companies.

[19] *Industrial Commission,* VII, 395–396, also, I, 861, 876, 926–928.
[20] Amalgamated Association, *Proceedings* (1901), p. 6046; *Iron and Steel Trade Journal,* July 21, 1900, p. 58.
[21] *Labor Conditions,* III, 120–121; Amalgamated Association, *Proceedings* (1901), p. 6046, (1902), p. 6297.

The formulation of a union policy had occupied the Executive Committee of the Steel Corporation from its first meetings. Three factors shaped its decision. Most important, the Corporation inherited the antiunion bias of the economizing movement; many of the operating executives were extremely hostile. As a whole, the Executive Committee believed that "a concern operating with a union was pretty badly handicapped." It recognized, secondly, that the Amalgamated Association was "very strong" in roughly one-third of its holdings. Finally, strikes had to be avoided in the precarious early months: "A policy of antagonism . . . might be disastrous. . . . We must not lose sight of the financial interests of the Corporation and must keep clear of anything that might be prejudicial to these interests." These considerations determined the compromise resolution adopted on June 17, several days before the first conference with the union.

That we are unalterably opposed to any extension of union labor and advise subsidiary companies to take firm position when these questions come up and say that they are not going to recognize it, that is, any extension of unions in mills where they do not now exist; that great care should be used to prevent trouble and that they promptly report and confer with this corporation.

The subsidiary presidents were instructed to sign reasonable scales for the union mills — but only for these.[22]

The issue was joined, therefore, as soon as the conferences began. The tin plate officials refused to sign for the Monessen mill, pointing to the nonunion sheet mills. Concession would hurt their reputation at the New York office. The Tin Plate Company, it appears, agreed orally to give up the Monessen mill if the union won a contract covering all the sheet mills. The American Sheet Steel Company rejected outright the Amalgamated demand. Relations with the company had deteriorated during the year. There had been a bitter organizing strike at the Dewees Wood mill in

[22] The minutes covering these meetings, April 20–July 12, 1901, are fortunately available, having been secured in the course of the federal investigations of the steel industry. They are printed in *Stanley Hearings*, VI, 3819–3833, and in *Labor Conditions*, III, App. D, 497–506.

McKeesport. Sheet officials now refused to concede this mill. Even worse, they would not renew the contract for the union mills at Saltsburg and Scottdale, Pennsylvania. The sheet company, instead of offering a compromise, was demanding a further surrender from the union. President T. J. Shaffer came out of the final conference in a rage. The company spokesman, P. F. Smith, had not even attempted to negotiate. "He sat there like a great judge without a jury. . . . No matter what we said, it had no effect." [23] Shaffer had maneuvered himself into a corner. He had no choice but to order a strike in the sheet mills for July 1. The men in the hoop mills were called out also, although at that point only some Ohio plants were organized.

The union strategy was to apply pressure on the sheet company through the Steel Corporation. Shaffer informed the tin plate subsidiary that, in compliance with the constitution, he would be obliged to shut down its mills unless the sheet and hoop strike was settled within a week. Shaffer had measured the position of U.S. Steel with fair accuracy. "This is the very worst time of the very worst year to have any trouble," warned Chairman Elbert H. Gary on July 2 in apprehension of a widened strike. The union leaders had also judged rightly the embarrassment of the Executive Committee over the hostile attitude of the sheet officials. When twelve men were discharged at the Wellsville, Ohio, mill for forming a lodge during the first week of the strike, the Executive Committee finally decided to overrule the management of the sheet company. The Committee voted on July 8 to compromise with the union, settling "the matter on the very best terms possible and as quickly as possible and have no row now." [24]

[23] *NLT*, July 4, 1901. The *National Labor Tribune* is indispensible for following the course of the strike. The important documents are printed in Amalgamated Association, *Proceedings* (1902), pp. 6297 ff.; *Labor Conditions*, III, 122 ff.

[24] U.S. Steel, Executive Committee Minutes, July 2, 8, 11, 12, 1901, *Labor Conditions*, III, 501–506. Chairman Gary complained, among other things, that the sheet officials were holding back information and misleading the Executive Committee. He did not know, for example, about the strike at the Wood plant at McKeesport in April.

At the Pittsburgh conference of July 11–13 company representatives offered to sign for the sheet mills at Scottdale, Saltsburg, McKeesport, and Wellsville. This was a considerable concession, reducing as it did the number of nonunion mills to five out of twenty-three. The technique of starving out the union mills would be rendered less effective, and the safeguarding of the sheet mill membership — the chief aim of the union in the struggle — would be nearer to accomplishment.

President Shaffer, unfortunately, was unable to capitalize on his apparent success. He had unwittingly initiated forces that he could not control. An ex-minister of oratorical ability, he had built the issue of the nonunion mills to overriding importance. Now the men, having struck to attain a company-wide scale, would settle for nothing less.[25] Moreover, the strike call had brought out the workmen in all but one of the nonunion hoop mills. They were being formed into lodges and could not be deserted. The controversy became both a bargaining and organizing strike. It was a disastrous combination.

The U.S. Steel offer was perforce rejected. Another compromise was still possible. Company representatives had argued that they had no right to force nonunion men into the Amalgamated Association by signing a scale for them. Shaffer replied that, without company opposition, they would immediately join up. "If the manufacturers will . . . allow us to quietly work, unmolested, among them . . . we will ask nothing further." But, he concluded, the only guarantee for this was the scale. There was an obvious compromise: a contract for all mills whose men, by answering the strike call, had indicated their desire to be unionized. However, this suggestion was not taken up until too late. At the Pittsburgh conference the overconfident union leaders refused to budge from their demand for all hoop, sheet, and tin mills. The meeting broke up without reaching an agreement, and Shaffer gave the fateful order to the tin plate men to strike starting July 15.

[25] See, for example, the estimate of opinion in *NLT,* July 11, 1901; also, the shrewd observations in John R. Commons, *Myself* (New York, 1934), pp. 86–87.

Negotiations were resumed two weeks later, this time with the final authority of the United States Steel Corporation — J. P. Morgan. At his instance, President Shaffer and Secretary John Williams came to New York on July 27. Morgan asserted his sympathy with organized labor and his willingness to see the mills of U.S. Steel unionized. It was necessary, however, to go slowly because of the many complications.[26] Persuaded by his assurances, the labor leaders agreed to Morgan's terms. They were clearly impressed by the great banker. Williams had thought that "a man of his immense wealth and power would be distant and difficult to talk to. I found, to my great surprise and joy, that he was quite the reverse. . . . Our conference was one of the pleasantest I ever attended." The two officers returned to Pittsburgh amid rumors of important concessions gained from the Steel Corporation.

The members of the Executive Board, meeting on Tuesday, July 30, to ratify the agreement, were dismayed when they heard the terms. Shaffer and Williams, it turned out, had accepted a scale covering only those mills under contract at the end of June, not including even the four additional plants offered on July 13. After two days of hot debate, the proposal was voted down. The entire Executive Board then journeyed to New York on August 3 to see Morgan and President Charles Schwab. The union made a counter offer: a scale "for none but those [mills] which are organized and where the men by ceasing to work have signified their desire to be associated with the Amalgamated Association." This meant most of the hoop mills, the sheet mills signed for the previous year plus Wellsville and McKeesport, but not Saltsburg or Scottdale, and all the tin mills except Monessen. But Morgan was adamant. It was his view, in fact, that the agreement signed the week before by Shaffer and Williams was binding on the union. The talks were thereupon broken off and, as one union official said, "the strike from now on is to be a fight to the finish."

[26] This is based on Gompers' account, derived from conversations with U.S. Steel President Charles Schwab, who was present, and with Shaffer and Williams. *American Federationist,* October 1901, p. 428.

The members of the Executive Board, before leaving New York, instructed Shaffer to call a general strike against U.S. Steel. There were several reasons for this final act of foolhardiness. The ability of the Steel Corporation to withstand the strike of finishing mills was already becoming apparent. The unions in the steel plants, moreover, were considered of only secondary value to the Amalgamated; it was worth the gamble. Finally, although the basic steel plants were only partly and weakly organized, the steelworkers might answer the strike call with the same enthusiasm as had the men in the hoop mills. "We have some great surprises in store for the trust," said Shaffer. "The men have been organized in some of their plants that they never dreamed could be touched. We have the sympathy of the workmen." [27]

His hope was short-lived. Called out on August 10, the Amalgamated men at the South Works refused to strike at all, insisting on honoring their contracts, and at other Illinois Steel plants the men came out in scattered numbers under protest. The union mills of the National Steel and National Tube companies struck more effectively. There was also some activity around unorganized plants, particularly at Duquesne. But the total response was too weak to affect significantly the operations of the Steel Corporation. Meanwhile, strikebreakers were being imported and struck plants opened. By mid-August the union's cause was obviously lost.

The strike in its last weeks was a sorry affair. Shaffer did not know how to extricate himself. He asked Samuel Gompers on August 8 to call a national labor conference to make the steel strike "the central fight for unionism." Gompers of course refused. He waited until early September to see what terms could be gotten by Gompers, John Mitchell, and the Conciliation Committee of the National Civic Federation. The Steel Corporation was by then willing to sign only for mills still on strike. This was too hard to accept. Shaffer then expected (so he claimed afterward) the Miners and Trainmen to go out in sympathy. Finally, the strike came to an end on September 14, the union agreeing to a settlement far

[27] *NLT*, August 1, 8, 1901, covers in detail this period of negotiation and reprints the proposed settlements.

worse than had been offered ten days before. In the well-known epilogue to the strike, Shaffer accused Gompers and Mitchell of indifference and untrustworthiness, only to back down when they offered to place themselves before a jury of labor leaders and resign if found guilty.[28]

The strike of 1901, in addition to the blunders attending its execution, involved a final miscalculation. The Amalgamated Association had assumed the indispensability of its experienced men. The improved machinery in the sheet and tin mills, although not comparable to the advances in steel manufacture, did lessen the degree of required skill. The "incredibly short space of time" to train raw country hands astonished English visitors at the Vandergrift, Pennsylvania, mill, the most modernized of the sheet mills. The superintendent boasted he could make a roller of an untrained man in six months. The strikebreaking strategy could be applied to the sheet and tin plants. The Steel Corporation decided to open as many of the struck mills as possible. At the Hyde Park sheet plant, for example, new men and two experienced rollers started operations on August 3, and did not lose a turn thereafter. The loyal Monessen men were instrumental in opening a number of tin plate mills. The union itself ascribed the strike's failure very largely to the Corporation's "evident willingness to spend millions to teach green labor to become experienced and skilled." The history of the steel mills was recurring to a lesser extent in the sheet and tin plate industries.

U.S. Steel shrewdly played its advantage in settling with the union. It refused to sign the scale for any mill that had successfully started during the strike. Not only did the union thereby lose fifteen mills, but the remaining ones were largely inefficient and unim-

---

[28] The later period of the strike and the subsequent recriminations are fully recounted in *American Federationist*, October 1901, pp. 415–431; Marguerite Green, *The National Civic Federation and the American Labor Movement, 1900–1925* (Washington, 1956) pp. 24–36; Selig Perlman and Philip Taft, *History of Labor in the U.S., 1896–1932*, Vol. 4 of John R. Commons et al., *History of Labor in the U.S.* (4 vols., New York, 1918–1935), pp. 101–109; Philip Taft, *The A.F. of L. in the Time of Gompers* (New York, 1957), pp. 136–142.

proved, and some were soon dismantled. Out of the total, the Amalgamated Association retained but eight first-class tin mills. The Corporation had started only one of the union sheet mills and no union hoop mills, but many of these under Amalgamated contract were backward anyway. The best tin, sheet, and hoop mills were mainly nonunion. These were sufficient in normal times to handle the bulk of the trade. To insure its position, the Corporation required the union to pledge not to extend, or even accept, organization in any plant then not under contract.

Not merely falling short of its objective, the Amalgamated Association found its basis of strength, seemingly secure at the outset, shattered by the strike's end. It was a settlement from which the union never recovered.

The later history of the Amalgamated Association is a melancholy tale. The union subsided into submissiveness, hoping thereby to conserve the remnants of its former glory. After a lifetime of conflict, President Shaffer lectured convention delegates in 1905, "I enter my most vigorous protest against any strike which does not emanate from the employer." Unnecessary belligerence would mark a "union as unreflecting, jejune and vicious." Toward the Steel Corporation the Association assumed a humble stance. Hearing rumors of Corporation plans to break with the union, Shaffer repeatedly "sought expressions from those in charge of Trust interests." Reassured, he reported hopefully that "the Trust prides itself upon its willingness to keep its contracts. Also that it is ready to continue its relations and do business with us if we keep ours." [29] This the Amalgamated Association fully intended to do.

For its part, the Steel Corporation preferred to maintain a benevolent aspect, avoid a final conflict, and gently dislodge the union. Until 1909 only one notable strike marred the process. Corporation officials had planned to consolidate the National Steel and American Steel Hoop Companies into the Carnegie organization, but its officers objected because this would mean dealing with the Associa-

---

[29] Amalgamated Association, *Proceedings* (1905), pp. 7262–7264, (1904), pp. 6940–6942.

tion. When the merger did occur in 1903, the antiunion Carnegie men agreed to sign the hoop mill scale only in the name of the nonexistent hoop company.[30] In 1904, a depression year, the Carnegie Company peremptorily demanded sharp reductions. The union had little alternative but to call its men out. The strike continued effectively until December, ending in defeat, and losing to the union the Corporation's Western hoop mills.

Elsewhere the Amalgamated lodges fell without a struggle. The last of the steel mills surrendered its charter in 1903, and the remaining tube mills followed in 1907 and 1908.[31] U.S. Steel continued the policy of idling the union mills. Consistently these received less work. The Corporation, Amalgamated men charged, used a "starvation and petition method." After prolonged unemployment, mill officials would suggest that if the workmen circulated a "voluntary petition" to leave the union, they would get work. That was the source, the Association claimed, of the loss of many of its lodges.[32]

Although clearly irresistible, the Steel Corporation was not eager to force the issue with the union. Amalgamated members remained valuable in many places. The superintendent of the Elwood, Indiana, plant, for example, wrote a convention delegate that the mill had not been up to full production since his departure.

> You have been away from here about five weeks attending to Amalgamated matters, during which time another roll turner quit, and the fact that the roll turner's place is a hard one to fill, as we never have any spares. All these things taken into account, I don't see how [Shaffer] can refuse to let you come home at once.[33]

Such men could offer formidable resistance in a contest. Equally important, a strike always risked driving them to other firms. The

[30] Carnegie Company Minutes, June 4, 1901, *Stanley Hearings,* VI, 4054, June 4, 1901, *Government Exhibits,* II, 465; *ITR,* June 25, 1903, p 39; *EMJ,* June 27, 1903, p. 987.

[31] Chicago *Daily Socialist,* July 16, 1909.

[32] Amalgamated Association, *Proceedings* (1906), pp. 7555, 7560; *Amalgamated Journal,* September 26, 1912, p. 13; *ITR,* August 20, 1903, p. 43; *IA,* October 6, 1904, p. 8.

[33] Amalgamated Association, *Proceedings* (1904), p. 6892.

American Rolling Mill Company, for instance, had thus benefited from the 1901 strike.

The Steel Corporation derived also a certain competitive advantage from its limited recognition of the union. Independent firms, entering the sheet and tin plate fields after the consolidations, were generally obliged to become Amalgamated mills. By insisting on uniform standards for all union plants, the Steel Corporation had in its unorganized mills a clear advantage over its competitors. The lead was largely erased, however, when the union weakened in depressed times.

Output limitation had always been a feature of Amalgamated contracts, designed to protect the men from overwork, rate cutting, and unemployment. Employers bitterly opposed the restriction on their output. The members themselves often ignored the rules. "Year by year," complained the president, "the men, by violations, have proved to the manufacturers that greater outputs could be obtained and that the committees lied." Pressed, the union gradually raised the limit. Even so, output restriction hurt union mills. The unorganized U.S. Steel tin mills produced 11.7 per cent more per turn in 1902 than was permitted in Amalgamated shops. The disadvantage became insupportable during periods of stiff competition. In 1903–4 the union was forced to discard almost entirely the restrictive rules.[34]

United States Steel similarly lost its wage differential. Despite their contract, the independents in early 1904 clamored for a 20 per cent reduction to match the lowered rates at the Steel Corporation's unorganized mills. At many places tonnage rates were cut illegally. U.S. Steel thereupon demanded that the Amalgamated Association force the independents to uphold their agreements; or, failing that, give *all* union mills the reduction. Aware of its helplessness, the union agreed on March 19, 1904 to a 20 per cent cut,

---

[34] U.S. Commissioner of Labor, *Regulation and Restriction of Output*, 11th Special Report (Washington, 1904), pp. 255 ff.; Shaffer, in Amalgamated Association, *Proceedings* (1904), pp. 6902 ff., and (1905), p. 7246; *EMJ*, April 11, 1903, p. 579; *ITR*, August 27, 1903, p. 38, September 3, 1903, p. 71; *IA*, February 16, 1905, p. 584.

and then put it to the lodges for ratification. Rejection, officials warned, would mean a strike and in the end "the destruction of the Association so far as the Sheet and Tin trade were concerned." The men nevertheless voted down the reduction. Finally, the union agreed in April to a cut of 18 per cent, and the conflict was avoided.[35] But, from U.S. Steel's viewpoint little justification remained for the continuance of the union contract.

The weakness of the Amalgamated Association was manifest. Handicapped in depressed periods by their contracts, independent firms found it relatively easy to break with the Association at a time when many skilled men were unemployed and eager for work. The union lost altogether about thirty lodges and four thousand men in the 1904 recession. The months after the panic of 1907 were equally disastrous. When prosperity returned in the spring of 1909, the Amalgamated Association had the strength neither to benefit the Steel Corporation nor effectively to oppose it.

On June 1, 1909, workmen read a notice posted at the twelve union mills of the Steel Corporation.

> After a careful consideration of the interests of both the company and its employees, the American Sheet and Tin Plate Company has decided that all its plants after June 30, 1909, will be operated as "open" plants. The scale of wages . . . until further notice will be as follows . . . [a detailed scale with reductions ranging from 2 to 8 per cent].

The sudden action shocked Amalgamated officials, who thought they had purchased security by "giving way to every request."[36] The Amalgamated Association had to fight. Complete submission would probably have been fatal in many independent mills. In fact, the largest concerns — Youngstown Sheet and Tube and LaBelle Iron Works — and several lesser firms followed the Cor-

[35] Amalgamated Association, *Proceedings* (1904), pp. 6925–6935, includes also correspondence with companies.
[36] *NLT,* June 10, 1909. U.S. Steel notice printed in *Labor Conditions,* III, 130–132.

poration's lead. At a Pittsburgh meeting union representatives agreed on a strike unless U.S. Steel relented.

Amalgamated officials met with unexpected determination from the lodges. Despite the recent emergence from depression, the men were ready to resist the summary dismissal of their union. At the pivotal New Castle, Pennsylvania, mill less than half the eligible men were members; few were paid up in dues. Yet on July 1, the entire force came out. Of all the Amalgamated mills, only the Cambridge, Ohio, plant did not close down — it was said because the men had been promised steady work. Heartened by the unexpected response, the officials promised an "aggressive fight." [37]

They dispatched organizers to nonunion mills. Significantly, they focused on the large Vandergrift plant. The 1901 strike had taught them that strength lay in control of the modern mills. U.S. Steel also understood the high stakes. The organizers were not permitted to hold meetings in Vandergrift, were mobbed and driven from the town. The attempt failed. [38]

The strike continued strong through the summer. Assistance came from unexpected quarters. No strike benefits were payable for July and August. Thereafter, the men counted on four dollars a week. On September 4 the secretary-treasurer confessed that the union was unable to meet its obligations. But contributions then began to pour in from unions and sympathizers, and an assessment was leveled on all working members. Early in October the secretary could report the union stronger financially than before the strike, and able to assist every needy person.

Meanwhile United States Steel brought to bear the advantages of its extended structure. The Wheeling district was the center of resistance. The Corporation shifted its orders elsewhere and reopened plants "that had been practically abandoned." It attempted to import strikebreakers, touching off considerable violence in Wheeling and New Castle. But some plants were successfully

[37] *NLT*, June 17, 24, 1909, July 8, 1909; Chicago *Daily Socialist*, October 13, 1909. On the effort to negotiate later in the strike, see Gompers' letter to John Williams, October 16, 1909, Gompers Papers.

[38] See affidavits in *Labor Conditions*, III, 507–509.

opened, and production was increasing. By mid-September the sheet and tin plate company claimed to be up to 69 per cent. Yet the strikers continued to resist doggedly through the next winter. Only when the crucial New Castle lodges surrendered in late August of 1910 did the union finally call a halt. The strike had lasted fourteen months.[39]

The Amalgamated Association had expended the energy of a last stand. Just as the logic of economical steel manufacture made inevitable the conflict, so did the strength of the Steel Corporation assure the union's ultimate defeat. Technological improvement, lessening the importance of hand skills, had undermined somewhat the Association. But it was the great resources and multiple units of U.S. Steel that really overbore the craft union in sheet and tin plate making.

The strike left the Amalgamated Association with little power among the independents. At next year's negotiations they rejected outright the union request for the wage increase granted by U.S. Steel on May 1, 1910. In the depression of 1915 the Amalgamated was forced to accept sizable cuts during the contract year. Only a score of small firms with perhaps a fifth of the total sheet and tin plate capacity remained to the union. The Amalgamated Association had rightly foreseen the consequences of defeat.

For different reasons the puddling section of the union fared little better. Ironmaking continued to be highly skilled work. The *National Labor Tribune* observed in 1913 that "the puddler is the most independent man in the iron and steel mills. He has no fear of ordinary men without skill being shipped into the forges to take his place. . . . A green hand could never turn out a pound of muck bar." He was treated in accord with his strong position. When in 1909 Republic broke with the Association, the union questioned the decision.

> We feel convinced that it is impossible for a company to win on a strictly iron proposition as this is. If the Republic intended

[39] *NLT*, July 15, 22, August 5, October 20, 1909, April 28, August 4, 1910; Chicago *Daily Socialist*, October 26, 1909; *IA*, August 25, 1910, p. 431.

to give up the manufacture of iron it might be a different proposition. But it does not.

Republic did reverse its stand. Youngstown Sheet and Tube likewise excluded the iron mills from its open-shop announcement.[40] And the puddlers were better able to maintain their scale than the sheet and tin division.

Yet the Association derived little strength from the puddlers; the iron division counted only 2,239 men in 1911. The wrought iron trade had greatly declined; the small iron mills, dispersed and isolated, were difficult to keep organized; and in the East and around Pittsburgh the antiunion bias excluded the Association. Only in Ohio was the union well entrenched.

A puddlers' revolt occurred in 1907. Long dominant, they were angered by the deterioration of their position. They claimed the union ignored their interests. Conservative in outlook, they objected also to the benefit system then being introduced. The rebels assumed the name of the old puddlers' union, the Sons of Vulcan, and adopted bodily the Amalgamated constitution, omitting the benefit feature and sliding scale. At their first convention they claimed 1,265 members in fifteen lodges.[41] Although often plagued, the Amalgamated Association had never before been seriously injured by secession.

Now a bitter conflict ensued, gravely damaging to the cause of organization. The Lockhart Iron and Steel Company of McKees Rocks, Pennsylvania, for example, agreeably recognized the new union. In 1910 the Vulcans demanded a radical increase. A strike resulted. Because of pressing orders, the company hired Amalgamated men. The Vulcans then ended their strike. But they demanded the discharge of the new men. Fighting broke out in the plant. The company pleaded that there were jobs for all, and that the Amalgamated men had been promised permanent work. It was willing to take back the strikers, but was proceeding mean-

[40] *NLT*, June 24, July 22, 1909, June 26, 1913.
[41] *Labor Conditions*, III, 129; *NLT*, April 22, August 5, 1909; Robinson, pp. 54–55. For earlier disputes, see Robinson, pp. 47–56; *EMJ*, November 11, 1893, p. 562.

while to find replacements.[42] Thus was organization weakened, and in some plants destroyed. In 1913 the Vulcans lost both the A. M. Byers and Youngstown Sheet and Tube companies, its largest employers. Added to internal dissension, this heavy blow ended the union, and the seceders drifted back to the Amalgamated Association.

A quarter century earlier, the Association had been the model craft union, and, by Gompers' estimate, probably the strongest organization in the American labor movement. Inflexible before revolutionary industrial progress, the union subsided into impotence. Its contracts covered only a small portion of the skilled men in the puddling and sheet and tin plate segments of the industry. The Amalgamated membership amounted in 1914 to only 6,500.[43] Despite its insignificance, the union retained one source of importance: it had jurisdiction over all ironmaking and steelmaking occupations. The future of labor organization in the steel industry would have to include the Amalgamated Association.

The fortunes of other union men in the industry depended on the Association. When employers signed the Amalgamated scale, they were likely to recognize the unions in the mechanical, building, transportation, and mining trades. The reverse was true also. Declining to deal with the Amalgamated Association, companies became hostile to all trade unions. Once the steelworkers became unorganized, it was not usually difficult to eliminate the unions of other employees.

Mechanical and building craft workers, constituting a small segment of the labor force in the mills, were too weak to dispute the efforts of the steel companies. Intransigent union men were discharged, or driven out by substandard conditions. The South

[42] *NLT*, October 6, 1910.

[43] On the operation of the Amalgamated Association during this period, see H. E. Hoagland, "Trade Unionism in the Iron Industry: A Decadent Organization," *Quarterly Journal of Economics*, XXXI (August 1917), 674–689. Hoagland argued that the Amalgamated remained in existence only at the sufferance of the employers, who considered the Amalgamated to be insurance against the formation of a more effective organization.

Works, for instance, in 1906 replaced six hundred union brick-layers, earning sixty cents an hour, with others at a lower rate. On occasion, employers had to hire union labor because of the unavailability of adequate nonunion men.[44] But, in general, companies dispensed with other craft unions with jurisdiction in the steel mills along with the Amalgamated Association.

The tin house workers suffered a similar dismal fate. Organized in 1899, they prospered and declined with their parent organization. Striking in sympathy in 1909, they were forced out of the Steel Corporation together with the Amalgamated Association. The remnants merged with the Association in 1913 after being dislodged at the important Weirton, West Virginia, mills.

Manufacturers had special objections to the unions of structural workers, dockers, lake seamen, and transport men. These outside employees, strategically situated, added constant uncertainty to operations. The Carnegie Company had for years stored an immense pile of coke at its Edgar Thomson Works as a safeguard against a coal or railroad strike.[45] Fearing trouble with the seamen and dockers, the Steel Corporation in 1902 shipped down the Great Lakes one-quarter more than its immediate ore requirement. "The possibilities of trouble have been increased" by the growing strength of the Lake unions, feared the *Iron Age*. Strikes occurred in 1904, and again in 1906. Fabricating companies were similarly plagued. A strike of structural workers in 1903 forced the Steel Corporation's American Bridge Company to pay a forfeit to the Wabash Railroad for an unfinished bridge spanning the Monongahela River. The structural men appeared especially prone to embarrassing strikes.[46]

Employers therefore were eager to destroy the organizations of

[44] Chicago *Daily Socialist*, October 29, 1906, February 25, 1910; *ITR*, July 9, 1903, p. 42; Amalgamated Association, *Proceedings* (1904), pp. 6936–6937.

[45] *Iron and Steel Trade Journal*, July 28, 1900, p. 82. Every long-term contract included this clause: "Strikes, differences with workmen, or other contingencies beyond control of the respective parties hereto, shall be sufficient excuse to either party for failure to make or accept deliveries." *Government Exhibits*, X, 2487–2493.

[46] *EMJ*, March 21, 1903, p. 463, and April 25, 1903, p. 651; *IA*, May 24, 1906, p. 1689; *ITR*, May 21, 1903, p. 38.

outside workers. The Association of Erectors of Structural Steel won its bitter struggle for an open shop in November 1906. Led by the Steel Corporation's Pittsburgh Steamship Company, the Lake Carriers' Association in 1908 began forcing the Lake Seamen's Union from its ships. The dock laborers' union, only fully established in the Corporation's mills in 1902, succumbed to improved unloading machinery. Frick had broken permanently the coke workers' union in 1889, and the coal and ore fields were unorganized. The unionizing drives of the United Mine Workers met vigorous resistance. The strategic and conservative railroad brotherhoods alone escaped the antiunion reaction. Otherwise, the steel industry was by 1910 effectively unorganized from the ore to the finished product.

The destruction of labor organization capped the drive for economy. Hitherto, the unions had impeded the minimization of labor costs. Steelmasters had been obliged to negotiate at annual conferences and with standing mill committees for a division of the benefits of improved operation. The employees' bargaining power ended with the union. Now the determination of labor expenses rested solely with the steel men.

Occasionally, the bargaining forms remained for a time. When the union was broken at the Edgar Thomson Works, the Carnegie Company agreed to a sliding scale for three years. Workmen's committees would examine monthly the books to figure the wage scale, which depended on current prices. A similar agreement followed the Homestead strike.[47] The Amalgamated Association itself insisted on the continuance of mill committees as a condition to opening nonunion plants to its men.[48] Companies that were anxious to retain their union workmen often accepted the stipulation. But even when the form remained, the substance did not. Without the

[47] *Senate Report 1280*, pp. 165, 167–168. The sliding scale continued in use in Carnegie mills for a number of years, and was observed in the Braddock Works in 1907. It was also continued in the American Steel and Wire Company in 1900, where the agreement was signed individually.

[48] Amalgamated Association, *Proceedings* (1905), pp. 7257–7259, (1906), pp. 7565–7567.

union, committees carried little weight, and did not long outlast organization.

The practice of simply notifying workmen of the conditions of employment became the rule by 1910. Minor variations existed. Some plant superintendents allowed workers' *ad hoc* committees to be heard on all matters, others on specified subjects. One large independent customarily received many petitions, and had as a result several times changed the hours. Steelworkers in practice rarely formed committees, and, at best, employers considered them a means of communication, not of bargaining. More often, managers forbade any collective activity. The superintendent of the Standard Steel Car plant at Hammond, Indiana, reflected a common attitude when he seized the spokesman of a grievance committee and ejected him violently from the office.[49]

The worker had but one bargaining right. "If a man is dissatisfied," said President F. N. Hoffstot of the Pressed Steel Car Company, "it is his privilege to quit." Frick explained the change since 1892. Before, decision had been reached "by an agreement." But now "it was brought about by our fixing the wages that we felt we could afford to pay, and they agreeing individually to accept them."[50] The terms of their employment were out of the hands of the steelworkers.

Unencumbered, the steelmaster could base his labor decisions on the objective criteria of what minimized his cost and maximized his profit. He could with impunity manipulate the wage rate, step up the work, and extend the twelve-hour day and the seven-day week. The antiunion triumph completed economical steel manufacture.

The accomplishment, however, much widened the area of labor relations for the industry. The union, despite its drawbacks, had been the basis of a stable and viable labor system. That structure was shattered with the union organization. Labor stability had to be built anew. The burden, once the function of the union ma-

[49] Chicago *Daily Socialist,* January 20, 31, 1910.
[50] Hoffstot quoted in *Survey,* August 7, 1909, p. 665; Frick, in *Senate Report 1280,* p. 166.

chinery, passed to the steel men. In addition, since the unorganized state was basically involuntary, they constantly had to be prepared to smash employee impulses toward reorganization. New and troublesome problems were opened up by the destruction of trade unionism.

Chapter IV

The Sources of Stability:
The Skilled Workers

The success of the economizing system left shattered the labor equilibrium of the industry. Steel men now had to devise means to insure against continuing discontent and a union resurgence. The laboring men, for their part, had to adjust to the terms of work dictated by the cold logic of economy.

In time a nonunion pattern of stability emerged. Its sources were varied. The social and economic alignments of the mill towns buttressed the employers' dominance. Among unskilled workers an accommodation already existed, based on the special nature of the immigrant influx from Eastern Europe. The chief problem was the skilled men. They accepted the new situation because, firstly, mechanization had much weakened their role, and, secondly, steel men shrewdly made it seem to their interest to do so. The immediate necessity, of course, was to eradicate completely the influence of trade unionism in the industry.

The cleansing process was accomplished chiefly through the elimination of rebellious workmen. After the failure of a strike, employers normally used the opportunity to cut away the active union men. "Those members of the Amalgamated that have not made themselves obnoxious are given employment, as others are, after they have denounced the association," reported the local Steelton press after the 1891 conflict.[1] The end of the Homestead strike left many participants at the Carnegie plants jobless. Numerous strikers

---

[1] Quoted in *Report on Immigration*, VIII, 646.

suffered a similar fate in 1909 at the mills of U.S. Steel and Youngstown Sheet and Tube.

Some firms, such as Cambria and Colorado Fuel and Iron, openly opposed organization of their men. "A 'union' is talked of being formed among the Wire Drawers," recorded the secretary of the Waukegan Works of Washburn and Moen in 1897. " 'Woe be unto them' in this vacinity [sic]." His prediction was accurate. He noted soon after that the leaders "were today called in to sign papers to the effect that they would not join the 'Wire Drawers Union' which they all agreed to." The use of "ironclads" was widespread in the early days. John W. Gates required his men in 1891 to sign this agreement:

> I will not become a member of any labor organization. . . .
> I will not enter into or participate in any manner in any strike
> or labor trouble with the St. Louis Wire Mill Company . . . and
> should I agree to do so I hereby agree to forfeit ten days wages.

The company, for its part, promised to pay a like amount if it discharged any "efficient workman without sufficient cause for doing so." [2] The Bureau of Labor found even in 1910 one large independent employing a similar document.

After 1900, however, most steel companies denied discrimination against union members. "We do not ask them whether they are union men or not," asserted a Jones and Laughlin official. In practice, isolated card-holders might be tolerated. But, when trouble brewed, employers, even those of the open-shop persuasion, did not disguise their aversion to unions. During organizing campaigns foremen were customarily stationed outside the halls to warn workmen away from the meetings. That proving inadequate, superintendents would resort to the effective antidote of discharge. Carnegie workmen were fired for union activities at Braddock after

[2] Entries, March 29, 1897, April 3, 1897, Waukegan Works Diary, Washburn and Moen, American Steel and Wire Collection; Gates to A. R. Whitney, April 9, 1891, St. Louis Wire Mill Co., American Steel and Wire Collection. The practice had been sufficiently prevalent to impel the Amalgamated Association to offer a resolution at the A.F.L. convention of 1893 for state laws forbidding ironclads. A.F.L., *Proceedings* (1893), p. 72.

1889, at Homestead in 1895, 1899, and 1901, and at Duquesne in 1901. The manager of the U.S. Steel sheet mill at Wellsville, Ohio, Schwab reported, dismissed "twelve men who were endeavoring to institute a lodge." [3] Usually, the punishment of leaders discouraged the rest. When "example" failed at the Cambria Works in 1919, however, hundreds of employees were summarily dismissed.

Discharge was an extreme measure. Companies preferred to prevent potential union leaders from entering their mills in the first place. Employment managers were wary of troublemakers. At the Youngstown Sheet and Tube Company, for instance, all applicants were questioned about union affiliation. Except for puddlers (the company recognized the Sons of Vulcan), no jobs were offered to union men. Those who did slip through the screening were retained if they agreed to work under open-shop conditions. [4] When the union threat subsided after 1901, hiring offices no longer felt the need to inquire about union membership.

There were, moreover, more accurate sources of information. U.S. Steel maintained, as did the independents, a central list of men dismissed "for cause." Such records were available on request on a reciprocal basis. In troubled times companies circulated black-lists, such as those in use at Monessen in 1919. The Lake Carriers' Association devised an ingenious plan in 1908. Every seaman received a "discharge book." He surrendered it upon finding a berth, and retrieved it when he left. It was not returned to union men. Since jobs required the book, the undesirables were gradually eliminated from Association boats. [5] Blacklist, in varying forms, was an effective tool against labor reorganization.

The antiunion animus inevitably fostered espionage. Pinkerton's Detective Agency early offered firms the services of "a detective suitable to associate with their employees." The Illinois Steel Company employed operatives in 1885 at Bridgeport and Joliet, as did Frick in 1892. Workmen secretly reformed a lodge at Homestead

---

[3] U.S. Steel, Executive Committee Minutes, July 8, 1901, *Labor Conditions*, III, 503–504; *Industrial Commission*, XIII, 503.

[4] *Labor Conditions*, III, 143–144.

[5] *Stanley Hearings*, IV, 2995–3031, V, 3419–3431.

in 1899. "Then, like a bolt from the blue sky," a Pittsburgh paper wrote, "the company let the newly made union men know that it was cognizant of every move that had been made." A similar debacle in 1895 had led the Amalgamated Association to surmise that every tenth man at the works was a spy.[6]

The Steel Corporation established secret-service departments of astonishing efficiency. Llewellen Lewis, an Amalgamated official, related an incident during a wage conference at New Castle. Unable to attend, he had instructed an assistant to call him as soon as the scale was settled. Before the message came, a U.S. Steel district manager across the river at Wheeling telephoned with the correct scale and the vote by locals. During a Cleveland unionizing campaign in 1913, Steel Corporation officials planted loyal employees in the newly formed unions to report on the meetings. Independents had equally effective methods. At times of serious unrest, steel companies usually supplemented their permanent forces with detective agencies, in later years more respectable and circumspect than the old Pinkertons.[7]

The effects of espionage were immediately evident to investigators. John Fitch of the Pittsburgh Survey found himself repeatedly suspected of being a company agent. Friendly workmen immediately became reticent when he shifted the talk to the plant. "Concerning the most patent and generally known facts," he ruefully observed, "intelligent men display the most marvelous ignorance." Steelworkers were silent even among themselves. One

[6] *IA*, October 8, 1885, p. 18; *Senate Report 1280*, pp. 90–91, 171, 198; Pittsburgh *Dispatch*, August 4, 1901; Amalgamated Association, *Proceedings* (1895), p. 4882.

[7] *Survey*, April 6, 1912, p. 25; *Amalgamated Journal*, April 25, 1912, pp. 1–2; Commission of Inquiry, Interchurch World Movement, *Public Opinion and the Steel Strike* (New York, 1921), pp. 1–85; Sydney Howard, "The Labor Spy," *New Republic*, February 16–March 30, 1921. Scrapbook, Volume 16, American Steel and Wire Company, American Steel and Wire Collection, contains a foreign-language leaflet with a letter of translation, dated April 2, 1913, Cleveland, announcing a union meeting, and below this penciled comment to the superintendent: "R. W. Ney. The enclosed letter translation above was received by Louis Eppich Fine Wire Drawer who did some work for us but who has dropped out of the union at our request. (signed) Putnam."

Vandergrift man wrote anonymously in 1901: "A man must not think loud here, as even the trees have ears. When any two or more men get together, since the sheet workers went on strike, there is sure to be some Judas . . . not far off. . . . The men dare not trust one another." [8] There was a common phrase: "If you want to talk in Homestead, you must talk to yourself." The spy system effectively stifled the men.

Any collective action in steel plants became suspect. The Colorado Fuel and Iron Company, for instance, had decided on an increase for its switchmen. Impatient, the men sent a delegation. The company thereupon discharged all of them. At Homestead in 1895, at Jones and Laughlins in 1900, and at Gary, men were dismissed or threatened for meeting together. Workmen told investigators of the suppression of petitions. According to the Steel Corporation, the New York office was glad to receive the views of the workmen. The head investigator asked a department supervisor, known to oppose Sunday labor, to, pass a petition among his men for its abolition. He refused, and so did others. They doubted that the New York office could protect them from their immediate superiors.[9] In any case, steelworkers knew that it did not pay to speak out.

Defeat after bitter conflict crushed the union spirit. Following the Homestead strike, Frick wrote to Carnegie with keen insight:

> We could never have profited much by any of our competitors making and winning the fight we have made. We had to teach our employees a lesson, and we have taught them one that they will never forget.

Joe Reed, for example, had been a strike leader. Afterward, he left the mills. Finding a job later in an unorganized plant, he vowed never to join a union again. By the estimate of the Amalgamated president, not more than two or three 1892 strikers joined

[8] *NLT,* July 11, 1901.
[9] *Survey,* February 3, 1912, p. 1718; Fitch, pp. 214, 217–219.

in the organizing attempts at Homestead later in the decade. After the 1909 conflict some lodges in the Wheeling district voted to retain their Amalgamated charters. But the New Castle men, who had put up the stiffest fight, were finished with the union.[10] Men who "had gone through the mill" abandoned hope. They appeared permanently lost to the union cause.

Everywhere the sense of despair spread, usually less abruptly than in the wake of conflict. To workmen the implacable Steel Corporation and the large independents were too powerful to oppose. The manufacturers would rather "let the grass grow green over the furnaces" than accept organization, a Jones and Laughlin blower observed.[11] Repressive measures effectively cowed the steelworkers; but discharge, blacklist, and espionage would not by themselves create labor stability.

Two patterns of adjustment evolved after the destruction of the union. They followed opposite courses for the skilled and unskilled, but both worked toward the same end: acquiescence in employer control and accommodation to the terms of work.

Once, skilled steelworkers had been strong, even arrogant, in their indispensability. Then, steel men observed, "the roller could be an autocrat." John Gates recalled angrily the "uncouth, treacherous irishman who worked for the Braddock [rod and wire mill] in the capacity of boss roller for a number of years." [12] Such a man counted himself free, beholden to no one, and he acted accordingly. That sharp sense of independence disappeared in the later years

[10] Frick quoted in Harvey, *Frick*, p. 178; *Industrial Commission*, VII, 388; *NLT*, September 1, 1910.

[11] Personal Interviews with Workers in the Steel Industry, David Saposs Papers, University of Wisconsin Library, interview with James Coon, Jones and Laughlin blower, also, heater in U.S. Steel plant in McKeesport, July 19, 1920.

[12] Gates to J. C. Fleming, August 9, 1892, St. Louis Wire Mill Co., American Steel and Wire Collection. Gates stated that he was especially anxious to see the Amalgamated beaten by the Carnegie Company because the boss roller was then employed in Carnegie's Beaver Falls mill.

of the industry. Increasingly, the steelworker's livelihood rested, not on his mastery of a difficult trade, but on the sufferance of the company. Its approval became the key to his success. He learned, therefore, to accept without complaint whatever was meted out to him. And steelmasters were acute enough to appear openhanded. The skilled force was enticed, not hammered, into dependence.

Chiefly, the steelworker's role was undercut by mechanization. The modern steel mill developed a clear line of promotion. Each man was training for the next higher job and usually capable of filling it. No workman was irreplaceable. The altered situation had two effects. Job tenure lost its certainty. And, second, the opportunities for promotion sprang open. On both counts, the employer's good will took on first importance. The decline of skill made insecure the workingman's present place and whetted his ambition for advancement.

As a group, intelligent steelworkers had always been eager to rise. Horatio-Alger-type stories were popular in the columns of union periodicals. Superintendents were customarily recruited from the ranks. The lodge correspondence of the *Amalgamated Journal* carried frequent congratulatory notices of brothers who had taken managerial positions. All but one Amalgamated president left office to enter politics or business, often with firms dealing with the union. Indeed, Gompers believed this eagerness to leave the laboring class was the Association's chief weakness.

But a spirit of solidarity had tempered ambition. Although without apprenticeship rules, the union had supervised promotion procedures and limited the training of new men. Advancement, moreover, had depended on experience and the acquisition of specific skills. Now, lacking the difficult test of performance and the restraint of the union, competition for promotion became fierce.

"Each man is out for himself," interviewers were told repeatedly. "The men here have lost any spirit of working together," said a McKeesport workman. "They look out for their own interest." One worker observed of the higher paid men during the 1919 organizing campaign: "Naw, they won't join no union; they're all after every other feller's job." [13] To encourage this spirit, managers held out unlimited prospects for advancement. "This should inspire every honest man," stated the *Joliet Works Mixer,* to help "along everything for the best interests of the Company." [14] Steel hands found this to be good advice. Insecure and ambitious, they came to identify their fortunes with the good will of their particular boss, and they behaved accordingly.

The nature of the steelworker's skill also limited his independence. Unlike a machinist or bricklayer, his training was valuable only in a steel mill, frequently only those turning out the same product. Moreover, steel plants were largely isolated. Even in the Pittsburgh district, mills were too distant for a man conveniently to live in the same residence after changing jobs. "There is no other place [in McKeesport] to find work of that kind," said a tubeworker, "so a man cannot afford to be independent." Home ownership compounded the problem. "When you can't get work here you must leave, and if your property is not paid for you can lose it," observed a Vandergrift sheet worker.[15] Recognizing this, employers commonly threatened during labor troubles to remove their plants to more tractable communities. In 1900 one-quarter of families in Homestead owned their homes. The Immigration Commission in 1908 found a similar situation for the entire industry. These men of substance, mainly skilled workers, had a strong reason to be model employees.

Companies consequently urged employees to buy property. Carnegie early offered low-interest loans to be repaid by deductions from pay envelopes over a long period. Shortly after the 1892 strike, the company acquired the site of the Pittsburgh City Poor Farm

[13] Samuel Gompers, *Seventy Years of Life and Labor* (2 vols., New York, 1925), I, 340; Whiting Williams, *What's on the Worker's Mind* (New York, 1920), p. 152; Saposs Interviews, Henderson, McKeesport, August 2, 1920, J. Maturch, McKeesport, July 30, 1920, American mechanic, McKeesport, August 3, 1920, and Mary Senior's analysis after speaking to many men.

[14] *Joliet Works Mixer,* April 1914.

[15] Saposs Interviews, Harry Meredith, McKeesport; *NLT,* July 11, 1901; Youngstown *Labor News,* August 16, 23, 1901.

adjoining Homestead and erected there houses for sale to employees. The building-loan plan was continued and extended in the Steel Corporation. The Apollo Iron and Steel Company, laying out the town of Vandergrift in 1895, sold land and advanced money to employees for houses. "The system of this company in the lot and building line has many really good men tied up," said a union man. Complaints were heard that only men who accepted the offer found jobs in Vandergrift.[16]

Most steel men had not been eager to become involved in housing. "We are manufacturers, not real estate dealers," said the head of a large Pittsburgh firm in 1908. "In an old, settled community let the laboring man take care of himself."[17] Johnstown, Pittsburgh, South Chicago, and Youngstown all suffered from inadequate, expensive housing. The Lackawanna Company at first made no provision for its workmen when it erected its immense works outside of Buffalo. But the difficulties in recruiting labor forced the company to build 575 houses. Bowing to necessity, companies that established plants at Midland, Aliquippa, Ambridge, Gary, and elsewhere undertook large-scale programs. The Bureau of Labor found in 1911 that 56 of 74 establishments were active in housing their employees, although often on a small scale.

Reluctant to enter the field, companies nevertheless saw the uses of their realty ventures. Profit was not an objective. Jones and Laughlin limited the net return on its Aliquippa land company to 5 per cent. The Granite City Steel Company sold its houses to employees at cost plus 6 per cent. The means were seized to encourage workmen to become property owners.

Rented houses also strengthened men's attachment to the employer. Company houses were almost always a bargain. The Cambria Company built in scattered sections of Johnstown primarily to hold down rental levels. Carnegie dwellings at Munhall rented for one-third under other houses. The receipts of the Steel Cor-

---

[16] Jeans, *American Industrial Conditions*, pp. 572–577; *NLT*, July 25, 1901.
[17] *The Pittsburgh District Civic Frontage*, Vol. V of *Pittsburgh Survey*, ed. P. U. Kellog, p. 121.

poration averaged only 1.5 per cent of the construction cost —
"tantamount to an addition to wages." Company houses were,
moreover, the best available in mill towns. They were, as a rule,
sturdily built, in good repair, large, and with sanitary conveniences.
Gas, electricity, and water were often provided free or at cost. There
were usually waiting lists for vacancies, and, for those with leases,
strong reasons for staying with the company.[18]

Employers began to develop other means of fostering loyalty
among the skilled men. The Steel Corporation inaugurated in
1903 a stock subscription plan by which employees could buy preferred stock on monthly installments at prices slightly below the
market. Besides the regular dividend, holders were to receive for
each share five dollars a year extra for five years, provided they
were employed continuously during the year by the Corporation,
and, as indicated by certification, had "shown a proper interest in
its welfare and progress." The five-dollar rewards left undistributed
each year went into a special fund which accumulated for the five
years. "The Corporation will then by its own final determination
award to each man whom it shall find deserving thereof" the part
equal to his shares. Here was tangible compensation for being a
model employee.

There were variations. The U.S. Steel sheet and tin plate subsidiary paid a bonus of 4 per cent for "faithful service" to the men
of the Monessen Works, the only tin plate mill to run continuously
through the 1901 strike. The Youngstown Sheet and Tube Company, starting in 1909, gave an annual bonus to every employee who
had worked for the entire year.[19]

Other innovations also placed a premium on loyalty and continuous service. The American Steel and Wire Company began a

---

[18] Doris R. H. Beuttenmueller, "The Granite City Steel Company," unpublished Ph.D. thesis, St. Louis University, 1952, pp. 32, 38; *Labor Conditions,* III, ch. 16; A. W. Mitchell, "Industrial Backgrounds of a Large Steel
Plant (Aliquippa Works)," unpublished M.A. thesis, University of Pittsburgh,
1932, p. 18.

[19] Fitch, App. 5; *IA,* May 29, 1902, p. 27, October 27, 1904, p. 63; *Labor
Conditions,* III, 462–463.

pension system in 1902; and the Relief Fund of four million dollars, donated by Carnegie on his retirement, provided modest pensions, as well as injury and death benefits, to employees of the Carnegie Company. These were consolidated in 1910 into one plan to cover the entire Steel Corporation. The pension was "a purely voluntary provision for the benefit of employees superannuated or totally incapacitated after long and faithful service and constitutes no contract and confers no legal right upon any employee." The pension plans of Wisconsin Steel (a subsidiary of International Harvester) and Midvale Steel and Ordnance contained a similar limiting clause.[20] Other firms cared for faithful employees in less formal ways. The promise of old-age assistance was in every case a a powerful incentive toward company loyalty.

Employers made deliberate efforts during hard times to hold their skilled men, frequently offering lesser jobs. The Immigration Commission found the percentage of skilled steelworkers employed regularly during the 1908 depression significantly above the average. Chairman Elbert H. Gary in late 1913 instructed U.S. Steel subsidiary presidents to keep as many men as possible working on repairs and improvements.

The Steel Corporation led the movement to strengthen the ties of the skilled ranks to management. Gary explicitly instructed the company presidents: "Take special pains to conciliate and promote the best interests of your employees. . . . We have little, if any, [organized] labor . . . and I am glad that your employees are pleased with that fact." His strategy was clear. "So far as you can, cultivate a feeling of friendship and influence your men to the conclusion that it is for their interests in every respect to be in your employ." [21]

Through promotions, housing, bonuses, pensions, and steady

[20] *Labor Conditions*, III, 455–461; *IA*, April 5, 1917, p. 841, July 17, 1919, pp. 182–183.

[21] E. H. Gary, Address to Subsidiary Presidents, October 11, 1911, and December 17, 1913, *Addresses and Statements by E. H. Gary* (8 vols., compiled by the Business History Society, November 1927, and located in the Baker Library of Harvard School of Business Administration), I.

work, corps of company retainers were developed. The skilled workmen entered an orbit of dependence, induced to accept without dispute the terms of employment set by the steel companies.

Room for adjustment existed. Wages barely kept pace with the rising cost of living in the two decades after 1890. But earnings were sufficient to support families in varying degrees of decency. On a weekly income of twenty dollars in the Pittsburgh district, investigators found in 1907, a workingman's family could live in comfort. He could rent or own a six-room house distant from the din and smoke of the mill. There was money enough for a healthy, varied diet; for furniture, clothes, and small pleasures; and for insurance and some savings.

The wages of the semiskilled man were less adequate. His house usually consisted of four rooms, two on a floor, the "front room" opening directly on the street. Such gray frame structures stretched innumerably in monotonous rows within sight of every works. They rarely had inside toilets. Nine of twenty-three Homestead families lived in dwellings lacking running water, and nine crowded two or more persons into each room. Yet these houses offered some comfort, and also the respectability of the musty parlor. Except for large families, the semiskilled workman's wages provided adequate food and clothing. But to lay aside appreciable savings meant scrimping on recreation and other expenses. The income of skilled labor, therefore, provided at least minimal decency at the lower levels and substantial comfort at the upper.[22]

In misfortune, the steelworker was badly situated. Until after 1910 the burdens of hazardous and unhealthy work rested primarily on him. Liability principles required proof of the employer's fault for an accident victim to receive compensation. And judicial interpretation steadily narrowed the application of liability. Earlier, companies had employed liability insurance firms, who were even

[22] Margaret F. Byington, *Homestead: The Households of a Mill Town*, Vol. IV of *Pittsburgh Survey*, ed. P. U. Kellogg, chs. 3–6; *Report on Immigration*, VIII, 95–103.

less concerned with seeing justice done. But by 1900 most major steel manufacturers preferred to work directly through their own claims departments. Injured workmen could sue. But the procedure was lengthy, abused by lawyers, and in the end highly uncertain. In the six years prior to 1912 the Steel Corporation had lost not more than six verdicts, the attorney handling its injury cases in Pittsburgh estimated. "Under our common law the employee has not a chance of recovery in two cases out of a hundred." Knowing the odds, workmen were likely to accept whatever the employer awarded.

Steel companies were not unduly generous. During the year ending July 1907, Jones and Laughlin paid nothing to the families of seven, funeral expenses for ten, and over a thousand dollars to only two families of its toll of twenty-five dead. In Allegheny County 88 out of 158 injured married men received no compensation, and 23 of 33 men permanently disabled were given less than one hundred dollars. A few companies were consistently more liberal. The American Steel and Wire Company paid adequate benefits for temporary disability, and compensated the family of every killed workman an average of five hundred dollars. The Carnegie Fund awarded a like amount, plus one hundred dollars for each child. The company itself, however, was no more generous than most others. Employers always assumed hospital expenses. But workmen had to look elsewhere for ways to ease the worst hardships of injury and death.

Benefit associations operated in 27 of 84 plants surveyed by the Bureau of Labor. Workmen contributed a specified amount, deducted from their wages, and in turn received accident insurance. For two cents a day the employees of the McClintic-Marshall Company in Pittsburgh were insured for one hundred dollars at death and three to five dollars a week for disabilities for a half year. The company made up deficiencies in the fund. Employers generally guaranteed payment, and contributed office space, clerks, and some funds, rarely totaling a third of the costs. In many cases, the relief associations enabled employers to avoid legal responsibility. Cambria required every member of its association to sign a release. In effect, the benefit organizations shifted the burdens of industrial accidents from the employer. But if workmen had to pay, mutual insurance was the most effective means of assuming the charges.[23]

The men themselves recognized the need for protection. In 1903 the Amalgamated Association instituted a death benefit, and in 1908 expanded the program to cover sickness and accidents. The insurance system became an important function, and in the end, as much as anything, kept the Association in existence.[24] Steelworkers flocked into Royal Arcanum, Modern Woodsmen, Odd Fellows, and other fraternal orders that offered generous benefits at low rates. Over 3,600 men belonged to twenty-three such organizations in Homestead in 1907. To a lesser extent, steelworkers patronized insurance companies. Thirty-seven of forty-two Homestead families with incomes over $15 a week carried some form of insurance, and many were able to bank money. Of 115 skilled men killed in Allegheny County in 1902, 32 left nothing, 33 under five hundred dollars in savings and insurance, and 33 over $1,000.[25]

No provision against calamity ever equaled the earning power of a vigorous workman. Sickness, injury, or death inevitably spelled lost savings, lowered living standards, even poverty for the unfortunate family. The attempted provision was, nevertheless, a rough adjustment to the hazards of steelmaking.

Workmen accepted exhausting labor, heat, fumes, and danger as part of the job. Long hours, however, were a continuing grievance. Fitch transcribed his impressions after interviewing a twelve-hour man.

[23] Crystal Eastman, *Work-Accidents and the Law,* Vol. II of *Pittsburgh Survey,* ed. P. U. Kellog, pt. 3; *Labor Conditions,* IV, 239–241, 276–277, app. H; Byington, app. 11; *Stanley Hearings,* V, 3402–3403; *Industrial Commission,* VII, 99.

[24] Robinson, *Amalgamated Association,* ch. 5; letter of R. H. March of Newport, Kentucky, August 29, 1912, in *Amalgamated Journal,* September 5, 1912, p. 5.

[25] Byington, pp. 90–92, 113–114; Eastman, p. 134; B. H. Meyer, "Fraternal Beneficiary Societies in the U.S.," *American Journal of Sociology,* VI (March 1901), 646–661.

He cannot go out and feel much like work the next day. He usually goes to the lectures at the Carnegie Library, but to little else. No man who works twelve hours, he says, has time or energy to do much outside of his work. His life is lived in the mill.

Steelworkers invariably described their lives as a continual round of toil: "A man works, comes home, eats and goes to bed, gets up, eats and goes to work." The trolley ride home after a fourteen-hour night shift showed the heavy toll on the men.

Nobody was talking. . . . They held their buckets on their laps, or put them on the floor between their legs. 6 or 8 were asleep. The rest sat quiet, with legs and neck loose, with their eyes open, steady, dull, fixed upon nothing at all.[26]

More than anything else, the grinding schedule disgruntled the skilled workers. But mitigating circumstances gave room for accommodation even here.

The work had become, as employers claimed, less arduous; and rest spells eased the tougher jobs. Recurrent repair and slack periods gave opportunities for recuperation. Steelworkers frequently arranged to work a fourteen-hour night and ten-hour day turn, providing more living time on alternate weeks. Sunday labor, moreover, did not extend to the upper ranks to a great degree because continuous departments required relatively few skilled men. Shorter hours, finally, meant slimmer pay envelopes. Particularly where wage rates were falling, steelworkers preferred the extra hours. Nothing mattered more than the maintenance of accustomed living standards. On occasion, workers actually requested the return of a longer schedule. Men grew accustomed even to the eighty-four-hour week and to the twenty-four-hour turn on alternate biweekly changes in the shift. They worked slowly and, through weariness, without interest; became surly on the long turn; and in the end accepted their lot.

A stable, peaceable nonunion relation thus developed with the

[26] Fitch, p. 204; Saposs Interviews, Harry Meredith, McKeesport, August 2, 1920; Charles R. Walker, *Steel: The Diary of a Furnace Worker* (Boston, 1922), p. 44.

skilled steelworkers. The employers offered tolerable wages and conditions, buttressed by the threat of repression. But the solid basis of accommodation was the workman's increasing dependence and loyalty to the company. The unskilled laborers likewise adjusted to the industrial situation; their accommodation, however, rested on change, not permanence.

Chapter V

The Sources of Stability: The Immigrants

Before 1880, "English-speaking" workmen had manned America's iron and steel plants. Then immigrants from South and East Europe began to arrive in increasing numbers. More than 30,000 were steelworkers by 1900. The newcomers soon filled the unskilled jobs in the Northern mills, forcing the natives and earlier immigrants upward or out of the industry. In the Carnegie plants of Allegheny County in March 1907, 11,694 of the 14,359 common laborers were Eastern Europeans.[1] The recent arrivals dominated the bottom ranks of the steel industry.

The Slavic influx shaped the labor stability at the unskilled level. A lowly job in the mills, however ill-paid and unpleasant, was endurable if it enabled the immigrant to leave in a few years with funds enough to resume his accustomed place in his native village. That was his original purpose. The majority, who in time decided to stay in America, usually had by then risen into higher paid jobs. In either event, the acceptance of the hard terms of common labor was the necessary prelude to a better life. Immigrant mobility was at the center of the peaceable adjustment of the unskilled steelworkers.

Fixed for centuries, by 1900 the peasant society of Eastern Europe had begun to disintegrate. The abolition of serfdom gave the peasant the right to mortgage and sell his land, and, later, to subdivide it. The falling death rate upset the ancient balance between

---

[1] *Stanley Hearings,* IV, 2889–2893. For the general movement of Eastern Europeans into the industry, see second chapters in all the sections of *Report on Immigration,* VIII, XI.

population and acreage, leaving sons unprovided for or with insufficient land. Manufactured goods destroyed the peasant's self-sufficiency, raised his living standards and costs, and emphasized the inefficiency of his farming methods. When misfortune struck — a destructive storm, a drought, an outbreak of phylloxyra in the vineyards or disease in the livestock — he fell into debt, or, already mortgaged, lost his farm.

The peasant was linked to a chain of family inheritance and tradition. He had a name, a reputation, and a posterity. His self-esteem went with property, independence, and an assured social position. All this rested on his land, located in a certain village and held by his family from the immemorial past. The peasant with mortgage payments he could not meet faced an intolerable decline into the dependent, propertyless servant class. Rooted to the land, he saw his salvation only in emigration to a country from which men returned with money.

Inhabitants of the Western provinces of Austria-Hungary had long been accustomed to migrate seasonally to Germany for the harvests. To supplement meager farm incomes, Slovaks had peddled goods or followed wandering trades as wiremakers, pot-menders, and glaziers. From the peasant viewpoint the longer move to America differed from seasonal migration only in degree. Men went to Germany to add to a slender livelihood. In America they would save enough to pay off the mortgage or to buy the land that would restore their social position. A Polish immigrant expected to "remain for some years and return with something to our country, so that later we might not be obliged to earn [as hired laborers]." [2] The Atlantic crossing meant a heavy investment, a long absence, unaccustomed work in mill or mine; but the essential purpose did not differ from seasonal migration. The immigrant hoped to earn a stake and return to his village. With this end Slovaks, Poles, Croats,

[2] Raczkowski Series, April 8, 1907, W. I. Thomas and F. Znaniecki, *The Polish Peasants in Europe and America* (2 vols., New York, 1927), I, 771, as well as similar statements in other series, I, 454, 1023, 1041, and letters to the Emigrants Protective Society in Warsaw, II, 1504–1509. The immigrants quotations in this chapter come from the collections of letters in these volumes, unless otherwise stated in the footnotes, and will not be individually cited.

Serbs, Magyars, and Italians made the passage to America, and many found their way into the steel mills.

They entered the mills under the lure of wages. Earnings of $1.50 or $2.00 a day, it was true, would not support a wife and children. In the Pittsburgh district, where a family required $15 a week, two-thirds of the recent immigrants in the steel plants made less than $12.50, and one-third less than $10. The Pittsburgh Associated Charities in 1910 found that, if a steel laborer worked twelve hours every day in the year, he could not provide a family of five with the barest necessities. Every steel center had large numbers who earned much below the minimum for family existence.

But the immigrant steelworkers had not expected to support families in America. The vast majority came alone. One-third of those surveyed by the Immigration Commission were single, and roughly three-quarters of the married men who had been in the country under five years reported their wives abroad.[3] The minority with families supplemented its income by lodging the others.

A "boarding-boss system" developed, benefiting all except perhaps the overburdened women. The workmen paid the "boss" $2.50 or $3.00 a month for lodging, including cooking and washing. The wife, or occasionally a hired housekeeper, bought the food for the household, and at the end of each month the total bill was divided among the adult males. There were variations. The boss might charge a flat monthly rate, or provide only a specified amount of food. In Granite City, Illinois, the Bulgarians economized by doing their own housework. But the system was essentially the same. A boarder could live for about $15 a month, and even after spending another $10 on clothing and trifles, could put aside $15. The boarding boss increased his income usually by more than half his mill earnings, and, in addition, was likely to be made a foreman.

[3] *Report on Immigration,* VIII, 139–151, also, III, 47, for numbers of males and females coming to the United States, 1899–1910. The bulk of the statistical data in this chapter comes from vols. VIII and IX of the invaluable *Reports* of the Immigration Commission, covering the iron and steel industry, and will hereafter not be specifically cited in the footnotes.

The immigrants, moreover, counted the value of their hoards in terms of the increased buying power in their native villages. Mentally converting dollars into roubles, they estimated carefully that a few years of steady work would bring enough to buy a piece of land. "If I don't earn $1.50 a day," figured a prospective immigrant, "it would not be worth thinking about America." He could surely get that much in a steel mill. The large sums deposited in banks or sent home during prosperous years like 1907 verified the calculations. America, a Polish workman wrote home, "is a golden land as long as there is work." The wages in steel mills appeared to enable the peasant to achieve his purpose.[4]

The newcomers harbored no illusions about America. "There in Pittsburgh, people say, the dear sun never shines brightly, the air is saturated with stench and gas," parents in Galicia wrote their children. A workman in the South Works warned a prospective immigrant: "if he wants to come, he is not to complain about [reproach] me for in America there are neither Sundays nor holidays; he must go and work." Letters emphasized that "here in America one must work for three horses." "There are different kinds of work, heavy and light," explained another, "but a man from our country cannot get the light." An Hungarian churchman inspecting Pittsburgh steel mills exclaimed bitterly: "Wherever the heat is most insupportable, the flames most scorching, the smoke and soot most choking, there we are certain to find compatriots bent and wasted with toil."[5] Returned men, it was said, were worn out by their years in America.

Knowing about the taxing labor awaiting them, only the hardier men immigrated. Letters cautioned, "let him not risk coming, for he is still too young," or "too weak for America." The need to borrow for the trip tended to limit the opportunity to those who

[4] In 1907 immigrants in Johnstown and Steelton sent abroad $1,400,000. In September 1907 one bank on the South Side of Pittsburgh had on deposit $609,000 in immigrant accounts. See Emil Lengyel, *Americans from Hungary* (Philadelphia, 1948), pp. 182–185, for functioning of Transatlantic Trust Company set up by the Hungarian Postal Savings Bank.

[5] Peter Vay de Vaya und zu Luskod, *Inner Life in North America,* reprinted in Oscar Handlin, *This Was America* (Cambridge, Mass., 1949), p. 410.

expected to make "big money." [6] This selectivity gave the steel mills the best of Europe's peasant population.

Accustomed to village life, the adjustment to the new world of the steel mills was often painful. An Austrian Jew recalled his first day in a plant.

> The man put me in a section where there was [sic] terrible noises, shooting, thundering and lightning. I wanted to run away but there was a big train in front of me. I looked up and a big train carrying a big vessel with fire was making towards me. I stood numb, afraid to move, until a man came to me and led me out of the mill. [7]

Most weathered the first terror, the bewildering surroundings, the shouts in an unknown tongue. Appearing passive and unflinching, they grew used to the tumult and became skillful in their simple tasks.

A fat pay envelope overshadowed heavy labor and long hours; a few years' hardship was a cheap enough price for the precious savings. "I should like to have piecework, for work is never too hard," wrote a Polish peasant. "The work is very heavy, but I don't mind it," a brick factory worker informed his wife, "let it be heavy, but may it last without interruption." Russian steel laborers in Pittsburgh told an investigator they were glad to work extra days. A majority voluntarily reported on Sundays in 1907 to clear the yards and repair equipment. [8] An immigrant characterized his twelve-hour position: "A good job, save money, work all time, go home, sleep, no spend." [9] Thus did the immigrant's purpose match the policies of the employers.

The hazards of the mill alone troubled the workmen. Dangerous to experienced men, steelmaking was doubly so to untutored peasants. The accident rate for non-English-speaking employees at the South Works from 1906 to 1910 was twice the average of the

---

[6] Emily G. Balch, *Our Slavic Fellow Citizens* (New York, 1910), p. 186.

[7] Saposs Interviews, anonymous.

[8] *Pittsburgh Survey,* ed. P. U. Kellog, VI, 39–44.

[9] Walker, *Steel,* p. 28.

rest of the labor force. Almost one-quarter of the recent immigrants in the works each year — 3,273 in the five years — were injured or killed. In one year 127 Eastern Europeans died in the steel mills of Allegheny County.[10] Letters told, sometimes in gory detail, the sudden end of friend or relative. The debilitating effects of industrial life took their quieter toll on the health of the immigrants.

In misfortune, the peasant had depended on his kin and parish, whose obligations to assist were defined and certain. He left this secure web of mutual help when he came to America. A Pole explained to his wife the hard lot of an immigrant.

> As long as he is well then he always works like a mule, and therefore he has something, but if he becomes sick then it is a trouble, because everybody is looking only for money in order to get some of it, and during the sickness the most will be spent.

Illness meant expenditure without income; a lengthy convalescence drained his savings and completely frustrated his ends.

Accidents were equally catastrophic. Illiterate, ignorant of the law, unable to speak the language, the immigrant had small likelihood of successfully presenting his compensation claim. If he was killed, the chances of his dependents were even more dubious. The Pennsylvania courts had ruled that the liability statute did not extend to nonresident aliens. Whatever the company's negligence, the victim's family in Europe was helpless. More than one-fourth of the men killed in Allegheny County in the year ending July 1907 had left their dependents in Europe, and the families of a score more departed soon after the funeral. Destitution awaited them. Friends learned from letters that "the widow begs, and the children are in rags," that the woman "works in the fields" or has "gone out to service," or that the family returned to the grandparents "who are old and have nothing." [11]

Very early, the immigrants sought to ease the heavy individual risks. As soon as a number gathered in a mill town, they set up an

[10] Eastman, *Work-Accidents*, p. 14.
[11] Eastman, pp. 132, 185; *Pittsburgh Survey*, VI, 44.

informal mutual help society obligating each member to assist at sickness or death. These became local insurance associations, in time affiliating with national benefit societies which were able to provide better and cheaper coverage. For example, the National Slovanic Society for monthly dues of 60 cents paid a death benefit of $1,000 and a sick benefit of $5.00 for the first thirteen weeks and $2.50 for another thirteen weeks. Immigrant steelworkers joined in large numbers. The Polish National Alliance had thirty locals in Pittsburgh in 1908. In Homestead 421 men belonged to the Greek Catholic Union, 363 to the National Slavonic Society, 460 to the First Catholic Slovak Union, 130 to the National Croatian Society.[12] In much the same way as the native steelworkers, the immigrants partially coped with the hazards of the new world.

Bleak prospects faced the newcomers outside the mill. They settled on the low ground never far from the smoke and clamor of the plant, but also within easy walking distance to work. At Lackawanna they occupied the marshy land surrounding the works, living in houses on "made ground" surrounded by stagnant, filthy pools. In the older mill towns they pushed the inhabitants of the dreariest streets into better neighborhoods. They huddled apart in enclaves often called Hunkeyvilles — in Gary, the Patch; in Granite City, Hungary Hollow; in Vandergrift, Rising Sun.[13]

Flimsy, dilapidated structures lacking the most elementary sanitary facilities sheltered the immigrants. The Pittsburgh Bureau of Health reported after its 1907 inspection of tenement houses:

> The privy vaults were often found to be foul and full to the surface, sinks without trap or vent, the rain conductor serving

[12] Byington, p. 162; Thomas and Znaniecki, II, 1517–1521, 1570, 1577 ff. See also "The Slovaks in America," *Charities and the Commons,* Dec. 3, 1904, p. 242, on the history and functioning of the National Slavonic Society. Also, A. A. Marchbin, "Hungarian Activities in Western Pennsylvania," *Western Pennsylvania Historical Magazine,* XXIII (Sept. 1940), 163–174.

[13] Map of Johnstown showing immigrant settlements in *Report on Immigration,* VIII, 329; map of Steelton in *ibid.,* p. 659, and description of settlement process, *ibid.,* pp. 659–660; *ibid.,* p. 767, on Lackawanna; *ibid.,* IX, 44–45, on Granite City.

to carry off waste water; damp, dark, and ill-smelling cellars used for sleeping purposes; cellers filthy; leaky roofs causing the walls and ceilings to become watersoaked, rendering the rooms damp and unhealthy; broken and worn floors; broken stair railings . . . plaster broken and paper torn and dirty.[14]

Conditions were little better outside urban centers. Croatian workmen in Johnstown occupied frame houses edging a courtyard. A low four-room closet serving over fifty groups stood in the center directly over an exposed cesspool. The houses were dark, poorly ventilated, and in bad repair. Similarly, families depended on outside hydrants in the dismal immigrant courts of Homestead's Second Ward.

The inadequate dwellings were greatly overcrowded. The boarding boss and his family slept in one downstairs room in the standard four-room frame house. The kitchen was set aside for eating and living purposes, although it, too, often served as a bedroom. Upstairs the boss crammed double beds which were in use night and day when the mill was running full. Investigators came upon many cases of extreme crowding. Thirty-three Serbians and their boarding boss lived in a five-room house in Steelton. In Sharpsburg, Pennsylvania, an Italian family and nine boarders existed without running water or toilet in four rooms on the third floor of a ramshackle tenement. According to the Immigration Commission report, the number per sleeping room in immigrant households averaged around three; a sizable portion had four; and a small number six or more.

Ignorance compounded the living problems. Country people, the immigrants could not fathom the ways of urban life. Before the Pittsburgh filtration plant went into operation in 1908, many contracted typhoid fever. Doctors complained of the refusal to boil water. Despite warnings, men persisted in going to the river to quench their thirst as they had at home. Nor did they easily adjust to crowded, indoor life. Investigators found their rooms filthy, windows shut tight, sanitary facilities neglected and clogged.

[14] *Pittsburgh Survey,* V, 90 ff.

The occasional indoor bathrooms were left unused or served as storerooms.

The landlords, for their part, considered the immigrants fair game. When the newcomers invaded neighborhoods, property depreciated and frequently passed into new hands. The speculators ignored housing regulations, made no repairs or improvements, and in the continuing housing shortage and animus against immigrants, charged exorbitant rents. In some instances they received an extra dollar a month for each boarder. For much inferior accommodations, immigrant steelworkers paid an average 20 per cent more per room than did English-speaking tenants.

The local courts also fleeced the immigrants. The "squires" of the aldermanic courts in Pennsylvania received no salary, but were entitled to the fees incident to minor criminal and civil cases. Untutored in the law, they were usually brokers or real estate agents who regarded their office as a source of easy profit. And their prey were the foreigners, ignorant, inarticulate, and frightened. On pay nights the aldermen reaped handsomely from the workmen corralled into their dingy "shops" on dubious charges. An investigation of two aldermen revealed that only a small part of their criminal cases justified indictment. A Ruthenian boarding boss who had been fined $50 for disorderly conduct commented scornfully:

> Huh! The police are busy enough all right stopping disorder when the men have got money. But when there's hard times, like there is now, a man can make all the noise he pleases. . . . It ain't law they think about. It's money.

Indiana, Ohio, and Illinois justice was equally corrupt.[15]

Harsh as life in the mill towns was, room still remained for a happier side. The newcomers went usually to friends and relatives, and worked with men from their own villages. The benefit societies were convivial, and from them sprang other social organi-

[15] *Pittsburgh Survey,* V, 139–152, VI, 72, 378–379; E. A. Steiner, *The Immigrant Tide* (New York, 1909), pp. 250–251.

zations. Priests arrived as soon as there were people enough to support a church. The parish emerged to unite the activities of the ethnic, religious group into a coherent community. The later arrival in steel towns found his social needs relatively well satisfied.

There were other means of consolation. Intemperance, particularly during pay nights and marriage and birth celebrations, dismayed social workers. The immigrants had ready money, beer and whiskey cost little, and saloons served as social centers. Investigators counted 30 saloons in Duquesne, 65 in Braddock, 69 in McKeesport. Gary had one saloon for less than every hundred inhabitants; barrooms lined solidly the immigrant end of the main thoroughfare, known locally as Whiskey Row.

But the main consolation was the knowledge that the hard life was temporary, a few years' sacrifice in exchange for a competence at home.

The one essential was not wages, working conditions, or living standards, but employment itself. "When there is none," wrote one Polish laborer, America "is worth nothing." Prospective immigrants wanted to know only "whether work is good and whether it is worth while to go to America." Favorable reports emptied the villages. "An awful multitude of people are going from here to America," a Polish peasant informed his brother during the high prosperity of early 1907. The peak years of American industry — 1892, 1903, 1907, 1910 — matched the heights of immigration.

The newcomer's stay depended directly on his employment. "I have had no work for four months now," a workman wrote his brother in February 1904. "If conditions don't improve by Easter, we will go back to our country, and if they improve and I get work, I will immediately send a ship ticket and you will come." In depressed years immigration dropped sharply; one Polish woman reported in 1908 "whole throngs of people coming back from America." More Austro-Hungarians and Italians departed than arrived that year.

The effects of trade fluctuations were, if anything, exaggerated in the unstable steel industry. And the immigrants were the first to be let go. Non-English-speaking men constituted 48 per cent of the South Works labor force in 1907, 37 per cent in 1908.[16] Thirty per cent of the immigrant steelworkers surveyed by the Immigration Commission in 1908 worked less than six months, almost two-thirds under nine months. Approximately 2,425 recent immigrants left Steelton, where only half the normal work force had employment. By the end of the depression, nine-tenths of the Bulgarians, the chief unskilled labor of Granite City, had departed.

Unemployment frustrated the immigrant's aims in much the same way as illness or injury. If the depression was prolonged, he might be reduced to real want. Granite City's Hungary Hollow came with reason to be called Hungry Hollow during 1908. But the boarding boss system mitigated the worst of extreme hardship; the fortunate boarders shared with the others, and the boss rarely forced a penniless workman to leave. In every case, nevertheless, the lost job meant the collapse of the immigrant's plan. Not only did his savings stop, but his accumulation quickly drained out. Unemployment, impossible to accommodate within the immigrant's purpose, alone disturbed the unskilled labor pattern. Otherwise, the Slavic steelworker found entirely acceptable the terms of work imposed by the system of economy.

The immigrants intended to return to their villages, and many did. From 1908 to 1910 (including a bad, middling, and prosperous year) forty-four South and East Europeans departed for every hundred that arrived; altogether, 590,000 left in the three years. But more remained.

Many forces turned the immigrant away from his homeland. He saw little enough of the new country, but he was nevertheless influenced by it. He at once discarded his peasant garb, and he sensed, despite the hard life and the hostility of Americans, the disappearance of clear lines of class and status. Nothing revealed more of the American influence than the complaints of the gentry that immigrants, when they returned, were disrespectful.

Migration weakened the familial solidarity of peasant society,

[16] *Labor Conditions,* IV, 108, 166.

clouded the purposes and inherited values of the immigrant, and, particularly after the wife arrived, dimmed the image of the home village. Moreover, the presence of friends and relatives and the developing social institutions began to meet the needs of the immigrants. They in time regarded their jobs, not as temporary chances, but as their careers, and their goal became promotion rather than property at home.

The crucial fact was that in the steel mills immigrants did rise. Thomas Huras, for example, came to America in October 1910 and the following February found a job in the open-hearth department of the Gary Works. He transferred to the merchant mill, where there was more opportunity, gradually rose, and in 1918 was a catcher in the ten-inch mill. Walter Stalmaszck, at fifteen going to work on a blast furnace in the South Works, eventually became a straightener on No. 1 rail mill. When in 1914 the Joliet Works picked out men to serve as safety supervisors for their sections, many immigrant workmen received their first chance to advance.[17]

Statistics showed the process. At one large Pittsburgh mill in 1910 none of the recent immigrants with under two years' service had skilled jobs, 56 were semiskilled, 314 unskilled; between two and five years, 17 were skilled, 243 semiskilled, 544 unskilled; between five and ten years, 79 were skilled, 441 semiskilled, 475 unskilled; and over ten years, 184 were skilled, 398 semiskilled, 439 unskilled.[18] The income of immigrant steelworkers increased steadily. Less than one-tenth of any ethnic group resident less than five years earned over fifteen dollars a week; between 13 and 25 per cent resident from five to ten years; and 20 to 33 per cent resident over ten years. Altogether, 13 per cent of the recent im-

[17] *Gary Works Circle,* October 1918; *South Works Review,* June 1918, also, February 1918; *Joliet Works Mixer,* July 15, 1914. For example, Samuel Starkovitch, employed for five years in the yard now was promoted to safety man in the yard department. Many other issues give squibs on such safety workers, almost invariably immigrants.

[18] *Labor Conditions,* III, appendix C, 480 ff.; *Stanley Hearings,* IV, 2889–2893. See also *Report on Immigration,* VIII, 395–399, for figures on Cambria Works.

migrants in the industry held skilled jobs, another 42 per cent semiskilled.[19]

The pattern of life changed with lengthening residence and rising earnings. The immigrant steelworker sent for his family; two-thirds in America under five years reported wives abroad, one-third from five to nine years, and one-seventh after nine years. His living standards rose; more money went for food, clothing, and luxuries. He was willing to pay higher rent for better lodging, frequently moved his family out of the densest immigrant sections, and abandoned the boarding boss system. Habitually saving, he often bought his house. One-sixth of 1,674 immigrant steelworkers in the Immigration Commission survey owned their homes. In time he learned to speak English with fair fluency. Steve Augustinovitch, a Croat who immigrated at the age of eighteen, was typical. Foreman of a repair crew at the Gary Works at twenty-eight, he owned his house, had savings, a large family, and his first citizenship papers.[20]

In short, he merged with other skilled steelworkers. Distinguishable ethnically and perhaps socially, within the plant he moved in the same orbit of dependence and repression. If anything, the immigrants were more susceptible to the employers' strategy, for the peasant mentality sharply distinguished between independent farming and hired labor. The immigrant felt less secure in his job than the native steelworkers, whose experience encompassed only hired employment, and he therefore became a more docile, loyal employee.[21]

The stability in the unskilled ranks thus rested on mobility. The newcomers either moved up into the skilled force; or they moved out at the first depression or with a satisfactory accumulation. Despite the harsh terms of work, therefore, steel companies enjoyed peaceful relations with their common laborers.

[19] *Report on Immigration,* VIII, 54–55. Lowering the figure to $12.50 a week added 25 per cent to each group.

[20] *Gary Works Circle,* February 1918.

[21] See, for example, Saposs Interviews, Mike Stephan in McKeesport, July 29, 1920; Julius Danko, McKeesport; and blast furnace labor foreman in McKeesport, August 2, 1920.

The employer's part in maintaining the pattern was essentially passive. He was generally ignorant of the reasons why the immigrants came to America. But he recognized them as a "floating supply of labor." [22] That simple, crucial fact governed his decisions.

Hiring and firing policies assumed the mobility of common labor. Employment officials did not investigate the immigrants, kept no detailed records, and observed individual capacity only for physical strength. When labor was plentiful, foremen usually picked likely men out of the jobless crowds that gathered before the mill gates at the changing of the shift.

To insure a steady supply, companies reached understandings with immigrant leaders. The employment manager, said the labor supervisor of the South Works,

> . . . must not only be aware of the location of all the groups of foreign settlement in the community, but he must become personally acquainted with the individual boarding bosses, steamship agents, clergymen, and other influential agents. . . . These are his supply depots, and only by perpetual, personal reconnoitering can he remain familiar with the quality and quantity of available applicants.[23]

The steel plants in Granite City, for instance, had an agreement to employ all the applicants of a Bulgarian leader. Boarding bosses, when they were gang foremen, could hire as well as lodge workmen. Before the immigrant channels to mill towns developed, steel companies had sent agents to New York City docks or employed labor agencies. That was rarely necessary in later years except during serious shortages.

Welfare efforts, designed to attach workmen to the company, did not extend to common labor. "The problem of maintaining a force of skilled workmen is realized by every employer" and "much attention has been given to" their welfare, observed the *Iron Age,* "but the unskilled employee of shop or foundry gets

---

[22] *IA,* October 30, 1913, p. 987.
[23] A. H. Young, "Employing Men for a Steel Mill," *IA,* November 16, 1916, p. 1108.

little attention." [24] The difference could be seen most clearly in housing programs. One company in the Eastern district provided excellent facilities at low cost for its higher paid men. For unskilled labor, the firm offered "shanties," an appropriate designation. Ten by fourteen feet, these were constructed of ordinary rough pine boards weatherstripped on the outside. Four men ate, washed, and slept in each shanty. Four "barracks," built like the shanties, housed twenty men each. All the structures were primitively furnished, and damp and cold in winter. According to the federal Bureau of Labor estimate, the rent amounted each year to more than 200 per cent of the company's original investment.[25] In less isolated areas employers generally ignored the housing problems of the immigrants.

The few efforts at improvement proved dismal failures. Lackawanna erected a village of monotonous but substantial houses around its new plant for low paid employees. And the Steel Corporation put up fifty dwellings — "double dry goods boxes" — for its laborers at Gary. But the men did not understand the need for sanitation and objected to the lack of amusements in the vicinity. The Gary houses were filthy, used as boarding houses, and greatly overcrowded. Within a few years the Corporation evicted the inhabitants of the notorious Hunkeyville and razed the houses.[26] The experiment was admittedly unsuccessful.

> The housing provided by the Corporation is perhaps better suited to the needs of the skilled workmen than to the wages of the unskilled laborers [who are] largely foreigners without families. . . . These men earn low wages, out of which they seek to save the utmost amount possible.[27]

[24] *IA*, February 19, 1914, p. 504.

[25] *Labor Conditions*, III, 420–426.

[26] G. R. Taylor, "Creating the Newest Steel City," *Survey*, April 3, 1909, pp. 20–36; J. A. Fitch, "Lackawanna," *Survey*, October 7, 1911, pp. 929–945; Gary *Post-Tribune*, May 23, 1923.

[27] U.S. Steel Corporation, Bureau of Safety, Sanitation, and Welfare, *Bulletin*, No. 5, p. 56.

The Steel Corporation thereupon left the immigrant steelworkers to their own devices, erecting housing designed only for the higher ranks. Other measures to reduce labor turnover — pensions, profit sharing, stock purchase — likewise bypassed the unskilled.

The steel manufacturers had ready answers for the criticisms of reformers. The immigrants, they said, were eager to work the long hours for the greater earnings. They received wages higher than for similar work in Europe. Their living conditions were worse than the skilled workers' not because of smaller income, but because their wages were dissipated in "debauch." However bad their life appeared, said a Pittsburgh employer, it "is probably somewhat better than that to which such foreign workmen were accustomed in their own countries." [28]

It was not that steel manufacturers undervalued the immigrants. Although claiming natives to be superior workmen, employers understood very well their good fortune. They dealt with the immigrant steelworkers as they did because nothing else was necessary. Developing without any effort on their part, the unskilled labor pattern of mobility fitted perfectly into the scheme of economical steel manufacture. The steelmakers were content.

[28] *IA*, March 24, 1910, pp. 670–671 (a series of short statements by Pittsburgh employers in reply to charges by the Federal Council of Churches).

Chapter VI

The Sources of Stability: The Mill Towns

While skilled and unskilled workmen made their separate accommodations to modern steel manufacture, a favorable setting
for stability was developing in the mill towns. Local support for
management was vital for the maintenance of the labor status quo.
The decline of union organization opened the way for an alliance.
Economic and social circumstances drew the citizenry into the
employer's camp. The connection rested, at bottom, on the central
place of the steel plant in the life of the community.

With the growth of the industry, urban areas had sprung up
around the great steel works that lined the rivers of the Ohio
Valley and the shores of the Great Lakes. Medium-sized in population, Lackawanna, McKeesport, Gary, and a score of other steel
centers were one-industry towns. There lived three-fifths of the
steelworkers. Steel manufacture dominated even cities, constituting
five-sixths of the industry in Youngstown, one-half in Pittsburgh,
and one-fifth in Cleveland. More important, even in these densely
populated regions, every major plant fostered its own community:
for instance, South Chicago or East Youngstown. The ruling
presence of the mill shaped the mentality of the steel centers.

It was a matter of self-interest. For years the South Works
built out onto Lake Michigan until a zealous public official enforced the law and ordered a halt. Two hundred South Chicago
citizens journeyed to Springfield, lobbied for two weeks, and won
a bill permitting U.S. Steel to fill in along the lake front for a
nominal sum. Nevertheless, the Steel Corporation erected its new
Gary Works. "The big plant would have been built here instead

of at Gary," grumbled an old South Chicago man, but "for that damn little cuss of a public works commissioner."[1] The profits of local enterprise rested on the existence of the mill.

The logic could be seen in reverse as well. The giant plant at Gary hugged the lake shore. Owning the land south to the Wabash Railroad tracks, the Corporation planned Fifth Avenue, running east-west north of the tracks, to be the main street around which settlement would grow. The realtors, limited to the territory to the south, desired development along the north-south artery, Broadway, and they began to improve its lower portions. The projected street railway became the crucial issue. U.S. Steel wanted the main line along Fifth Avenue. Its workmen would then settle in the surrounding area, easily accessible to the works. A bitter fight resulted. The business people captured the newly formed municipal government and awarded the franchise to one of their number to build the main car line on Broadway. Gary thus developed along Broadway, thwarting the Corporation's plans. One curious result of the victory was that the better section of town was closer to the mill than were the slums.[2]

The sharp clash of interests was highly unusual. Ordinarily, profit dictated agreement rather than conflict. Even at Gary, resentment quickly subsided. Mill officials and merchants soon joined together in a Citizens' Party to depose the mayor, who was trying to keep the antagonism alive. The outcome of the Gary conflict was equally uncharacteristic, for the mill held the strategic position as the source of the town's prosperity and, indeed, existence. Cognizant of this, the Real Estate Board had appointed a committee to induce new industry into Gary. The futility of the attempt no doubt intensified the eagerness to reach an accord with the mill officials, once the objectives of the realtors had been gained.

Troubled times exposed to view the local strength of the steel

[1] J. A. Fitch, "Illinois: Boosting for Safety," *Survey,* November 4, 1911, pp. 1146, 1159.

[2] Isaac J. Quillen, "Industrial City. A History of Gary, Indiana, to 1929," unpublished Ph.D. thesis, Yale, 1942, pp. 138–142, 208–216, 251–254.

companies. During the 1909 strike, the district manager of the American Sheet and Tin Plate Company invited to an informal meeting the leading businessmen of Wheeling. He read a letter from the president, E. W. Pargny. The company was withholding $200,000 for improvements planned for Wheeling plants. "I am not now prepared to say that it will ever be spent," Pargny warned. He repeated the remark of a high U.S. Steel official:

> . . . that unless our operations in that locality could be carried on with less trouble incident to labor, and more cooperation on the part of the community, the natural outcome would be the boarding up of the plants . . . and moving them elsewhere.

Afterward, the district manager handed the letter to the press. In the next weeks, rumors abounded that the Corporation planned to concentrate all the Wheeling district mills at Gary. Shortly, strikers were watching the apparent dismantling of plants at Wheeling and Bridgeport, Ohio, the machinery reportedly consigned to Gary.[3]

Similar events transpired in other mill towns during the strike. "Because McKeesport . . . has a population that is largely in sympathy with lawlessness, and has a mayor who will not use his police to protect the property of manufacturers and will not permit a nonunion man seeking work to enter town," an official announced, the W. Dewees Wood plant was being dismantled. The threat was common then, as well as in the earlier conflict of 1901.[4]

An opportunity did present itself to discard some old, inefficient mills. But the Corporation had not really intended in 1909 to dismantle its modern plants. The warning, some strikers recognized, was a "bugaboo." For many Wheeling people, however, "the opening of the mills came somewhat as a surprise."

[3] Chicago *Daily Socialist,* December 21, 1909; *NLT,* October 14, 1909, December 23, 30, 1909.
[4] Iron and Steel Association, *Bulletin,* August 25, 1910 (clipping in the American Iron and Steel Institute Library); Youngstown *Labor News,* August 16, 23, 1901; New York *Tribune,* August 15, 1901.

Possible beneficiaries of removal also took the threats seriously. In the 1901 strike shopkeepers and nonunion men at Vandergrift met to ask the sheet steel company to move the McKeesport mill there. Local businessmen in 1910 hoped for the relocation of some Wheeling mills in New Castle, "where it will be possible to operate its own plants at the least prospect of interference." [5]

The merchants' response was less clear while life was still in the local unions. At Elwood, Indiana, businessmen banded together at the warning, refused to give credit or employment to the strikers, and thus weakened the strike. The Businessmen's Exchange of New Castle passed a resolution of neutrality, but declared that either party had the right to carry on its activities unhindered; that picketing should be prohibited; and "that the mayor be commended for his action in enforcing the laws." [6] Beyond this, merchants feared to go until the union was definitely broken. They were deterred by the high wages and standing of the striking skilled men, as well as the damaging effect of an antiunion stigma on business.

Businessmen were not similarly fettered during an unorganized strike early in 1910 at South Bethlehem. They had at first sympathized with the men. Then the overzealous strike leaders petitioned Congress to halt the government armor contracts until the company improved working conditions. President Schwab threatened to close down the works unless the merchants rallied to his support. A committee rushed to Washington to counteract the petition. The Industrial Commission of business and professional men met to consider the differences between the company and "a number of misled men on strike." The Commission denounced "the unscrupulous and non-resident agitators" for arresting "the development of the town" to the "great pecuniary loss of the business interests and of the invested capital of our citizens." The meeting ended on a note of gratitude.

> We desire to express our appreciation of Mr. Charles M. Schwab for the great things he has already accomplished for

[5] *NLT*, August 15, 1901, September 1, 8, 1910.
[6] *Amalgamated Journal*, February 3, 1910, p. 8.

this community and trust he will not be diverted by the unfortunate industrial dissensions from continuing to carry out his great plans. We stand ready now as in the past to aid him in whatever way we can.[7]

The sense of dependence necessarily allied the business elements with the steel men.

Somewhat similar considerations directed the religious and service groups. Their main source of material assistance was the steel plants. The Pennsylvania Steel Company presented to Steelton a brick school building costing $100,000, and contributed to the unusually high salary of the school superintendent. The Colorado Fuel and Iron Company built and staffed the excellent hospital at Pueblo. The Steel Corporation erected the schools, library, hospital, and magnificent Y.M.C.A. building at Gary. Companies customarily followed this policy when they established plants outside settled areas.

Employers everywhere tended to be liberal and cooperative. When the First Hungarian Reformed Church was being built in Pittsburgh, the minister collected substantial sums from the steel companies in the vicinity. The Bethlehem Company deducted for their churches one dollar a month from the pay envelopes of its Catholic workmen. "It is a great thing to keep in touch with the priests and the clergy," Judge E. H. Gary told U.S. Steel subsidiary presidents. "The pastors are in contact with the families and the workmen themselves."[8] The Steel Corporation figured charitable contributions as a regular expense in the budget.

Generosity had its effect. Tom Girdler remembered from his years as superintendent of the Jones and Laughlin plant at Aliquippa "the habit of everyone to look to the company for anything the community needed. . . . The most anybody ever did

[7] *Report on Bethlehem Strike,* pp. 20, 48 ff., 130; J. A. Fitch, "Bethlehem: The Church and the Steelworkers," *Survey,* December 2, 1911, pp. 1289–1298.

[8] E. H. Gary Address to U.S. Steel Subsidiary Presidents, January 2, 1919, *Addresses and Statements by Gary,* III.

was to make a suggestion and immediately bracket it with a fulfillment by saying, 'We'll ask the company.' " [9] Thinking thus, men were unlikely to be critical of the steel mill.

During the Bethlehem strike, for instance, steelworkers' leaders complained that "the church as a whole . . . gave no aid to the men." "The Protestant Ministerial Association as a body practically championed the cause of the corporation." When the Federal Council of Churches inquired, Bethlehem clergymen asserted that they had appealed to the company against Sunday labor and had formed a strike mediation committee. But only one, a Catholic priest, openly supported the men, appeared at their meetings, and urged them on. A notice in the local press revealed the attitude of the others.

> Only the officials of the company can accomplish the righting of any existing wrongs. . . . Is it reasonable to expect that by attacking your employer, you can persuade him to deal generously and magnanimously with you?

Such statements, the Federal Council investigators judged, afforded "some warrant for the belief of the strikers that the ministers inclined to favor the corporation." [10] The chief concern was to end the conflict, not to consider the workmen's grievances.

Reforming zeal was similarly lacking among Pittsburgh pastors. An outcry had arisen in late 1898 from workmen and unions at the introduction of Sunday labor in steel mills. A committee of churchmen formed, and called meetings of the Pittsburgh clergy. But most hesitated before definite proposals, and the movement failed. [11] More than other cities, Pittsburgh enforced its Sabbath and liquor laws. In 1908 an effective campaign ended Sunday labor in drugstores and confectionaries. But the Sabbatarian spirit was never leveled against the seven-day week in the steel mills.

When the Y.M.C.A. secretary in a Pennsylvania steel town ex-

[9] Tom M. Girdler, *Bootstraps* (New York, 1943), p. 175.
[10] *Survey,* July 2, 1910, pp. 576-578, December 2, 1911, p. 1296.
[11] *Industrial Commission,* VII, 391-392.

plained that few steelworkers were members because of their long hours, the Survey investigator suggested that the Association campaign for a shorter day. The secretary hastily replied:

> O, no, we could not do that. In the first place, the association is the child, you might say, of the steel company. They are the heaviest contributors. . . . Probably [the State Association] couldn't touch it either. You see, we are backed up everywhere by the substantial businessmen of the various localities; they would not stand for any such movement.

Moreover, the company had donated the high school building to the borough and done more than anyone else to further public education. The Y.M.C.A. president was chairman of the school board; how could he oppose his benefactors? [12] The interests of the noncommercial groups, as with the merchant class, attached them to the companies.

The social alignments of the steel towns also buttressed the dominance of management. In this sphere, too, lack of diversity was the paramount factor. Company officials were ordinarily the leading citizens. The vice president of the Brier Hill Steel Company presided over the Youngstown Chamber of Commerce; the superintendent of the Carnegie Works was vice president. A high official of Illinois Steel belonged to the Chicago School Board, as did the head of the American Rolling Mill Company at Middletown, Ohio. The president of the Gary park board was the mill superintendent, and another official headed the Commercial Club. Tom Girdler was a Rotarian and a lusty vestryman in the Episcopal church at Aliquippa. The presence of company men set the tone of life in the mill towns.

The more substantial merchants and professionals recognized a kinship with the plant officialdom. They lived in the same sections, frequented the same clubs and churches, and shared its outlook on industrial and business matters. They had, investigators noted, small interest in the conditions in the mills. The Protestant

---

[12] *Survey,* April 6, 1912, p. 21.

clergy were likewise ignorant; they were, as one observer put it, "sincere but otherworldly." Social identity held together the inhabitants of the high ground that overlooked the grimy towns.

Closer to the works, the lawns became smaller and the houses plainer. Here dwelled the shopkeepers, the minor mill functionaries, and also the skilled workers. All belonged to the same fraternal organizations and churches. Living on the same careful scale, they held in common small ambitions and threadbare respectability. Middle class in outlook, they tended to turn to their betters for guidance and standards. The skilled steelworkers, laboring men as they were, were drawn into this orbit largely in response to ethnic tensions in the mills.

An unbridgeable gulf separated, in mill parlance, the "Hunky" and "English-speaking" workmen. The English, Irish, and Germans were distributed in the mills in roughly the same pattern as Americans, and grouped with them as English-speaking.[13] But the strange-tongued Slavic peasant repelled the native workers. "Here I am with these Hunkies," complained an old-timer whose friends had left the mill. "They don't seem like men to me hardly. They can't talk United States. You tell them something and they just look and say 'Me no fustay, me no fustay,' that's all you can get out of 'em." [14] The immigrants seemed an ignorant and degraded breed of man.

Widely differing situations contributed to the sense of distance. A skilled man complained of the laziness of the Rumanian stokers at the Fort Wayne Rolling Mill.

As soon as the night boss turns his back . . . they just drop down and sleep while the company pays them wages and gets nothing in return. If an American would do the same there would be no excuse taken from him that would save his job, no matter if he worked a double turn or not. [This was the boss' excuse for the Rumanians.] But what if he did, he might as

[13] See, for example, editorial in *NLT,* July 29, 1909; R. T. Berthoff, *British Immigrants in Industrial America* (Cambridge, Mass., 1953), ch. 5.

[14] Fitch, *Steel Workers,* p. 12.

well be home asleep as in the mill drawing pay for sleeping while the firm gets no results, and the men have to work a lot of cold blooms.

The weariness of the Rumanians on the twenty-four-hour shift meant to him lost tonnage, and harder work "without any more credit for it than they give those fellows that get paid for sleeping." [15] Workers in the same plant, skilled and unskilled men shared little more than a common employer.

Steelworkers widely held the belief that immigrants lowered labor standards and displaced natives, but few, if any, could actually point to personal suffering because of the newcomers. Rather, the influx combined with the industry's growth to push them upward into the skilled and supervisory ranks.

The presence of immigrants did limit the jobs socially appropriate for native workers. When an investigator requested employment on a blast furnace, he was informed that "only Hunkies work on those jobs, they're too damn dirty and too damn hot for a 'white' man." Laborers could not believe that another investigator was native-born. "No white American work in steel-plant labor gang unless he' nuts or booze-fighter." When the plant manager at Steelton offered his skilled men immigrants' jobs during the 1908 depression, he was surprised to find few takers.[16]

One consequence of this sense of superiority was a dwindling supply of natives to fill openings in the skilled ranks. "Many American boys fancy that they degrade themselves by entering into competition with a Slav for a job," observed John Fitch. They preferred "pencil jobs," another inquirer added, which they "apparently considered more gentlemanly." By 1910 steel men consequently noted the shrinking number of native steelworkers, even in the skilled jobs.

The English-speaking workman was in general content to ignore the immigrants. Outside the mill he rarely encountered

[15] Letter from P. W. Kohli, Fort Wayne Lodge No. 17, *Amalgamated Journal*, December 26, 1912, p. 12.

[16] Walker, *Steel*, p. 107; Williams, *What's on the Worker's Mind*, p. 33; *Report on Immigration*, VIII, 597.

them or entered their crowded streets. But indifference often edged
into animosity. The very term "Hunky" was contemptuous. A
heater who had worked in the Shenango mill during the 1909
strike described his experience.

> There is a . . . crowd of Negroes and Syrians working there.
> Many of them are filthy in their personal habits, and the idea
> of working with them is repugnant to any man who wants to
> retain his self respect. It is no place for a man with a white
> man's heart to be. The Negroes and foreigners are coarse,
> vulgar and brutal in their acts and conversation.[17]

Disdain could be read also in the stereotyped Dago and Hunky
in the short stories that appeared in labor papers, and in the
frankly hostile remarks of native workers to investigators.

Eager to dissociate himself from the Hunky, the skilled man
identified with the middling group of small shopkeepers and
artisans, and with them came to regard the merchants and
managers as his models. Whatever his interests may have been,
the English-speaking steelworker had a psychological commitment
in favor of his employer. As much for social as for economic
reasons, the citizenry of the mill towns aligned with the steel
companies.

In times of labor strife, the support of local government was
critically important. There had been much sympathy at first for
the unorganized strikers at South Bethlehem in 1910. The men
were given free use of the town hall, and left unmolested in their
meetings and activities; and the strike flourished. Once sentiment
turned against the strikers, however, the council closed the town
hall to them, and the sheriff called in the state constabulary. Soon
workmen were being arrested and beaten by the "cossacks."
Political assistance had strengthened the strike; opposition broke
it.

At its peak of power the Amalgamated Association had found
important sources of strength in the mill town government. Its

[17] Letter from August Arnold, *Amalgamated Journal*, October 28, 1909, p. 1.

domination of Homestead accounted for its strategy in the bloody strike of 1892. There and elsewhere union members held public office and directed the affairs of steel towns. Even when not including unionists, municipal administrations normally favored the cause of strong lodges. "I am with the Amalgamated Association men in this fight to the end," asserted Mayor W. J. O'Donnell of Mingo Junction, Ohio, during the 1901 dispute. The burgess of Braddock actually urged strikers to "run nonunion men out of town." Support came in equal measure from merchants and clergymen. At Canton, Ohio, for instance, ministers of all denominations prayed for a quick end to the strike in 1901. "The men have asked for nothing unreasonable," said one churchman, "and the only way to attain their demands is to show a perfect union spirit." [18] Steel towns were useful allies of the union, where it was entrenched.

Steel companies, too, utilized friendly municipal administrations. Public powers were even more effective in forestalling than in defending unionization. At Wellsville the mayor arrested union men during an organizing attempt in the 1901 strike. The burgess of Vandergrift ordered five Amalgamated organizers out of town during the 1909 strike, and prohibited even the Labor Day parade because it

> . . . would mar the peace and harmony which now pervades the entire community. . . . Marches, parades, meetings, and demonstrations by persons, mostly non-residents . . . could have no other effect than to engender ill feeling among our citizens and neighbors.

Similarly, the Morgantown, West Virginia, mayor informed the A.F.L. representative that "in view of his mission he was not wanted here." When workmen responded to union agitation,

[18] Youngstown *Labor News,* August 30, 1901; *NLT,* August 1, 1901; New York *Tribune,* August 3, 13, 1901; *Independent,* August 1, 1901, p. 1768. On unionists in office, see, for example, Arthur C. Burgoyne, *Homestead . . . the Struggle of July, 1892* (Pittsburgh, 1893), pp. 37–40; *American Federationist,* August 1909, p. 860, October 1909, p. 889.

authorities customarily prohibited meetings and countenanced violence against the strikers. Many towns in the Pittsburgh district had the power to restrict free speech and assembly. The ordinances were freely applied against labor organization.[19]

Considering its usefulness, steel men bent every effort to dominate local government. New towns were easy marks. One community in the Eastern district serving a medium-sized plant had no formal government. The justice of the peace, also school superintendent and coroner, considered himself "practically an employee of the company," as were the police. Aliquippa, Pennsylvania, had a municipal administration, but the real control rested in the hands of the plant superintendent. "In fact, I suppose I was a sort of political boss," recalled Tom Girdler. "I had considerable power without responsibility to the people." Company police supplemented the ineffectual town constabulary.[20] Such localities were completely under the company's thumb.

Steel officials frequently held public office in steel towns, just as Amalgamated leaders did where the union was strong. The vice president of Pennsylvania Steel and an official of U.S. Steel presided over the city councils of Steelton and Gary. In 1919 mill executives were president of the Homestead borough council, burgess of neighboring Munhall, and burgess of Clairton. The sheriff of Allegheny County and the mayor of Duquesne were brothers of important steel men. But an office holder needed no connection with the mill to be the company's man.

"The favorable or unfavorable attitude of the company toward candidates for office seems . . . to constitute the most important influence in local politics," observed an investigator in Steelton.[21] The pressure could be devious or direct. The plant magazine at the Gary Works ran photographs in support of employees running

[19] *Amalgamated Journal,* September 12, 1912, p. 13; Amalgamated Association, *Proceedings* (1910), pp. 8880–8927; A.F.L., *Newsletter,* February 1, 1913, August 16, 1913. The use of injunctions by sympathetic local judges could also be useful. See, for example, *IA,* September 22, 1904, p. 22, Chicago *Daily Socialist,* October 13, 1909.
[20] *Labor Conditions,* III, 420; Girdler, pp. 177–178.
[21] *Report on Immigration,* VIII, 582.

for city council. In Braddock the Steel Corporation intimated in 1908 that the works would resume if its candidates were nominated. Employees were often convinced that voting against the company meant discharge. An investigation in Duquesne heard repeatedly of such dismissals. One embittered Braddock resident charged: "There is not such a perfect political organization in the country as the steel trust. . . . You ought to see the way they line up their men at the polls and vote them by the thousands."

The primary of 1908 in Braddock evoked unusual bitterness. The main issue was local liquor option, for which a number of mill officials had become active. Then the superintendent received orders to support the Penrose candidates, opponents of local option. The Corporation "needed [Boies Penrose] in the Senate." Despite some muttering, the officials reversed themselves. Penrose carried Allegheny County.[22]

Ordinarily, steel companies did not find it necessary to press actively for their favorites. Because shopkeepers, clergy, and skilled men came to identify their interests with the mill, all were likely to unite on one ticket. (The political realignment after the clash of merchant and mill at Gary was a striking instance.) Political support was only the most concrete manifestation of the ties of the local groups with the steel mills.

Openly and actively in crisis, quietly but continuously in normal times, the mill towns exerted their stabilizing influence on the labor status quo as it had developed since the technological revolution in the steel industry.

[22] Fitch, pp. 229–231. The immigrant played a negligible role in steel town politics. In Indiana, however, aliens who declared an intention to become citizens were eligible to vote in a short time. In Gary the boarding bosses or foremen led them to the circuit court to signify their intention, and on election day herded them to the polls.

Chapter VII

Toward Industrial Unionism

Steel men of 1910 could congratulate themselves on the success of their labor efforts. They had overcome the last impediment of organized labor. Their policy of wages and hours conformed to the requirements of economy. And patterns of adjustment and stability had developed within the steel mills and towns. The very completeness of the achievement, however, set in motion countervailing forces in the American labor movement.

The defects of craft organization accounted for the easy victory of the steelmasters. Once the primary source of union strength had been the control of steelmaking skills. But an exclusive craft union became ineffectual in the face of industrial unification and mechanization. Only a union of all steelworkers could withstand the modern steel corporation. That hard fact was accepted when labor organization reached the edge of bankruptcy. U.S. Steel's open-shop announcement of June 1, 1909 — the final step in the construction of the system of economy — marked also the turning point away from narrow craft unionism in the steel industry.

The Amalgamated leadership had not wholly ignored the consequences of advancing technology. The membership had in fact been gradually widened from its narrow skilled craft basis until in 1889 even laborers were admitted "at the discretion of the Subordinate Lodge." This was, however, only a token recognition of the changing industrial situation. Few locals exercised their prerogative. A later president admitted that "the unskilled men have never received encouragement to join our ranks." [1] The Amalgamated Association sought to avoid the unpleasant prospect of opening its doors to the rabble of unskilled immigrants.

The union after 1901 staked its future on the goodwill of the Steel Corporation. Perhaps the steel trust would permit it to extend to all the sheet and tin mills, and eventually even to regain the ground lost among the skilled men since 1892. The open-shop declaration dashed that hope. The Amalgamated Association would have to rely on its own strength; and strength required the admission of the unskilled.

The U.S. Steel announcement "opened the way for a general attack on all of its plants by Amalgamated men," proclaimed Secretary John Williams.

> We were held in check more or less in the past because we did not want to injure our standing with the sheet and tinplate departments by pushing our organization in other unorganized mills. Now that restraint is off.

The union acknowledged that exclusiveness had undermined its vitality. "The self-centered aristocratic Amalgamated Association looked with contempt upon the unskilled workers," wrote a member, "and the manufacturers took advantage of the situation." That attitude, Williams admitted, "has in large measure been responsible for our lack of solidarity." [2] The 1910 convention amended the constitution to open membership to all ironworkers and steelworkers; the path was clear for the transformation of the Association.

In an official circular President P. J. McArdle had earlier invited all steelworkers to join the Association. "There is but one way to relieve [the] situation for the men in the iron and steel industry," he pronounced. "That is to organize them into a powerful or-

---

[1] *Amalgamated Journal,* August 22, 1912, p. 1, cited hereafter as *AJ.* During the dispute in 1888 with the Knights of Labor, who were taking in unskilled steelworkers, Secretary William Martin had urged the admission of these men to the Amalgamated. Robinson, *Amalgamated Association,* pp. 49–50.

[2] *NLT,* July 15, 1909; *AJ,* December 7, 1911, p. 1, August 22, 1912, p. 1.

ganization, embracing all branches of the steel and iron industry, beginning with the blast furnaces."

The Amalgamated Association is undertaking the task. . . . [It] asks you, as one of the workers, regardless of nationality or creed, to join with it in its fight for the emancipation of yourself and fellow workmen from the industrial tyranny of the steel masters of the country.

The union dispatched organizers to trust sheet mills, and tentatively attempted to interest furnace workers in the Mahoning and Shenango valleys.[3] But the job of reaching several hundred thousand steelworkers was beyond the resources of the Amalgamated Association.

The second effect of the open-shop announcement came into play at this point. Other unions had not been greatly excited by the fate of organization in the steel industry until 1909. Then their indifference came to an end.

The attitude of organized labor had been based partly on the earlier place of the Amalgamated Association among the strong A.F.L. unions. It had, as Gompers observed, usually given, rather than received, assistance. The Amalgamated had always seemed capable of protecting its own interests. The reputation persisted without basis in later years.

In addition, the union alienated potential support. President T. J. Shaffer's inept leadership isolated the Association during the 1901 strike, when the need for help was very clear. He had precipitated the conflict, recklessly broken contracts, and demanded sympathy strikes. After requesting Gompers' intercession, the union foolishly rejected the compromise offer won by his efforts. Further, before the strike Shaffer plotted against the A.F.L., during the struggle he appealed for assistance without its sanction, and afterward he accused Gompers and John Mitchell of indif-

[3] *AJ*, October 7, 1909, p. 1; Amalgamated Association, *Proceedings* (1910), p. 8841; Cleveland *Citizen*, August 21, October 13, 1909; *NLT*, September 30, 1909.

ference. Consequently, the Amalgamated Association was left to its own devices.[4]

The Steel Corporation, by contrast, emerged from the contest in a favorable light. J. P. Morgan and Charles Schwab had acted in a reasonable and even friendly manner. Union leaders afterward associated amicably with the heads of the Corporation on the National Civic Federation. Finally, U.S. Steel continued to deal with unions without apparent rancor. The Steel Corporation did not seem to threaten organized labor. If recognition was limited and gradually lessening, it was still more than union men found in other trusts. After the excitement subsided, they, like the Amalgamated Association, kept silent and hoped for the best.

When it came, the open-shop announcement shocked organized labor everywhere. The Amalgamated Association had held its convention of May 1909 in Cleveland. At its end the local labor paper congratulated the delegates on their happy relations with employers and their "splendid and progressive organization, of which they have a right to feel proud." In June, a month later, satisfaction turned to anger. The trust "proposes to crush labor" and "establish a feudalism," the journal cried. "When will the iron and steel workers display as much backbone as the miners and strike?"[5]

A torrent of criticism rained on the Steel Corporation. "Never was a more unjust contention instituted than the onslaught of the steel trust," charged the *American Federationist*. "The relentless war of extermination carried on by the gigantic Steel Trust," President E. F. Greenewalt told the Pennsylvania Federation of Labor, was "a shining example of the labor crushing tactics employed by the overgrown combinations." The debates of city centrals, meeting to consider the strike tax, were bitter. "The steel trust conducts the most vicious system of exploitation in existence," a Structural Workers official told the Chicago Federation

[4] On the bitter dispute precipitated by Shaffer's irresponsible charges, see *American Federationist*, October 1901, pp. 415-431, cited hereafter as *AF*; A.F.L., *Proceedings* (1902), pp. 127, 172-178; Taft, *A.F. of L.*, pp. 240-242.

[5] Cleveland *Citizen*, May 22, June 19, 26, 1909.

of Labor. The anger was translated into generous support, even from wholly unrelated unions.[6]

The Steel Corporation had become a generalized danger. Union men recalled now the long history of antiunionism in the industry. There were reports of actions against the remaining union men in Corporation plants. The Seamen's Union was fighting for survival against the Lake Carriers' Association. "The trust is stinking drunk," cried the Cleveland *Citizen*.[7]

The open-shop declaration killed any expectation for the peaceable unionization of the vast properties of the Steel Corporation. The United Mine Workers, for instance, coveted the coal fields and was reported "apprehensive" over the continual extension of Corporation holdings. In March 1910 a bitter strike broke out at the independent mines adjacent to U.S. Steel's coke lands in Westmoreland County, south of Pittsburgh.[8] Only a unionized steel trust would make possible the organization of this coal country, as well as other broad segments of the economy.

Finally, the plain hostility in the announcement frightened organized labor. No friction had preceded withdrawal of recognition; the Corporation simply did not desire to deal with the union. This endangered unions everywhere, particularly because of the leading position of U.S. Steel in American industry. Left unchallenged, President McArdle warned, the example would encourage "other corporations to begin conflicts with organized labor." There was little wonder that the unions unanimously recognized the Corporation "as the most formidable and aggressive enemy that the movement has to contend with."[9]

The Amalgamated Association was committed to organizing all

[6] *AF*, October 1909, p. 876; Lancaster, Pa., *Labor Leader*, August 7, December 4, 1909; Cleveland *Citizen*, January 8, 1910; Chicago *Daily Socialist*, October 7, 1909, January 4, 1910.

[7] Cleveland *Citizen*, August 28, 1909, July 3, 10, 1909; *Machinists' Journal*, October 1909, p. 891.

[8] S. M. Harrison and P. U. Kellog, "The Westmoreland Strike," *Survey*, December 3, 1910, pp. 345–366; United Mine Workers, *Proceedings* (1911), pp. 52–53, 41–47, 74–75.

[9] A.F.L., *Proceedings* (1909), pp. 226–227.

iron and steel workmen. And the labor movement was arrayed behind the endeavor. There remained, however, the practical problems of channeling the efforts and of handling the raw recruits.

Here the American Federation of Labor became important. The Federation leadership had always concerned itself about the unskilled and unorganized. "The constant aim of the union movement," Samuel Gompers had said in 1897, has been "to organize our fellow workers in unskilled labor." [10] The task in fields neglected by the national unions resided in practice with the A.F.L. Its organizing resources were slender, for the locus of power centered in the affiliated nationals. But the Federation retained a measure of strength from its tax on the affiliates and its ability to request their assistance. In the early years, the former was the more important for its unionizing work. In 1901 the A.F.L. employed a score of organizers who had been put on a permanent basis only a few years earlier. There were also over eight hundred volunteer workers, mainly local officials scattered across the country.

Organizational forms were devised. The unorganized in a locality were gathered indiscriminately into "federal labor unions." When a sufficient number in one occupation accumulated, they were drawn off and formed into locals (often over the protests of the federal union leadership). The newborn unions were promptly affiliated with the appropriate national union. Those locals falling outside all existing jurisdictions, as well as the federal unions, had the same connection with the A.F.L. as did ordinary locals with their national unions.

The A.F.L. was active in the steel industry in the 1890's. Organizers founded numbers of local trade unions of wire drawers, iron and steel workers, tin house men, and tube workers. The Federation representative at New Castle, Pennsylvania, reported in June 1895: "The blast furnace men are organized under the A.F.L., have secured an advance, and are getting along splen-

[10] President's Report, A.F.L., *Proceedings* (1897), p. 6.

didly." By the end of the summer charters were issued to four furnace workers' unions in Pennsylvania.[11]

Once established, these locals frequently developed considerable vigor. Amalgamated men during the 1901 strike found A.F.L. locals entrenched even in the antiunion National Tube plant in McKeesport. A notably strong organization formed at the Reading Iron Company plant, with over 2,000 members and "a good sum in the treasury." It had sufficient resources to wage an effective strike against the company for several months.[12]

The Amalgamated Association, despite its broad charter, rejected most of these local unions. Even when the A.F.L. organization was acceptable, the Association would not issue a charter until the local had won recognition. The union at the Reading Iron Company, including puddlers, clearly was such a case. The other locals, covering the relatively unskilled fields, stood no chance with the Amalgamated.

Rather than maintain numerous isolated locals, the A.F.L. formed them into national unions, limited to one branch of the industry and to areas ignored by the Amalgamated Association. The Federal Association of Wire Drawers was chartered in 1896, the Tin Plate Workers' Protective Association in 1899, the International Association of Blast Furnace Workers in 1901, and the International Association of Tube Workers in 1902. A number of A.F.L. federal and local unions struggled along here and there. The Amalgamated's exclusiveness and Gompers' unwillingness to set up a strong rival union thus fragmented organization in the industry.

A.F.L. representatives, in addition to organizing in neglected places, worked also directly with national unions, particularly the new affiliates. The Tube Workers, petitioning for assistance, pleaded that they were too poor to keep a man in the field. The

[11] A.F.L., *Proceedings* (1901), p. 11; *AF,* June 1895, p. 174, September 1895, p. 129, December 1902, p. 925, December 1905, pp. 940–942. See L. L. Lorwin, *American Federation of Labor* (Washington, 1933), pp. 305 ff., for discussion of varieties of A.F.L. unions.

[12] *AF,* April 1901, pp. 143 ff., July 1901, pp. 279 ff.; *NLT,* June 27, July 18, 25, 1901.

organizer assigned was later ordered to help the Blast Furnace Workers also. Even the Amalgamated Association sought aid from the Federation. The union had the valuable services of an A.F.L. organizer in its 1905 campaign in the Eastern district.

The A.F.L. efforts in the steel industry bore little immediate fruit. The Wire Drawers' Association had collapsed in 1899, followed by the Tube Workers. The Blast Furnace Workers experienced limited success for a short time. Covering mainly the easier merchant furnace field, the union was established in the Mahoning and Shenango valleys of Ohio and spreading along the Great Lakes. Although it reported a membership of 4,000, it never had strong bargaining power, and disbanded in 1905. Only a few local unions remained on the fringes of the industry.[13]

Yet these abortive efforts shaped the response to the challenge of the Steel Corporation in 1909. The interest and obligation of the Federation in the unorganized industry was established. Before leaving for Europe in June, Gompers put A.F.L. organizers at the disposal of the Amalgamated Association. In October, Vice President James Duncan urged affiliated unions to send representatives into places where U.S. Steel operated plants, "there and then organizing the unorganized workers in the vicinity."[14] The Amalgamated Association, for its part, had learned to look to the Federation for help, and the entire labor movement to expect a large-scale organizing campaign to operate through the A.F.L. machinery.

When the A.F.L. convention opened in November 1909, Amalgamated President McArdle was on the floor to introduce the first resolution, calling for "the thorough organization of all branches of [the steel trust's] business." The resolution passed unanimously. At the direction of the convention, forty-six union

[13] *ITR*, May 14, 1903, p. 35, May 28, 1903, p. 48, July 30, 1903, p. 38; *EMJ*, April 11, 1903, p. 579, May 2, 1903, p. 690; *IA*, March 2, 1905, p. 754.

[14] *AF*, October 1909, p. 877, December 1909, p. 1078; Gompers to J. Williams, October 16, 1909, Gompers Papers.

leaders met in Pittsburgh on December 13, 1909. After two days, they issued a "Plan of Action and Appeal" for the "complete organization of every wage earner in the iron, steel and tinplate industry." They called upon every national union to put at least one worker into the campaign; the A.F.L. to contribute as many commissioned organizers as possible; and the central bodies in mill towns to appoint special committees. To assist the strikers, the conference directed the A.F.L. Executive Council to issue circulars to all unions for financial support, the first on January 1, 1910 for not less than ten cents per member.

Within a week, organizers were at work at the Carnegie plants in Bellaire and Mingo Junction, Ohio. Others appeared in Homestead and the area to the south after the new year. President McArdle himself went to Chicago to hold meetings near the South Works, and expected then to proceed to Joliet and Milwaukee. At some steel centers, local unionists were recruiting around the mills. But the campaign hardly left the ground.

Enthusiasm quickly cooled. Gompers on January 19 appealed to the affiliates for the promised support. "The response so far to send organizers has been so meager as to render effective work impossible." Despite his plea, only a mere half dozen organizers were forthcoming. McArdle himself had only reluctantly agreed to direct the campaign.[15] He grasped the excuse. Without consulting Gompers, he dismissed the organizers in early February and called off the drive.

Gompers was dismayed. United States Steel was, of course, "a formidable concern, and the work of organization beset with difficulties." But even with an inadequate organizing force, "some effective work could have been performed. . . . Any moment might have developed into the psychological time . . . the workers themselves might have been reached." Despite his sore disappointment, however, Gompers refused to give "up hope in this

[15] Gompers to Presidents of A.F.L. affiliates, January 19, 1910, and Gompers to McArdle, January 15 and 20, 1910, Gompers Papers; Amalgamated Association, *Proceedings* (1910), pp. 8931–8932.

fight for the Amalgamated Association." [16] When at that moment a call came from South Bethlehem, he seized it.

A spontaneous strike had broken out at the Bethlehem Steel plant and had spread quickly. Notified of the failure of settlement efforts, the A.F.L. dispatched a crew of organizers. Aroused, the men flocked into the hastily formed organizations. At the peak officials counted 3,800 men in twelve unions. Appeals for assistance went out.

> For years the thousands of men employed by the Bethlehem Steel Company have suffered under the iron heel of the most crushing institution known to the civilized world. . . . AT LAST THEY REVOLTED. . . . The A.F.L. has full charge of the situation, organizing and protecting the interests of the suffering men, and unionizing all the trades interested.

The executive committee sent its demands to Schwab on March 4. Knowing the company's policy, it did not ask for recognition. Schwab answered through the Bethlehem *Times* that he would ignore the communication. "Under no circumstances will we deal with men on strike or a body of men representing organized labor." The strike dragged on for a time, but Schwab was prepared to compromise on the original overtime issue. The men gradually drifted back to work, and the remnants of organization rapidly disappeared.[17] The campaign ended without visible result.

Yet the experience of 1909–10 held enormous future importance. The question of union structure was settled. All steelworkers — skilled and unskilled — and every branch of the industry would be under a single jurisdiction (except the blast furnaces, which would be covered by the Mine, Mill and Smelter Workers after it affiliated with the A.F.L.). The Pittsburgh meeting of December 1909, recommending the merging of the tin house workers and the Amalgamated Association, contemplated a single union for "which all workers in the iron, steel and tinplate industry would be eligible." The stipulation, however, was that "this proposed

---

[16] Gompers to George Perkins, February 25, 1910, Gompers Papers.
[17] *Report on the Bethlehem Strike, passim.*

amalgamation shall not interfere with jurisdictions already recognized." Here was the sticking point. A steel union could include all the jobs peculiar to the industry, plus common labor, but craft workers such as bricklayers and machinists belonged to their own appropriate national unions. This was in keeping with the Scranton Declaration of 1901, and with the plan employed in organizing the meatpacking houses before 1904. The A.F.L. henceforth accepted the necessity for organizing the steel industry on a semi-industrial basis.

Several other important consequences followed from the events of 1909–10. The open-shop announcement made U.S. Steel the foremost enemy of organized labor and the prime target for unionization. The steel trust would never again rest easy.[18] The responsibility for leading the attack was shifted to the A.F.L.; the Amalgamated Association had demonstrated its inadequacy. Finally, the Bethlehem strike provided an invaluable lesson on how to go about organizing steelworkers.

The central fact facing a unionizing drive was that the mass of unskilled steelworkers were Eastern European peasants. Poor union material, indeed, these seemed. "The Poles, Slavs, Huns and Italians," complained the *National Labor Tribune,* "come over without any ambition to live as Americans live and . . . accept work at any wages at all, thereby lowering the tone of American labor as a whole." Flooding the labor market, they gladly worked for starvation wages. They were, concluded an A.F.L. newsletter, "ignorant of American standards and of industrial ways."[19]

Observers frequently noted the docility of the peasant workmen: "their habit of silent submission, their amenability to discipline and their willingness to work long hours and overtime without a murmur." Discussing the steelworkers inhabiting Pittsburgh's South Side, the Pittsburgh *Leader* said that the Eastern European made "a better slave than the American." He "wants oh so

---

[18] *AF* printed no less than eighteen articles attacking the steel trust in the five years after the open-shop announcement.

[19] A.F.L., *Weekly Newsletter,* November 22, 1913; *NLT,* July 29, 1909.

little to keep him alive and he doesn't belong to any labor organization and he doesn't want to belong to any." [20] He was a happy victim of the steel companies.

Employers, union men believed, preferred immigrant to native labor. During the 1909 strike, the Steel Corporation had advertised for nonunion experienced tin workers, "Syrians, Poles and Rumanians preferred." Afterward, company officials explained that they had sought these over other immigrants after exhausting the supply of native workmen. But the charge that employers wanted the docile immigrants, long suspected, stuck. The A.F.L. asserted in 1911:

> It has been the policy pursued in the past to exclude English-speaking employees so far as it has been possible. . . . It is more advantageous to the company to employ men who are unfamiliar with the moral and living standards of this country.

Moreover, steel manufacturers deliberately hired "foreigners of different nationalities, in order that there may not be free-speaking intercourse between them." "Directly or indirectly," Gompers said, the employers were channeling immigrants into the industry to keep wages down and workmen tractable.[21]

In fact, the mass of peasant workmen were, as they appeared, unpromising union material. Nothing in their agriculturalist past prepared them for collective activity in industrial America. Uncommitted to a permanent life in the mills, moreover, the immigrant did not find the arguments for joining a union persuasive. He knew that unions spelled dismissal or at least a prolonged strike. "As to work," a Polish laborer wrote home, "I have had no work for two months, since they had a strike. It means that they do not want to work for the same money, but they want more wages." [22] What was a dubious small increase compared to several months of

[20] Reprinted in *AJ*, April 25, 1912, pp. 1–2.

[21] A.F.L., *Newsletter*, July 8, 1911; Gompers, in American Academy of Political and Social Science, *The Annals*, XLII (July 1912), 58; Gompers, *Seventy Years*, II, 155, 160.

[22] Raczkowski Series, December 18, 1909, Thomas and Znaniecki, *The Polish Peasant*, I, 727.

idleness, when each day out of the mill added two days to his exile?
There was no interest in trade unionism among recent immigrants
in steel towns.

In addition, organizers would have to contend with the bias of
the English-speaking workmen. When immigrants served as
strikebreakers, the hostility deepened. During the 1909 strike the
National Labor Tribune, whose readership was largely among the
skilled steelworkers, sensed a powerful feeling against foreign
workers. The *Tribune* urged a twelve-dollar tax on all immigrants
to protect Americans from hordes of cheap labor. The organization envisaged by the A.F.L. faced impressive obstacles within
both immigrant and native groups.

One circumstance favored the organizing prospect. Above all,
the immigrant required steady employment, and this the steel
industry could not provide. Hard times invariably meant widespread idleness. Even the fortunate ones who retained their jobs
often worked irregularly. All faced an uncertain future. A lost
job meant drained savings or even debt — in either case a great
postponement of the return to the native village. Depression was
peculiarly disastrous for the immigrant.

The return of prosperity often brought with it a sharp psychological reaction. With work everywhere available for the asking,
immigrants lost the desperate sense of dependence on the boss.
And they harbored grievances stored up from the bad times just
past. The usual economizing measures of employers at this point
further aggravated the situation. Resentment was channeled generally into demands for more pay. Sometimes, however, the accumulated anger exploded into unexpected strikes, occurring
mainly during the initial upswing in business.

"The disposition of workmen to strike appears to be a necessary
accompaniment of high prices and excessive demand for labor,"
observed the *Iron Age* during the rash of strikes in the resurgent
prosperity of late 1899. Four hundred men in four wire mills in
Cleveland struck for higher wages, followed next summer by
Slavic furnace men at Mingo Junction and others at McClintic-
Marshall's Braddock plant. As production reached a new peak, a

general strike of blast furnace men threatened, but was quickly settled.[23]

After the 1904–5 recession, unrest again appeared. Immigrant laborers quit work at the Republic plant in East Chicago because they were denied a twenty-five-cent a day increase. A riot broke out when a foreman fired into an approaching crowd of strikers. The foreman was beaten senseless and twenty-one men were arrested. The following day the plant shut down. Meanwhile, 600 employees of the Interstate Steel Company at nearby Hammond struck, and Inland workmen at Indiana Harbor were reported on the verge of going out.[24] The discontent then subsided. No further immigrant strikes occurred until after the severe depression of 1908, when for the first time they began to draw attention.

The employees of the Pressed Steel Car Company at McKees Rocks, near Pittsburgh, had been idle for eighteen months when they finally returned to work early in 1909. During the depression the company had overhauled its operations. An ingenious pooling arrangement was introduced whereby wages were determined by the output, not of the individual, but of the entire assembly line. In addition, the system set a fixed rate on each car, and, whatever the cause of a stoppage, paid no more for the work. "The pool's paying for it," the men muttered at every breakdown. Also, the company put the rates considerably below 1907 levels. Finally, the exact rates were not revealed to the men.

For several months these grievances compounded the resentment of the prolonged idleness. Saturday, July 10, was payday. On Monday complaints abounded. About forty men refused to work unless they were told their wage rates. They were discharged the next day. Six hundred then walked out, others followed, and by Wednesday the plant was closed down. The strike had started among the immigrants, but the skilled Americans, about one-fourth of the total force, came out also. Although separate com-

---

[23] *IA*, quoted in *Iron and Steel Trade Journal*, May 19, 1900, p. 406; *NLT*, August 1, 1901; Youngstown *Labor News*, August 30, 1901; *EMJ*, January 3, 1903, p. 45; *ITR*, May 21, 1903, p. 38.

[24] Chicago *Daily Socialist*, March 18, 20, 1906.

mittees were formed, the Americans cooperated actively with the immigrants.

The strike was completely effective. Some trouble occurred, apparently fomented in part by the company; but in general the strikers exercised remarkable restraint. The inexperienced leaders — the "Big Six," they were called — proved exceedingly resourceful, gathering sufficient funds to keep the strikers alive, enlisting public opinion, and checking violence. The struggle lasted into September. Finally, after the company had shown itself both inept and ruthless, the strike ended in the apparent favor of the men.[25]

The unrest spread. Shutdowns occurred at the Standard Steel Car plant in Butler, Pennsylvania, and Hammond, Indiana, and at steel plants in the Chicago district. Trouble at many places was forestalled only by offers of wage increases.[26] The great Bethlehem strike capped the wave of discontent.

The reputation of the immigrant workman was altering. "The foreigner takes on a new, higher aspect after this demonstration of good qualities," reported a Pittsburgh *Sun* correspondent at the end of the McKees Rocks strike. The description of a strike meeting at Hammond appeared in a Chicago paper.

> The lights of the hall were extinguished. A candle stuck into a bottle was placed on a platform. One by one the men came and kissed the ivory image on the cross, kneeling before it. They swore they would not scab.[27]

Immigrants, it seemed, did have the capacity to carry on a prolonged strike.

The principles of collective industrial activity had not suddenly

[25] P. U. Kellog, "The McKees Rocks Strike," *Survey*, August 7, 1909, pp. 656–665; R. D. Smith, "Some Phases of the McKees Rocks Strike," *Survey*, October 2, 1909, pp. 38–45.

[26] Cleveland *Citizen*, August 7, 1909; Chicago *Daily Socialist*, June 20, 29, 31, 1910.

[27] *Sun* quoted in M. T. C. Wing, "The Flag at McKees Rocks," *Survey*, October 2, 1909, pp. 45–46; Chicago *Daily Socialist*, January 31, 1910.

dawned on the immigrant. Rather, his ability as a striker sprang from his European background. The peasant looked on himself primarily as a member of a family and a village. He could not conceive of differing with group decisions, unanimously reached. Moreover, nothing mattered more than communal approval. Immigration weakened, but did not destroy, group consciousness. When, therefore, immigrant workers were driven to strike, they were likely to persist until the general sentiment turned. They were effective strikers because they were peasants.

The second lesson of 1909–10 was that at certain points the steelworkers were ripe for organization. The immigrant's docility came to be regarded as the deceptive cover for underlying "unrest and discontent." "The trust is standing over a veritable Vesuvius," warned one bitter critic. "One spark . . . will send the trust and its hirelings to the depths of hell." Having "succeeded in crushing out labor organization," Gompers believed, the Steel Corporation was lulling itself "into a fancied security."

> But some day [the immigrants] will protest. Probably not in the same way as American trade unions, . . . the Anglo-Saxon plan. But if the great industrial combinations do not deal with us they will have somebody else to deal with who will not have the American idea.[28]

The crucial question, not fully answered at Bethlehem, was whether the immigrants could be channeled into the conservative labor movement.

Gompers' strategy was to gear the A.F.L.'s organizing effort to the next peak of discontent. By 1912 business recovery was evident. Steel mills were complaining of labor shortages. In mid-June a strike broke out at the National Tube plant in the Soho section of Pittsburgh — "a spontaneous outburst," a local citizen described it. Except for a few skilled men, the entire force was out. Soon

[28] American Academy of Political Science, *Annals*, XLII, 18, 50–51, 58; *AJ*, October 17, 1912, p. 1.

after, Jones and Laughlin men struck in protest against the Taylor efficiency system. The *Survey* reported "wild rumors in circulation as to sympathetic strikes" and "the feeling that the whole steel district might turn into a tinderbox once there was a flare-up at one point."[29] The time appearing opportune, the A.F.L. announced on August 2, 1912 an organizing campaign in the steel industry.

The second part of Gompers' plan rested on the view of immigrants as industrial workers. They were, he told the A.F.L. convention, "untutored, born in lands of oppression, surrounded by squalor, inured to hardship, reaching manhood without that full mental development which makes for independence and self-preservation." They "cannot be blamed for knowing little or nothing" of union principles and for being "a menace, not only to the iron and steel workers, but to the trade union movement in general." Moreover, "the light of our civilization but slowly dawns upon them. . . . Comprehension of the rights to which they are entitled comes as an exceedingly slow process." The A.F.L., therefore, had to educate the immigrant before undertaking to organize him.[30]

The campaign opened with two circulars explaining the purposes of organization. "Circular No. 1" began:

> Now is the time when you, the wage earners in the iron and steel industry, must feel and know how helpless you have become. You have acted as individuals. Do you know and feel how powerful you could become if you were to unite and become organized?

The hard conditions in the steel mills were compared to the eight hours and high wages in the coal mines and building trades. The powerful steel companies would bow only to collective strength. "Circular No. 2" concluded:

[29] *Survey,* July 6, 1912, pp. 487–488, August 3, 1912, pp. 595–596.
[30] A.F.L., *Proceedings* (1912), p. 385; A.F.L., *Newsletter,* November 16, 1912; Gompers to John Williams, July 17 and 25, 1912, Gompers Papers.

If you want more money for your labor — organize!
If you want shorter hours — organize!
If you want better working conditions — organize!

The A.F.L. would accept all steelworkers, "regardless of their mechanical ability, their creed, color, or nationality." [31]

The circulars were translated into all the languages spoken in the mills, printed in great quantity, and spread broadcast through the steel towns. City centrals, locals, volunteer and general organizers distributed the literature. The educational attempt was serious and thorough.

Having prepared the workmen, Gompers expected to get on with the actual organizing drive. The first circulars promised "No. 3," which would set the date for rallies for every steel center in the country. Simultaneous meetings would render retaliation against the steelworkers impossible. This ambitious scheme was partly diverted by a promising "Labor Forward Movement" which utilized revivalist techniques to recruit workers. After the Movement had proved successful in Minneapolis, the A.F.L. launched it tentatively on a national scale in October 1912. The earlier plan was overshadowed; Circular No. 3 never appeared.

Instead, Federation officials decided to await the response of the steelworkers, and to concentrate their efforts where discontent reached the combustible point. Union men found encouraging signs that the campaign was "injecting considerable more independence into the workmen." A short strike broke out among the unskilled men at the Rankin wire mill near Pittsburgh in October. Carnegie trainmen walked out in late November, and again early in the new year, closing down the Homestead plant for the first time since 1892. Then trouble erupted again in Rankin. Workers at the Braddock wire mill joined them, and both plants closed down.

Union representatives converged on the two towns. The strikers met on Saturday afternoon (February 1, 1913) in the Lithuanian Hall in Braddock. A.F.L. Secretary Frank Morrison came from

[31] Circulars printed in A.F.L., *Newsletter,* October 5, 12, 1912 and later.

Washington for the meeting. The Federation, he said, was beginning the organization of the entire industry here.

> The fight will not be confined to Pittsburgh. It will be carried everywhere where steel workers are working. . . . It so happens that yours are the first two mills to strike. It is up to you. The federation will do its part and hopes that you will do yours.

The men responded enthusiastically, raising their hands and shouting. They vowed to stay out until their demands were won.

For its part, the American Steel and Wire Company was eager to end the strike. It even received committees of the men. Only on the question of unionism was it adamant. "You will have to decide whether you want to work for us or for the labor agitators," the general manager told the strikers. When, during the second week, the company offered a pay increase, the men of Braddock and Rankin voted to return to work.[32] The A.F.L. proclaimed "Victory No. 1," and pressed the campaign elsewhere.

Organizers reported the formation of three unions in Indiana Harbor and Chicago Heights. Early in March the Inland mill was shut down. For four weeks the strike was complete. Then the company conceded the men's demands, and they came back to work. This, said the A.F.L., was the second victory.

Elsewhere prospects appeared bright. Organizer Thomas H. Flynn of the A.F.L. arrived in Cleveland in mid-February from the Braddock success to take charge of the campaign at the city's nine steel plants. The first meetings at immigrant halls were enthusiastic. The *Clevelandska Amerika* urged its readers to support the drive: "The union does not want any strikes, she only wants you to organize, that you are strong in multitudes, not separately for yourself." But the immigrant steelworkers were soon frightened off. Despite precautions for secrecy by the unions, the steel plants clearly had their intelligence sources. Soon men were being discharged. Within the immigrant community, in addition, opposition developed against the campaign. When Flynn departed in May, he did not leave permanent organizations in Cleveland.

[32] *NLT*, February 6, 13, 1913.

The response was small in other centers. A major "Labor Forward" effort opened in Pittsburgh in April under the joint auspices of the cental labor body and the A.F.L. A circular in thirteen languages, entitled "All Hail, The Union," was distributed throughout the area. The campaign established numerous organizations, but only one was reported in the steel plants. There were sporadic strikes elsewhere, and minor successes at Syracuse and on the Great Lakes.[33]

By the summer of 1913 the drive was stalled. When mills began closing down later in the year, the achievements of spring slipped away. The depression carried into 1915 and left no organizing opportunity before the outbreak of war.

The effect of "education" on the immigrants was, of course, impossible to gauge. Afterward there was no sign of permanent results. The circulars had argued on purely practical terms of the benefits of organization. The logic was not persuasive to immigrants eager to return home or to move into the skilled ranks. The literature, moreover, betrayed ignorance of the immigrant's motives.

> You could give much assistance in the movement, started in your interest, if when writing to your friends and relatives across the water, you advise them it would be to their advantage if they did not come to America for a year or two.

Nothing was better designed to alienate the newcomer.

The request, in fact, pointed to a chief liability of the A.F.L. Its leaders had unfortunate nativist leanings. The Federation had long favored immigration restriction. While carrying the organizing circulars, the *Newsletter* contained an article on the "Influx of Foreigners," and later warned that "Foreign Immigration Threatens to Submerge English-Speaking Workmen." The deep-rooted

---

[33] Numerous clippings of Cleveland newspapers, including translations of foreign language items, Scrapbook, Vol. 16, American Steel and Wire Collection; A.F.L., *Newsletter,* February 15, March 1, March 29, May 3, 1913; *IA,* May 1, 1913, p. 1092.

distrust of the immigrant, shared with the skilled workmen, corrupted any crusade to unionize the steel laborers.

It explains also a crucial gap in the A.F.L. strategy. Except in crisis, American workers had no sympathy for the immigrants. Tolerance was the prerequisite of any union including the two groups. It did not occur to A.F.L. officials that education of the Americans was as vital for organization as education of the immigrants. In the end, this blindness would have grievous consequences.

The Amalgamated Association meanwhile had settled back into its old track. Its part was minor at best in the 1912 campaign. The members were urged "to lend every assistance in their power to help the A.F.L. organizers. . . . *Agitate, Educate, Organize.*" The chief purpose of the "live committee" appointed at each lodge, however, was to reach indifferent members rather than to recruit new men. "We must first get right ourselves," explained President John Williams, "then we can with consistency seek the aid of those now outside the fold of unionism." [34] Little effort in the end actually went into the organizing drive.

The union remained, of course, aware of the plight of the unorganized. The Amalgamated convention of May 1912 roundly applauded the president of the Chicago Federation of Labor when he emphasized the necessity of organizing the immigrant workmen in the South Chicago mills. President Williams also dwelt on the subject. Yet, despite the imminent A.F.L. campaign, he said nothing of serious organizing plans. In fact, Vice President Ben F. Jones thought that Canada and Nova Scotia offered the most promising fields!

The Amalgamated Association had reverted to its pre-1909 attitude. The union quietly buried the opinion that strength required the recruitment of the unskilled. Although the U.S. Steel mills had been lost, the lodges in the small independent plants found their situation secure and unchanged. The weekly correspondence to

[34] Letter of President John Williams to the lodges, August 3, 1912, *AJ*, August 22, 1912, p. 1.

the *Amalgamated Journal* reflected the earlier conservatism. This letter from East Chicago, written in the midst of the 1912 unionizing campaign, represented the general sentiment.

> We have plenty of work now, and that makes a man feel good, for you can buy your wife or sweetheart a Christmas gift, to say nothing of being able to make the kiddies happy. This, with the prospects for next year, makes a man willing to spend a few dollars to make others happy.[35]

Combined with the normal disdain for the immigrant, such thinking deadened any interest in the unskilled. The Amalgamated membership was content.[36]

Comprising a scant few thousand workers, the Amalgamated Association would have held small future importance, but for the fact that it had legitimate jurisdiction over the mass of steelworkers. The A.F.L. would have to involve the Association in any future campaign and to channel any success into it.

Notwithstanding its liabilities, the labor movement after 1909 posed a continuing, real threat to the steel manufacturers. The seeds were sown for the reorganization of the steelworkers along the lines of industrial unionism. Before the open-shop announcement, the unions had been satisfied to conserve their limited position on a skilled craft basis. Afterward, organized labor was bitterly hostile and committed to seize every opportunity to organize all the men in the mills.

It was consequently expedient for the industry to soften the treatment of its employees, and fortunate that a new situation was developing to make possible a liberalization of labor policies.

---

[35] *AJ*, December 19, 1912, p. 13; also, Lancaster *Labor Leader*, January 8, 1910.

[36] There was, however, a minority which urged the organization of the unskilled and the creation of a "militant progressive organization." Discontent with the conservative leadership resulted in two insurgent movements in 1912–1913, one of which formed a dual union. See *AJ*, October 3, 1912, p. 13; Robinson, *Amalgamated Association*, p. 55; Hoagland, *Quarterly Journal of Economics*, XXXI, 683–685.

Chapter VIII

The Genesis of Labor Reform

The labor system of the steel industry was formed in the years of relentless competition. The aim of lower cost operation had governed decisions on labor, as on everything else, in the steel-making enterprise. Economy had shaped the hard terms of employment in the mills.

The competitive era ended in 1901, and with it the necessity for the economizing labor policy in its undiluted form. No basic alteration occurred, but the steelworker's situation improved considerably in the succeeding years. A leaven of benevolence was introduced, bringing an added measure of stability to the labor system.

The change accompanied the inauguration of the new period of "cooperation." The leadership of the industry passed to financial men, whose concern was not primarily with manufacturing costs. Espousing fair play in competition, they desired to apply their enlightened principles to labor also. They were, in addition, sensitive to public opinion and hastily responded to criticism of conditions in their mills. The restriction of competition provided new criteria for the treatment of labor.

The cooperative movement began with the return of prosperity in 1898. By 1900 nearly all the finishing firms were joined together into sheet, tin plate, hoop, tube, wire, and construction steel trusts. The conclusion of competition outside the basic industry inaugurated greater trouble. For the finishing combinations were allied with steel producers under the same financial control. Faced with the loss of his market, Carnegie threatened to establish his own finishing facilities. To avoid a disastrous war of giants, J. P. Morgan set about forming an organization to take in the major producers — the Carnegie, Federal, and National Steel companies — and the finishing companies. The United States Steel Corporation, a holding company, was the result.

The promoters of the combinations were essentially middlemen. Strategically situated in the financial world, they arranged the underwriting syndicate, bought out the competing firms, and floated the stock issues. Their services were amply compensated.[1] But the connection did not end here. Although he did not choose all the officers of the Steel Corporation, said J. P. Morgan, none were appointed without his approval. Three partners became directors, and one, Robert Bacon, headed the Finance Committee. Morgan himself had the final word in the counsels of the Corporation.[2] By the single promotional maneuver, control of the industry passed into the hands of the financiers.

Judge Elbert H. Gary was Morgan's man actually in charge of U.S. Steel. A Chicago corporation lawyer, Gary had been active in the early wire consolidations of the buccaneer John W. (Bet-A-Million) Gates. When Morgan became interested in steel, he took note of the lawyer's prowess, retained him to organize the Federal Steel Company, and then appointed him its chief. At the formation of the Steel Corporation, Gary became chairman of the Executive Committee.

By then, Judge Gary subscribed completely to the Morgan rationale. Consolidations, claimed the great financier, had a constructive purpose: namely, to bring order to industries "demoralized" by destructive competition. As Morgan's disciple, Gary aimed at ending in the steel industry "bitter, relentless, overbearing, tyrannical conduct, calculated to drive out the weak." Properly

[1] J. P. Morgan and Company received $12,500,000, plus its share as subscriber in the syndicate that underwrote the Steel Corporation. Commissioner of Corporations, *Steel Report*, I, 243–249.

[2] Ida M. Tarbell, *Elbert H. Gary* (New York, 1925), pp. 126 ff. For instances of Morgan's influence, see U.S. Steel, Executive Committee Minutes, July 1 and 2, 1901, *U.S. v. U.S.S., Government Exhibits*, II, 569, and *Stanley Hearings*, VI, 3791.

led, the Steel Corporation would attain for the entire industry Morgan's goal of "fair" competition.

As a lawyer, Gary saw also the legal dangers for United States Steel in aggressive policies. At a time of sharpening rivalry, the Judge pleaded with the subsidiary presidents: "make it certain your conduct is so high-toned, so fair and reasonable, that you cannot justly be charged with attempting to drive out of business . . . any of your competitors."[3] The fact was that the Steel Corporation was too strong for its own legal good. Only by exercising restraint, Gary believed, could it avoid prosecution under the Sherman Act.

Besides his legal acumen, Judge Gary brought another valuable asset to the Corporation. A Methodist and a moralist, he had a reputation of unshakeable rectitude. In the Waldorf crowd, Bernard Baruch recalls, he was a sort of saint among the sinners. That uprightness was brought to bear on the excesses of cutthroat competition. He insisted, according to Ida Tarbell, "that the Sunday school precepts . . . should be preached . . . in the board room as well as the church." "From the standpoint of morality," said Gary, earlier competition "was a shame and a disgrace."[4] Ethics as well as commercial and legal interest dictated moderation.

The Gary outlook did not go unchallenged. The "practical" men in the Corporation, veterans of the competitive era, felt that "the attitude of the Corporation was entirely too Christian." "I thought that we ought to use our power," recalled a former Carnegie partner, "more largely to secure business, — to be more aggressive."[5] The opposition of the top operating officials was immediately evident. President Schwab by-passed the Executive Com-

[3] Gary, in American Iron and Steel Institute, *Yearbook* (1912), p. 20; Gary Address to the Subsidiary Presidents, October 19, 1911, *Addresses and Statements by Gary*, I.

[4] Ida Tarbell, *All in the Day's Work* (New York, 1939), p. 368; Tarbell, *Gary*, pp. 137–138; Bernard Baruch, *My Own Story* (New York, 1957), p. 162; Gary Address, October 15, 1909, *U.S. v. U.S.S., Defendants' Exhibits*, III, 354.

[5] J. H. Reed and H. P. Bope, *U.S. v. U.S.S., Testimony*, XIV, 5679, XXVII, 11488.

mittee. Challenged by Gary, he responded that committee control was impracticable; he wanted to function unhindered as he had under Carnegie. The subsidiary officials were largely in Schwab's camp.

But, supported by Morgan and the financial group on the Board of Directors, Judge Gary gradually gained ascendancy. Schwab resigned in 1903, and his replacement, the Carnegie man W. E. Corey, was more effectively circumscribed. The same issues led to a conflict with Corey, and only after he was replaced at the end of 1910 by J. A. Farrell, a sales specialist, did all the top executives subscribe to Gary's views. Gary became eventually chairman of the Board, also of the Finance Committee, and finally by amendment of the by-laws "chief executive officer." The troublesome Executive Committee, constituted chiefly of subsidiary presidents, was abolished.

At first, executives had been able to keep Judge Gary ignorant of their normal sharp practices. He found it necessary long after to lecture the sales managers on the need for obedience to his directives, based as they often were on considerations not immediately apparent to operating officials.[6] The actions of the Steel Corporation began to correspond to Gary's views. After the early years the independents invariably testified that U.S. Steel was the "best competition we have."

The second half of Gary's task was to convert the rest of the industry. In the early years few companies were in a position to antagonize the formidable Steel Corporation. The pools started in 1899 continued to function effectively, although more informally after 1904. The creation of "Pittsburgh plus" also limited competition by fixing a standard price for steel based on Pittsburgh mill prices and transportation charges. A decline in 1903 did force general price cuts. But the mild recession passed before the end of 1904, and the steel market resumed its healthy activity.

The independents meanwhile "grew and flourished like a green

[6] Gary Address to Sales Managers, November 16, 1910, *Addresses and Statements*, I.

bay tree." Soon they equaled the Steel Corporation in integration, equipment, and raw material supplies. Opinion was divided
on whether or not the giant could crush them. But no one doubted,
as Julian Kennedy remarked, that "it would not be a forenoon's
job." Moreover, their disadvantages might lead the independents
to disregard Gary's precepts in hard years. The testing time came
in the autumn of 1907.

In the midst of booming prosperity, financial panic suddenly set
in. Overnight, the heavy demand for steel dropped to nothing.
Then Judge Gary issued a call for a meeting in New York for
November 20. He exhorted "us like a Methodist preacher at a
camp meeting," steel men recalled. He urged them "to avoid losing
their heads and giving away their business . . . by a sudden and
unreasonable drop in prices." Nobody would benefit from a price
war; not even sharp reductions would bring out additional orders
during a complete collapse. Persuaded, the steel manufacturers
agreed to maintain prices. Thus was launched a new departure in
the steel industry — cooperation.[7]

But the conversion came slowly. A few cut their prices, and
many who went along with Gary were openly skeptical. Backsliding
increased during 1908, and by early 1909 the Steel Corporation
appeared to be alone holding to the advertised price levels. Finally,
in February Judge Gary announced to the independents: "We will
go alone . . . we will make our prices to our customers, and . . .
try to get about our fair share of business."

The apparent failure of cooperation insured its ultimate success. U.S. Steel salesmen, long straining at the bit, "went out to
take business." Prices dropped, and orders began to flow. "Nearly
everything placed in the last week was taken by us," reported the
Carnegie sales manager in mid-March; and the next week: "The
other mills seem to think the pace we are setting is a little too fast
for them." Unrestrained, the Steel Corporation captured the lion's

[7] No stenographic record was made of this first Gary dinner, but in the
antitrust suit Gary and other prominent steel men gave their versions of what
had transpired. *U.S.* v. *U.S.S., Testimony,* VI, 2091, XIV, 5681, 5684–5685.

share of business.[8] Having learned their lesson, the steel manufacturers resumed their meetings.

The dinner of October 1909 marked the complete acceptance of cooperation. Charles Schwab, now chairman of Bethlehem Steel, publicly recanted his errors in his presentation of a loving cup to Judge Gary.

> I was wrong in most instances — indeed in all instances — and you were right. The broad principles you brought into this business were new to all of us who had been trained in a somewhat different school. Their effect was marvelous, their success unquestioned.[9]

Paying homage to Gary, the steel men acknowledged his leadership.

In part, the dinners were designed to dispel through "cordial intercourse" the hostile legacy of the Carnegie era. Prices, orders, and production were freely discussed. Thereby, said Gary, "everyone having a disposition to act reasonably . . . may determine his course with full information of all the facts." The Judge sought to instill a sense of common interest, for "we cannot make anything for our individual selves by injuring any other person, and we cannot assist . . . competitors in business without at the same time benefiting . . . ourselves." [10]

New organizational forms developed. At the first dinner a General Committee was established to guide the industry toward cooperation. Subcommittees briefed the lesser manufacturers. The creation of the American Iron and Steel Institute in 1909 formalized the functions of the Gary dinners. The necessary lines of communication were constructed.

In the course of convincing the independents, Gary perfected his case. Classical theory, he argued, was mistaken because it confused its terms. "Capacity to furnish does not create supply; nor does

[8] *U.S. v. U.S.S., Testimony,* XII, 4803, XXVII, 11465; Carnegie Company Minutes, March 15, 1909, March 22, 1909, *Government Exhibits,* II, 538–539.
[9] *Defendants' Exhibits,* III, 351.
[10] Gary Address, December 10, 1908, *Defendants' Exhibits,* II, 243; Steel Institute, *Yearbook* (1914), p. 284.

ability to purchase create demand." There had to be a *willingness* to buy and sell, and that could be rationally controlled. Unfortunately, steel manufacturers had only prices in their hands. But, since prices and demand were interdependent, holding one level would eventually steady the other. And stable prices would avoid bitter competition in the interim.

Schwab added the support of the practical men. Carnegie's competitive policies had rested on constantly increasing efficiency. "The day has gone by when those developments . . . can be made. There is little difference in the cost of manufacture as between different works to-day." The basis for unrestricted competition had disappeared.[11]

The years of conflict were at an end. The U.S. Steel antitrust suit, it is true, forced the discontinuance of the agreements established at the Gary dinners. Having reached an understanding, however, the steel men did not need to be obvious. They simply followed the price lead of the Steel Corporation. Ended in name, cooperation continued in practice.

The Gary movement inevitably made itself felt on the labor policies of the industry. Cooperation was too broad an idea to be confined to trade relations. If friendship and fairness "is a good doctrine for us," Judge Gary told the steel men, "it is equally as good for others. . . . We should have it in mind in dealing with our employees." Bitterness between workmen and managers was as deplorable as between business rivals. The solution was the same: to cooperate "with our men as we have . . . with our competitors." Nor would Gary's moral bent permit indifference. By fair treatment, "not only have we benefited ourselves pecuniarily, but what is more important . . . we have done the right thing." [12] Finally, the end of unrestrained competition lessened the necessity for a labor policy dictated by economy; survival no longer rode

[11] Gary Address, October 14, 1910, *Defendants' Exhibits,* II, 251; *Testimony,* V, 1857–1858; Schwab, in *Stanley Hearings,* II, 1290.

[12] Gary Addresses, October 15, 1909 and October 14, 1910, *Defendants' Exhibits,* III, 358, II, 254.

solely on the figures in the cost books (although the margin of profit did).

The first contribution of the financial men came in late 1902 in the form of the U.S. Steel stock subscription plan. Over 26,000 employees subscribed during January 1903. Republic, Cambria, and Youngstown Sheet and Tube adopted similar programs. To financiers like George W. Perkins, one of its originators, the "plan of cooperation and participation in the benefits and profits" seemed "the only way practically of helping to solve the relations of labor and capital." Judge Gary predicted that "the interests of capital and labor will be drawn more closely and permanently together."[13] Stock participation was the obvious application of their ideas to the labor field.

Wage policy also was affected by cooperation. "The elimination of wasteful strife," Gary had argued in 1904, "will enable employers to pay better wages." The onset of depression in late 1907 automatically reduced the rates of the independents, but despite their grumbling, U.S. Steel did not follow, and within a few months wages resumed earlier levels. The price break in 1909 tempted Corporation managers, but with Morgan's support Judge Gary held back until prices rose.[14] For the first time, in 1911, general wage cuts did not accompany a business decline. When stockholders complained of diminished profits in 1914, Gary retorted that he would pass the dividend before ordering pay reductions. Wage maintenance, like price maintenance, became the settled policy of the industry.

Judge Gary expected cooperation to steady employment also. Critics claimed the effect was just the opposite; the refusal to lower prices intensified the depression, for instance, in 1908. Gary

[13] *U.S.* v. *U.S.S.*, *Testimony*, XIV, 5492; *Harper's Weekly*, March 7, 1903, p. 404.

[14] Gary Statement to the Press, 1904, *Addresses and Statements*, I; U.S. Steel, Finance Committee Minutes, April 27, 1909, *Stanley Hearings*, VI, 3909 and 4406, for cables of Gary to Morgan, April 21, 1909. On the wage issue in 1909, see also J. A. Garraty, "The United States Steel Corporation Versus Labor: The Early Years," *Labor History*, I (Winter 1960), 24–26.

could only respond that in the long run steady prices would level demand for steel and hence for labor. Meanwhile, he urged subsidiary presidents in dull periods to employ as many men as possible on repairs and improvements. But unemployment was really beyond the Judge's control.

So too, in fact, were wages during labor shortages. Gary disapproved of bowing to the market. A workman's service to the Corporation, he told the subsidiary presidents, should determine his income. But in busy times labor exacted increases: 6 per cent in 1910, another 10 per cent in 1913. Consequently, observed the *Iron Age*, "since 1907 wage rates have only varied with improvements in trade." [15]

Although there were mutterings about flouted economic laws, steel men came to regard the Steel Corporation as the industry leader in wages as in prices. Manufacturers quite openly admitted that they followed its rates. The Colorado Fuel and Iron Company, hearing of an increase in the East, wrote for the details as a basis for its own adjustment. Youngstown firms in 1916 actually requested direction on wage decisions from the Steel Corporation.[16]

Judge Gary was unquestionably sincere when he said in 1904, "Our first concern is the welfare of our workingmen." But stock participation and steady wages were together a meager accomplishment. As yet, Gary had hardly touched the hardships of the steelworkers. Weighty obstacles blocked the way to reform.

Foremost was the opposition of the "practical" men. Labor policy they considered a technical matter, to be determined only with reference to the cost books and the production requirements. Gary's talk of labor betterment was mere sentiment. His directive in early 1907 to minimize seven-day labor had been ignored, as a stockholders' investigating committee reported, because of "that zeal of operating officials for output, exclusive of all other considerations."

---

[15] *IA,* December 11, 1913, p. 1345.
[16] Ben M. Selekman, *Employes' Representation in Steel Works* (New York, 1924), p. 90; *Survey,* March 18, 1916, pp. 711–712; G. P. West, "Industrial Relations Commission Report," printed in *NLT,* January 27, 1916.

Developed under the stress of competition, the rules of labor treatment, as of other aspects of steel manufacture, would remain binding through the era of cooperation.

For their part, Judge Gary and his associates were fatally hindered by ignorance. Well-intentioned, they knew neither the conditions in the mills nor the needs of the steelworkers. They had no easy access to information, located as they were in the Corporation's main offices in downtown New York. Percival Roberts, a director, voiced the general uncertainty even after a decade of effort. "We are feeling our way. . . . We are getting into grounds that have not been trodden before. We do not know where we are going." [17] Nor had the financial men compelling reasons for action. Indeed, nothing counterbalanced the inertia of the operating officials or defined the vague intentions of Judge Gary. The promise of the cooperative movement for labor came to little in the early years.

The formation of the Steel Corporation had, however, opened the industry to a new force that would in the end demolish the impediments to progress. Until then, public opinion had been beneath notice except in times of debate on tariff protection. Concerning their own affairs, steelmasters found secrecy the best policy. That was patently impossible in the case of U.S. Steel. The outcry at its birth demonstrated that the "steel trust" would never escape scrutiny.

Public approval was, moreover, of critical importance because of the precarious legality of the Steel Corporation. If it competed vigorously, it would be attacked for trying to create a monopoly. If, on the other hand, it made agreements, enemies would accuse it of acting in restraint of trade. The only sure defense, Judge Gary believed, was to persuade the public and the government "that the intentions of the managers are good." The Steel Corporation needed public favor.

So did the controlling financial men. Their function, as they conceived it, was in the national interest. J. P. Morgan "averted the

[17] *Stanley Hearings,* V, 3396.

threatened danger of one-man rule" by Carnegie, and "distributed the power of ownership" in the industry. "What is the essential difference," George W. Perkins asked, between the Steel Corporation "and a Department of Steel, as it might have been organized by the government?" [18] Judge Gary conceded the dangers inherent in the concentration of power in private hands. It went without saying (although it was repeatedly said) that the Steel Corporation recognized its grave responsibilities and acted always for the public benefit. Considering their work to be quasi-public, men like Gary and Perkins were as eager for "general commendation" as for dividends. "All of us must stand or fall," concluded the steel man Willis King, on the verdict of the public.

From the beginning, Judge Gary championed corporate publicity. Overriding considerable opposition, he published the annual reports, announced periodically the order backlog and price list, and opened the stockholders' meetings to full discussion. Abruptness with reporters gave place to Gary's amiable expansiveness; for, he frankly remarked, the press reached the American public. Several times, U.S. Steel considered establishing an advertising bureau for "disseminating proper knowledge of the corporation and its methods." [19]

Gary's assumption that publicity would dispel suspicion accounted in part for his insistence on corporate propriety and for the high moral tone of his public pronouncements. To "secure and retain confidence," he lectured the subsidiary presidents, "the people of power" must "consistently avoid giving any just ground for complaint." [20] The dictum applied to labor matters as much as to prices, competition, and monopoly. Gary's refusal to order pay cuts took into account public sentiment; to reduce wages while maintaining prices would have begged for attack.

The Steel Corporation was assiduous in urging its benevolent

[18] Quoted in Casson, *Romance of Steel*, p. 228.

[19] Willis King, *Western Pennsylvania Historical Magazine*, XXIII, 239; Arundel Cotter, *The Gary I Knew* (Boston, 1928), pp. 25, 60–62; U.S. Steel, General Managers of Sales Minutes, July 17, 1907, August 21, 1907, October 23, 1907, *Stanley Hearings*, VI, 3957–3961.

[20] Gary Address, June 25, 1914, *Addresses and Statements*, II.

intentions. "I do not know whether the public will believe it," Gary told reporters in 1904, "but a good deal of our time and thought is devoted to a careful and humane study of wages and hours. The welfare of our men can never be lost sight of no matter what happens." As a result of trade cooperation, "the relations of capital and labor will settle themselves on sensible and mutually satisfactory lines."

The stock purchase plan was persuasive evidence of the new labor outlook. United States Steel, as Gary informed a reporter, was spending several millions on the plan, "and expected no benefit in return except such as eventually results from a friendly and loyal feeling." Criticism arose when the stock declined before the end of the first year. But the Corporation's obviously good intentions — it offered to buy back the stock at the original cost or suspend payments during unemployed periods — quieted misgivings. In general, observers applauded the plan of "making partners, practically, of its workmen."

Gary, Indiana, presented another impressive spectacle. Not only was the Steel Corporation erecting the world's largest steel mill, but it was creating an "industrial utopia" where only a sandy waste had existed the previous year. Workers' houses, streets and landscaping, public buildings sprang up overnight. Widely publicized, Gary and stock subscription symbolized the capacity of U.S. Steel to do big things for labor.

Scrutiny was thus diverted during the early years from the realities of the steel mills. As the decade advanced, however, the air of national well-being changed to disquietude. Muckraking journalism was uncovering the seamier side of American politics and industry. Labor conditions in steel became one of the prime targets for attack.

The hardships of steelmaking had never passed unnoticed locally. Chicagoans, for instance, commonly believed that many men killed in the South Works were buried secretly. It was, the Chicago *Tribune* cried, a "Centre of Mill Horrors." [21] Possibly

[21] Chicago *Tribune,* May 13, 1906.

as a result of these rumors, William Hard investigated the South Chicago plant and published his findings in the November 1907 issue of *Everybody's Magazine*. Its title established the central point of the article: "Making Steel and Killing Men." There had been in 1906 46 fatalities, and probably 2,000 injuries. Six times coroner's juries had admonished the company. Graphically written, the article drew critical attention to the steel mills.

Meanwhile, the Charity Organization Society of New York with the financial support of the Russell Sage Foundation was launching its Pittsburgh Survey. A team of investigators worked through 1908 gathering material in the district. Their findings, grimly delineating the hard lot of the steelworker, appeared throughout 1909 in the Society's magazine *Survey,* later in book form, and were supplemented in 1911 and 1912 by a series of articles on other important steel centers.

The impact of the Pittsburgh Survey was quiet but profound. The facts uncovered gradually spread beyond the limited audience of *Survey* subscribers concerned with social service. The Federal Council of Churches of Christ urged the clergy to plead for reform from their pulpits. Some newspapers and popular magazines summarized the "appalling" facts.[22] But, unlinked to any dramatic event, the Survey had no immediately decisive effect. Its significance lay rather in the establishment of a fund of reliable information on the steelworkers.

U.S. Steel's attack on organized labor in June 1909 created a new source of criticism. "The Steel Corporation is going to find out some of the limitations of lawless wealth under our Government," vowed Samuel Gompers. The A.F.L. launched a publicity attack on the Corporation as a violator of antitrust laws and as an oppressor of labor. On January 10, 1910, labor spokesmen submitted both complaints to President Taft, and others approached state governors.[23] The legal attack ended without tangible result. But the Federation had drawn attention to labor conditions and,

[22] *Literary Digest,* January 15, 1910, pp. 100–101; *IA,* March 24, 1910, p. 669.
[23] A.F.L., *Proceedings* (1910), pp. 20–21, 111–112; Gompers to P. J. McArdle, December 27, 1909, March 12, 1910, Gompers Papers.

perhaps more important, had become the Corporation's avowed enemy. An influential voice in public places, it would seize every chance to injure the reputation of the steel trust.

Meanwhile, events were dramatizing the steel mills. The McKees Rocks strike provided the first impact. Appearing at first simply a spontaneous outbreak, it developed into a stubborn contest lasting through the summer of 1909. The strikers displayed remarkable restraint, and their leaders effectively argued their case before the public. The black conditions in the Pressed Steel Car plant were gradually revealed. Frank N. Hoffstot, the president, proved to be unusually arrogant. So far as the company was concerned, he announced, "there is no strike," and, moreover, "it's nobody's business how I run my affairs." He flatly rejected arbitration. Finally, toward the end of August, the fact was revealed that strikebreakers had been lured into the plant and forcibly kept there in utter misery.[24]

Angry disapproval, steadily rising, followed the course of the strike. After the strikebreaker revelations, criticism became unanimous. The *Wall Street Journal* found the company's methods "sordid and inhuman." The *Iron Trade Review* planned a series of articles to "prevent the occurrence of similar deplorable events elsewhere." The conservative New York *Evening Post* accused the company of "grinding out" profits "at the expense of its laborers." In Pittsburgh itself, at first the *Leader* alone had championed the strikers, but eventually the entire city was attacking the company. The district attorney called the strike "a shame and a disgrace." Sizable collections were raised for the men, and a delegation of stockholders waited upon the company officials and demanded immediate settlement of the strike.[25]

Pressed on all sides, the company surrendered. No immediate consequences followed the strike despite demands for a government investigation. Yet McKees Rocks was of immense im-

[24] Chicago *Daily Socialist,* July 21, August 26, 27, 1909; P. U. Kellog, "The McKees Rocks Strike," *Survey,* August 7, 1909, pp. 656–665.

[25] *Literary Digest,* August 7, 1909, pp. 188–189, September 4, 1909, pp. 525–527; *AF,* October 1909, pp. 871–876; *Outlook,* September 18, 1909, p. 84.

portance. It created an image of the autocratic employer and the downtrodden steelworker. It set the stage for the Bethlehem strike.

Spontaneous and complete, this stoppage generated a similar public response. As with the earlier conflict, its unorganized character struck observers; only the most desperate circumstances could have driven the Bethlehem workmen out.[26] In early March an A.F.L. representative led a strikers' committee to Washington to present the workmen's grievances and demand an investigation. The Pittsburgh Survey indicated the possibilities; public interest was aroused; and the Bethlehem Steel Company held important government contracts. On March 17, 1910 the Senate directed the Bureau of Labor to make a thorough inquiry, and soon federal agents descended on South Bethlehem.

The results, appearing in the press in mid-May, told of the twelve-hour day, seven-day week, speed-up, numerous accidents, and a wage too low to support the family of an unskilled laborer. Such conditions, said the *Outlook,* were "a reproach and a shame, not only to this company, but to the Nation and the State that allow them." The Federal Council of Churches, after making its own investigation, found the long day and week "alike a disgrace to civilization." Schwab protested angrily. The federal report was accurate enough, he admitted, but it gave the impression that conditions were peculiar to Bethlehem which were in fact common and imposed on him by the competitive situation. The entire industry stood implicated.[27]

The Bethlehem investigation bore immediate fruit in Washington. The Senate passed a resolution for a full-scale inquiry into the steel industry whose eventual result was a four-volume report of unprecedented thoroughness. The campaign for the eight-hour day on government contract work gained impetus. And the House, largely at labor's behest, directed the attorney-general to begin the

[26] New York *Herald,* May 23, 1910.

[27] U.S. Bureau of Labor, *Report on Bethlehem Strike* (1910); *Outlook,* July 16, 1910, pp. 544–545; *Literary Digest,* August 6, 1910, p. 204; New York *Herald,* May 23, 1910; New York *Tribune,* May 23, 1910; *IA,* May 19, 1910, p. 1191.

investigation of the Steel Corporation that would lead to the anti-trust suit. "Public opinion at the present moment," crowed the *American Federationist* in September 1910, "is arrayed against the working conditions in the steel industry."[28]

Criticism continued unabated. In March 1911 John Fitch published in the *American Magazine* a popularized summary of his findings for the Pittsburgh Survey: "a daily and weekly schedule of hours, both shockingly long; a system of speed-up that adds overstrain to overtime; and, crowning all, a system of repression that stifles initiative and destroys healthy citizenship." Fitch entitled the article "Old Age at Forty," a phrase that became the rallying cry of critics.[29]

The Stanley Committee hearings on the legality of the Steel Corporation provided another platform. Pittsburgh Survey men went over the ground that by then had become common knowledge. Louis Brandeis, admittedly not an expert witness, appeared for the public.

> How, in America, can you explain . . . in a great and conspicuous industry, a condition of work and of living, if living it may be called, affecting that large body of employees, such as we find here? . . . These horrible conditions of labor . . . are a disgrace to America, considering the wealth which has surrounded and flown out of this industry.

"We have got to consider what the effect of this is upon these American citizens and upon the rest of us through them."[30] What defense was possible against such charges?

Even stockholders became incensed. Charles M. Cabot, a Boston investment broker related to the prominent New England family, read an article in *Collier's* drawn from the Pittsburgh Survey. Feeling his responsibility as a small stockholder — a novel idea —

[28] *AF,* September 1910, p. 804.
[29] On response to Fitch article, see, for example, *Nation,* August 31, 1911, p. 193; *Chautauquan,* LXIV (November 1911), 305–306.
[30] *Stanley Hearings,* IV, 2835–2873.

he called on Judge Gary with a plan for interesting his fellow stockholders in the treatment of labor by the Corporation. John Fitch would set forth the evils in an article to be mailed at Mr. Cabot's expense to 15,000 owners of preferred stock. Somewhat to his surprise, Gary agreed. The article, reduced after much acrimony to a discussion of hours of work, was dispatched with a reply by Gary. Ninety of the 15,000 responded; one-fifth desired reduction in hours if possible; another seventh — "generally women and clergymen," Gary observed — preferred the reduction even at the cost of dividends. That was the slim result of Cabot's praiseworthy efforts.[31]

But they succeeeded in another direction. The genesis of the famous "Old Age at Forty" was Cabot's commission to Fitch for the piece to send to the stockholders. At the April 1911 stockholders' meeting Cabot interrupted the standard proceedings with a resolution for an investigation of the charges made in "Old Age at Forty." Pointing out his objections to the article and his control by proxy of a large majority of the stock, Judge Gary assented nevertheless to the appointment of an investigating committee of "able, substantial, reliable stockholders." Their report a full year later was in fact a whitewash, condemning evils already eliminated, hoping for further reform, and congratulating the management for its constructive attitude.[32] But Cabot's purposes were served. The odd spectacle of a corporation "investigating itself" caught public attention, and Cabot's complaints were amply aired.

Indignation reached its peak in 1912. The Stanley Committee censured the Steel Corporation for its labor policies. The Senate Committee on Labor and Education denounced its "brutal system of industrial slavery," and approved the eight-hour bill for government contracts which shortly became law. The New York *World*

[31] F. B. Copley, "A Great Corporation Investigates Itself," *American Magazine*, LXXIV (October 1912), 643–654; *Survey*, July 22, 1911, pp. 591–595. *Addresses and Statements by Gary*, I, gives copies of the letters and Stockholders' Meeting, April 15, 1912 (pamphlet) analyzes them.

[32] *Pittsburgh Survey*, VI, App. 1, 395–405, gives the full report. *IA*, June 27, 1912, pp. 1574–1575, gives Gary's letter accompanying the report.

ran a series of indignant articles on conditions which were "a crime against humanity." Even local newspapers found the steel mills exciting copy.

The Terre Haute *Post,* for instance, sent a reporter to South Bethlehem before the Christmas season. He described the life of an immigrant whose family lived in three meanly furnished, unheated rooms. The worn-looking mother had recently given birth without a doctor, and the baby had the only blanket in the house. The father, a seven-day-a-week man, had not been home at the birth, nor would he be on Christmas day. The article ended: "The Christmas spirit? Oh, I didn't see much of it around the mills of Bethlehem in Pennsylvania." [33] Such was the publicity that circulated the country in 1912.

The steel manufacturers did not take kindly to criticism. Always it distorted the facts, emphasizing the evils and relegating the good "to the fine type of a footnote." The reformers were either dishonest or "full of sentiment but with no experience." The Survey investigation, claimed an irate Pittsburgh employer, was the work of the "usual muckraker, and no one who knows anything about actual conditions has the least confidence in any statements they make." Politicians had their own reasons. An Ohio prosecutor, for example, indicted Youngstown steel companies for conspiring to give a wage increase. He was simply imitating ambitious federal attorneys, grumbled the *Iron Age.* The outrage was "legitimate fruit of many wrongs that have been perpetrated in the name of government" by "designing men in public life."

The presumption of the critics also angered the steel men. No one, stressed Judge Gary, had the welfare of the steelworkers more at heart than he. "If there are complaints theirs is the voice to speak, not that of the muckraker and the would-be philanthro-

[33] Reprinted in *AJ,* December 19, 1912, p. 1. See also the collection of Cleveland press clippings in Scrapbook, Vol. 15, American Steel and Wire Collection.

pists," a Corporation spokesman told the Rochester Chamber of Commerce. The knowledge rankled that the reformers, men of no personal importance, exerted great power. Their own efforts at reform, the manufacturers complained, made almost no impression. But "the attacks of government agents, political partisans, social workers . . . and writers who say the sensational things the average reader wants to hear — all these go to the far corners of the land." [34]

Handicapped as they were, the steel companies worked indefatigably to counteract adverse publicity. Spokesmen appeared on many public platforms, eagerly granted interviews, and wrote for popular magazines, even the troublesome *Survey. Leslie's Weekly,* edited by Colonel George Harvey and rumored to be under Morgan's control, consistently extolled labor conditions in the industry. In 1915 Arundel Cotter, a reporter on friendly terms with Judge Gary, published a highly sympathetic *Authentic History of the United States Steel Corporation,* later subtitled, "A Corporation with a Soul." According to Brandeis, the Steel Corporation maintained an effective "publicity bureau"; the *Iron Age* in 1911 referred to "the educational process now going on" to alter public sentiment. How far the industry's public relations machinery had developed was unclear; without question the steel companies ably presented their side. But only real accomplishment would silence criticism. The industry finally turned itself to reform.

Progress was made first to reduce the high accident rate — the prime target, significantly, of public attack. In May 1906 discussions at New York began among the casualty managers of the constituent U.S. Steel companies, to which safety work had until then been relegated. At the meeting of April 1908, shortly after the publication of the Hard article, Judge Gary announced: "We should like to take a prominent part in every movement that is calculated to protect employees. . . . We will not hesitate to make

[34] *Stanley Hearings,* V, 3300; *IA,* March 24, 1910, pp. 671–672, December 19, 1912, p. 1448, April 30, 1914, p. 1080; Gary Address at Pittsburgh University, February 26, 1915, *Addresses and Statements,* II.

the necessary appropriations." [35] The safety campaign was launched.

A Committee of Safety, appointed at the meeting, immediately installed an inspection system. On the basis of exhaustive reports, the Committee recommended changes to the subsidiaries, and required compliance or acceptable excuses within thirty days. The constituent companies meanwhile began their own campaigns. In every plant, safety committees searched for dangerous equipment, investigated accidents, and recommended improvements. Workmen were frequently chosen to make periodic inspections of their mills.

The movement went rapidly forward. As Gary had promised, the Corporation was unstinting; $750,000 was spent yearly on the work. U.S. Steel pioneered a wide array of safety devices and practices. Its education campaign preached safety on bulletin boards and pay envelopes, in short talks and competitions. Signs in several languages warned of danger spots. Accidents were reported candidly in plant magazines and, where justified, the fault was assigned to the company.

Visiting the Gary and South Chicago plants, John Fitch was greatly impressed by "the spirit that prevails among superintendents, foremen and men. . . . The slogan is 'Boost for Safety,' and everybody boosts." He came away from a meeting of the Illinois Steel Company's Safety Committee "with more faith in my fellowman" after listening to intense deliberations on matters that brought no "financial advancement of the company." [36] The results of the safety campaign could be measured precisely: in four years the number of serious accidents in Corporation mills declined 43 per cent.

The spirit swiftly spread. Safety managers of the Steel Corporation preached accident prevention and detailed their methods at the meetings of the Iron and Steel Institute and in the trade journals.

[35] U.S. Steel Committee of Safety, *Bulletin,* October 1, 1910.
[36] *Report on Labor Conditions,* IV, 187–236; Eastman, *Accidents,* App. 2, pp. 261–264; Steel Institute, *Bulletin,* April, 1916, pp. 113–121; Fitch, "Boosting for Safety," *Survey,* November 4, 1911, pp. 1148–1157.

The slogan "Safety First," originated in the Illinois Steel Company, became the industry's watchword. The "movement has become so general in the past few years," observed the *Iron Age* in 1914, that describing the efforts in any plant meant pointing out the slight variations. The achievements were as impressive outside as within the Steel Corporation. Inland Steel had reduced its accident rate 55 per cent by 1915, Jones and Laughlin 71 per cent.

The common-law concept of accident liability gradually fell into disrepute. The president of U.S. Steel's National Tube Company rejected the view that, because a man accepts the hazards of employment, "therefore the risk is his. I think the industry should bear that burden." [37] The Steel Corporation introduced its compensation plan on May 1, 1910. Injured employees or their families received payment irrespective of liability unless they sued the Corporation. The benefits were generous: for temporary disability, from one-third of the daily wage for single men up to two dollars per day for fathers; six to eighteen months' wages for permanent injury; at death, eighteen months' pay to the family, plus additions for long service and children to a maximum of $3,000; and free medical treatment in all cases. The cost to the Steel Corporation was roughly two million dollars a year.

More than public opinion was prodding the industry to shoulder this charge. When U.S. Steel announced its excellent plan, commissions in many states were already considering compulsory accident insurance. Most steel companies, unlike U.S. Steel, were content to await state legislation. The wave of enactments began in 1911. When Pennsylvania finally acted in late 1915, every industrial state protected its injured workmen to some degree. Only a few, including Ohio, however, were as generous as the Steel Corporation.

The safety movement and workmen's compensation had a close reciprocal relation. The reduction of its accident rate made feasible the insurance plan of U.S. Steel. Other firms reversed the logic. Compulsory insurance gave them an incentive to start safety programs, since premiums were based on the degree of hazard in the

[37] W. B. Schiller, Steel Institute, *Yearbook* (1912), p. 120.

industry. "As soon . . . as workmen's compensation laws transferred the burden of industrial accidents from the workman to the
industry the 'Safety First' movement began," observed the secretary
of the National Safety Council, and the *Iron Age* agreed with him.[38]
Safety and accident insurance were parallel developments.

Other efforts to mitigate insecurity were not forced by state
action. Many companies encouraged sick benefit clubs in their
mills. Often these were an outgrowth of the accident insurance
associations of the liability period. The Mutual Benefit Association
of the American Rolling Mill Company, for instance, continued
to function as a benefit society after the enactment of the Ohio
compensation law. In January 1917 the company, in addition, took
out a blanket life insurance policy for all its employees. At the
Lorain Works of the National Tube Company the workmen contributed fifty cents a month for sick benefits and the company
made up the difference. During the 1914 depression many plants
established Good Fellow Clubs through which all contributed to
assist needy members. The Steel Corporation started its pension
program in January 1911. Later, International Harvester's Wisconsin Steel Company and the Colorado Fuel and Iron Company introduced similar plans; and other concerns claimed to care for
aged workmen in less formal ways. All these measures made more
secure the lives of the steelworkers.

The health and comfort of the men at work were also vigorously
promoted. Steel companies purified the water sources at their
plants; improved sewage disposal; added sanitary fountains, water
closets, shower baths, wash basins, and lockers; and introduced
ventilating and heating systems. The Carnegie Company perfected
a standard plan for plant emergency hospitals costing about $10,-
000. Many mills provided plant restaurants and club houses. Even
gardens began to brighten the grim steel plants. "We make better
steel and more of it by raising flowers and having them in our
yards," Bethlehem's President Eugene G. Grace explained to a

[38] W. H. Cameron, *IA*, December 10, 1915, p. 1419, May 13, 1915, pp.
1077–1078.

curious visitor. The industry, as Republic's J. A. Topping said of his company, was extending "its welfare work in the broadest possible manner." [39]

Managers began to concern themselves even with the home lives of the workmen and their families. Some companies, following the example of the American Bridge Company, offered vacant land for gardens. These, said the secretary of the Steel Institute's Welfare Committee, not only cut living costs, but also "promote morality, keep the owner from the saloon and promote his self-respect." A number of companies expounded the virtues of "A Clear Brain." A notice posted at the Joliet Works urged abstention and promised the discharge of any man found drunk on the job. Other managers tried to prevent the location of saloons near the works.[40]

The National Tube Company pioneered in playgrounds. In 1910 it set aside a small plot of land, formerly used as a dumping ground, in a congested part of Pittsburgh. When this proved successful, the New York office urged other subsidiaries to do likewise. By 1914 over a hundred playgrounds were operating under the supervision of U.S. Steel companies, and the independents were following their example.

Visiting nurses were widely employed, especially to teach health and sanitation methods. Many plants opened small libraries and sponsored classes and athletic events. Finally, there was a wide array of activities to provide housing, to support the Y.M.C.A. and similar agencies, and to instruct the immigrants.

A spirit of service was developing. The Steel Corporation, said a spokesman, accepted its responsibility "to make up any local deficiencies for educational and social betterment." Companies had an obligation in direct proportion to their importance in the community, stated the *Bulletin* of the Steel Institute. Taking stock

[39] Grace, in Steel Institute, *Bulletin*, January 1913, p. 5; Topping, in *ibid.*, August 1913, p. 212.
[40] Steel Institute, *Yearbook* (1914), p. 251; *Joliet Works Mixer*, May 15, 1915, October 15, 1915.

after four years, the secretary of the Welfare Committee assured the Steel Institute of its success "in promoting the interests of humanity." [41]

The most noteworthy gains came in the reduction of the work week. Seven-day labor was indefensible. The U.S. Steel Finance Committee had recommended in April 1907 "that Sunday labor be reduced to the minimum." The order had some effect while business conditions were bad. But the press of orders in 1909 erased the progress. When the Bethlehem strike provoked government investigation of industry-wide labor conditions, Judge Gary hastily telegraphed the subsidiary presidents to observe fully the forgotten resolution of 1907.

The first annual session of the American Iron and Steel Institute met on May 27, 1910 under the shadow of public indignation over the seven-day week. William B. Dickson, First Vice President of the Steel Corporation, gave the major address. He warned his audience that it had no choice. The "tendency of the times" plainly indicated that failure to end voluntarily Sunday labor would result in "radical and ill-advised legislation." "True conservatism consists not in standing still and attempting to ignore public sentiment," he argued, "but rather in adjusting our methods of operating to meet the changing conditions of our time." His own experience as a steelworker, moreover, had convinced him that the eighty-four-hour week was "a reproach to our great industry and should not in this enlightened age be longer tolerated." Prodded by Dickson's forceful speech, the Institute voted to accept his suggestion for a committee to devise a plan to end seven-day-a-week work.[42]

A complicated rotating arrangement resulted. Unlike the earlier abortive attempt by the Steel Corporation, the scheme would eliminate seven-day labor where operations were continuous. Even

---

[41] Steel Institute, *Bulletin,* February 1914, p. 21; Thomas Darlington, "Present Scope of Welfare Work," Steel Institute, *Yearbook* (1914), pp. 240–252.

[42] Fitch, *Steel Workers,* app. 6, pp. 325–326, gives complete text.

men at blast furnaces, which had to run without interruption, were to have one day a week off. U.S. Steel immediately adopted the plan, and by early 1912 had essentially ended the seven-day week in its mills. Lackawanna, Youngstown Sheet and Tube, and a number of smaller firms accepted modifications of the Institute plan. In March 1912, 18,960 blast furnace men — 57.5 per cent — still worked every day, including the Bethlehem men. But the limited achievement, since it took in the Steel Corporation, quieted public criticism.[43]

Scrutiny shifted to the twelve-hour day — "the man-killing system," the New York *World* called it. An article in the January 1913 issue of *Metropolitan,* depicting the heavy labor in the steel mills, concluded: "Had you thought of doing that for one hour? And then for two . . . and finally for twelve hours? Had you? That is the barbaric twelve hour day which obtains in the steel industry." The *Survey* thought the abolition of the long day inevitable. The only question was whether "it can be done through voluntary action of the steel companies themselves. If they fail, the government will undoubtedly be forced to act, in behalf of the welfare of its citizens."

But twelve hours was entrenched as had been no other object of criticism. To steel men, the two shift system was integrally connected with efficient operation; its elimination would fly in the face of all sound principles of steelmaking. The difficulties raised, moreover, would be enormous. Three shifts, the only alternative, would require an addition of one-third in the labor force and necessitate general wage increases. By contrast, the day of rest had cost the companies nothing and had only slightly expanded the labor force.[44]

The manufacturers established their defenses. "The employees prefer twelve hours in order to receive a larger compensation," they claimed. Moreover, improved machinery made the long day bearable; workmen on blast and open-hearth furnaces actually

[43] *Labor Conditions,* III, 167–171, and app. H, 541–547.
[44] The federal Bureau of Labor, however, claimed eight hours would increase costs less than 6 per cent. *Labor Conditions,* III, 175–187.

were busy only for a few hours of their shifts. Finally, reflecting on his youth on an Illinois farm, Judge Gary found social and moral benefits in hard work. He was "not certain that twelve hours is a bad thing for employees." [45]

Without the leadership of the Steel Corporation, the prospects of the eight-hour movement were dim. Yet some progress was made. In early 1912 the Commonwealth Steel Company changed to three shifts in its open-hearth plant. The company gave a 20 per cent hourly raise and found its labor costs unchanged. The Cambria Steel Company, where three shifts had long been employed in the rolling mills, began in May 1912 to put its blast furnace men on eight hours. The Cambria plan substituted for the six-day week reforms, for the workmen did not get a day of rest. They worked fifty-six hours and received weekly an income only one-seventh less than under the eighty-four hour week. Because of increased efficiency, the company hired only one-seventh more men, thus not suffering financially from the plan.

The evident success of these experiments stirred criticism within the industry. R. A. Bull, Commonwealth president, commented caustically that the testimony on the easy work of steelmaking "by some captains of industry has amused me, as it doubtless has many others, by its misstatements of facts, possibly due to incorrect knowledge of working conditions." He deplored "the absolute injustice, humanly speaking, of the twelve hour shift," adding, "I hope I shall not be classified as a Socialist for having such a conviction." W. B. Dickson, the champion of the six-day week, became outspokenly critical of the long day after leaving the Steel Corporation. Aside from the likelihood of increased efficiency, the steel companies "can today afford to change." In the "remote contingency" that the cost would be too great at existing prices, the public would have to share the burden. The decision rested with the Steel Corporation, since "the conditions established by it must ultimately prevail in the entire industry." [46]

---

[45] *IA*, November 10, 1910, p. 1054, January 18, 1912, p. 1902; *Stanley Hearings*, V, 3262; *Literary Digest*, May 4, 1912, p. 921.

[46] Bull, in *IA*, October 3, 1912, pp. 808–809; also, R. A. Bull, "8 Hours vs.

But U.S. Steel, unmoved by public opinion, was unlikely to respond to the arguments of competitors. Twelve hours remained the standard day in the mills.

Taken all in all, considerable advances in working conditions had come about as a result of public criticism. In the area of trade unionism, however, steel men were immovable. They were equally as sensitive here as in other labor affairs. But labor organization was a matter too close to the sources of control to admit outside tampering. And, properly viewed, antiunionism could be effectively defended on grounds of principle.

There had been, initially, no certainty that the Steel Corporation would be hostile to trade unions. The financial men did not share the antiunion animus of the operating officials. Neither Morgan's experience in railroads, nor Gary's in the Federal Steel Company, had soured them on labor organization. Conceivably, cooperation with conservative unions could foster labor peace and stability. Uncertain, the financial group in the spring of 1901 compromised on a status quo policy.

The strike of 1901 quickly ended the possibility of accommodation. The Amalgamated Association acted too rashly. It rejected a reasonable compromise and, in extending the strike, dishonored its contract. After a fruitless month, Morgan himself intervened — in itself a notable concession. The union's rejection of his terms, already accepted by the Amalgamated executive officers under the assurance of his friendly intentions, seemed to Morgan to be the repudiation of an agreement. Angered finally by the intransigence of the union officials, he stalked out of the August 3 meeting "in a towering rage." [47] The Steel Corporation immediately took up the fight with increased vigor and quickly broke the resistance of the

12 Hours Shifts," *Engineering Magazine*, XXXIV (January 1913), 559–561; W. B. Dickson, "Can American Steel Plants Afford an Eight-Hour Turn?" *Survey*, January 3, 1914, p. 376.

[47] *NLT*, August 8, 1901; *Independent*, August 1, 1901, p. 1767; *Literary Digest*, August 10, 1901, p. 151. See, however, synopsis of letter of Ralph M. Easley to Louis D. Brandeis, November 4, 1912, in Green, *National Civic Federation*, pp. 33–34.

union. Thereafter, the hostile views of the operating officials on unionism dominated in the counsels of U.S. Steel.

The financial men were anxious, however, to avoid the onus for antiunion acts. During the 1901 strike, for instance, the Steel Corporation stated publicly that the constituent companies made their decisions independently. (In actuality, the New York office kept tight control throughout the strike.)[48] Afterward, the U.S. Steel officials reported:

> We might have exacted harsher terms with reference to the number of nonunion mills, but it was not thought wise by your Management to take the position of openly oppressing organized labor.[49]

Shrewdly handled, the Steel Corporation emerged from the strike without the blemish of antiunionism. Samuel Gompers himself testified to the good will of Morgan and Schwab.[50] To preserve that reputation, U.S. Steel would have to pursue its ends circumspectly.

The Steel Corporation bided its time. A canvass of plant managers showed the summer of 1909 to be propitious. Much weakened, the Amalgamated Association would offer slight resistance and stir only a ripple of outside interest. The open-shop announcement misfired, creating just the flood of disapproval Judge Gary had hoped to avoid. The miscalculation stamped the Steel Corporation as an oppressor of labor; thereafter, attacks almost invariably included that charge.

Its effectiveness was demonstrated in the indignant testimony of Louis Brandeis. "These horrible conditions of labor," he told the Stanley Committee, "are the result of having killed or eliminated from the steel industry unionism. . . . It is a condition of repres-

[48] Executive Committee Minutes, April 20, May 1, June 17, 1901, *Stanley Hearings*, VI, 3826–3828, 3830–3831.

[49] Quoted in Tarbell, *Gary*, p. 160.

[50] See, for example, *Independent*, August 22, 1901, pp. 1998–1999; *Outlook*, July 27, 1901, pp. 701–702; *Nation*, July 18, 1901, p. 44; *Literary Digest*, July–September 1901; *AF*, October 1901, p. 428.

sion, of slavery in the real sense of the word, which is alien to American conditions." Even assuming good industrial conditions, there existed "the fundamental question": "whether any men in the United States, be they directors of the Steel Corporation or anything else, are entitled and can safely determine the conditions under which a large portion of the American [people] shall live." [51]

The steel men marshaled their arguments against this powerful indictment. Unions were obsolete. "They may have been justified in the long past, for I think the workmen were not always treated justly," stated Judge Gary with characteristic judiciousness. But now "no necessity for labor unions" remained, and "no benefit or advantage through them will accrue to anyone except the union labor leaders." One spokesman catalogued the evils: "Unionism is opposed to efficiency. It destroys the esprit de corps . . . In its very essence it is antagonistic to the employer, it sets labor and capital into two distinct and inimical camps." "The existence and conduct of labor unions, in this country at least," Gary concluded, "are inimical to the best interests of the employes, the employers, and the general public." [52]

Even so, by what authority did employers deprive men of the right to organize? Steelmasters had long slipped by that painful question with the claim that their shops were "open" to workmen irrespective of union affiliation. Carnegie, for instance, wrote hurriedly to Frick in early 1892 to alter the notice ending relations with the Amalgamated Association:

I did not get it quite right, because I think it said that the firm had to make the decision of "Union" or "Non-Union." This, I am sure, is wrong. . . . We simply say that . . . we do not care whether a man belongs to as many Unions or organizations

[51] *Stanley Hearings,* IV, 2855–2856.

[52] Gary, "Principles and Policies of the U.S. Steel Corporation," Stockholders' Meeting, April 18, 1921, pp. 10, 12; *IA,* February 20, 1913, p. 479, February 22, 1912, p. 482; Arundel Cotter, *The Authentic History of The United States Steel Corporation* (New York, 1916), p. 126.

as he chooses, but he must conform to the system in our other works.[53]

Jones and Laughlin's Willis King explained to the Industrial Commission in 1901: "We find it more desirable to treat directly with our own men. We do not ask them whether they are union men or not." This defensive argument was employed in 1909.

Under the stress of sharp criticism, however, steel men found for the open-shop logic more effective uses. They began to charge that unions, through the closed shop, abridged the fundamental right of men "to work under such conditions as they may choose." The open shop was thus transformed into a compelling attack on organized labor. The Steel Corporation's refusal to deal with the union, claimed an official, was "in defense of the principle of the 'open shop.'"

> We do not believe it to be the wish of the people of this country that a man's right to work shall be made dependent upon his membership in any organization. We consider the principle of the "open shop" only another aspect of the principles upon which the government of this country was founded.[54]

The open shop, said the *Iron Age,* was "no more a debatable question than the right of property."

The maneuver was remarkably effective. From oppressors, the steel companies became the protectors of workmen's liberties. Labor leaders, losing the initiative, found themselves in the morass of open-and-closed shop debate. As for the charges of repression, leaders like Gary indignantly denied them; or, when occasionally confronted with the evidence, pleaded ignorance. Clearly, the open-shop argument won the battle for public opinion. And the steel manufacturers had learned an invaluable lesson. If it was necessary to placate the public, it was also possible to lead it in favorable, or at least irrelevant, directions.

[53] Quoted in Harvey, *Frick,* pp. 165–166.
[54] Raynal Bolling, American Academy of Political Science, *Annals,* XLII, 47.

By actual reform or by persuasive talk, the industry quieted public opinion. Its attackers, indeed, had been neither as extreme nor as indiscriminate as they had seemed. Many of the most outspoken critics eagerly applauded every sign of progress. The furor subsided. By 1914 Judge Gary was able to read signs of "a well developed sentiment throughout this country in favor of giving business — even big business — a fair chance. (Applause.)" [55] America's increasing involvement in the war left the industry at peace with its detractors.

Considering their handiwork, the steel men found little cause to regret the spur of public opinion. There was, firstly, "great satisfaction," as Judge Gary said, "to know that, activated by high motives, you have done the right thing." Welfare was "a simple duty that industry owes to labor." Such activity, added the chief surgeon of the Youngstown Sheet and Tube Company, "attached . . . the spirit of brotherly love" to the entire industry.[56] It was, after all, simply the extension of cooperation to labor that Judge Gary had espoused from the start.

The admitted danger of paternalism was "scrupulously and constantly avoided." But Judge Gary did succumb to the temptations of an attitude of *noblesse oblige*. "The man who has the intelligence and the success and the capital to employ labor," he stated at a Waldorf dinner, "has placed upon himself voluntarily a responsibility with reference to his men." "We have the advantage of them in education, in experience, in wealth, in many ways, and we must make it absolutely certain under all circumstances that we treat them right. (Applause)." This duty rested on the "big, broad employers of labor." [57]

Besides those noble sentiments, steel manufacturers, being practical men, were comforted by the knowledge that "in dollars and

[55] Steel Institute, *Yearbook* (1914), p. 13.

[56] Gary Address to Subsidiary Presidents, June 25, 1914, *Addresses and Statements*, II; Steel Institute, *Yearbook* (1914), p. 256.

[57] Gary Addresses, January 11, 1911, May 4, 1911, December 17, 1913, *Addresses and Statements*, I.

cents it pays to treat employees as we think they deserve." "It is good business to conserve life and health," observed John Topping of Republic Steel, for thereby "one of the most important items of economy in production is secured." [58] Safety, requiring a clean and ordered plant arrangement, became synonymous with economical operation. And, of course, efficiency was a prime argument of the proponents of shorter work schedules.

But the chief value of welfare work was to strengthen the labor stability of the modern steel industry. "A great many men," admitted Youngstown's J. A. Campbell, "try to get rid of [organized labor] in order to take advantage of their men. You will find always where that is done the employers are continuously in trouble. The way to keep out of trouble with your employees . . . is to treat them fairly." [59] Only the generous improvement of their conditions would gain the total acquiescence of the steelworkers.

Simple welfare, however, was not enough. It had to be applied so as to instill in its beneficiaries a sense of participation. American Rolling Mill, for example, called its program "Mutual Interest Work"; Commonwealth Steel, "Fellowship Work." "No man should feel that he is only a cog in a machine," explained the employment manager of Illinois Steel. Properly presented, the employer's good deeds would evoke the loyalty of his men. The company's liberality, stated the *South Works Review,* should increase "the spirit of cooperation and good fellowship between employer and employee. . . . So let each of us, from the highest to the most humble, show his esteem of the company's actions by an increased *Efficiency* in every thought, word and deed." "A body of loyal employees," observed the *Joliet Works Mixer,* could be created only by "square dealing. . . . Loyal service rests upon a foundation of mutual confidence and trust." [60] And that, in turn, depended on an effective welfare program.

"Considering their education and their experience," concluded

[58] Steel Institute, *Bulletin,* August 1913, p. 211.

[59] Campbell Address, May 4, 1911, *Addresses and Statements by Gary,* I.

[60] Steel Institute, *Bulletin,* April 1914, p. 95; *South Works Review,* October 1917; *Joliet Works Mixer,* March 15, 1914, January 1917.

Judge Gary, "our men have been very decent in their conduct toward us. . . . They are not at all blind to the fact that you [subsidiary presidents] have treated them on the whole better than employers ever before treated their workmen." [61] If employees were so persuaded, welfare projects were bargains indeed. They were a cheap solution to the problem of the "dishonest labor agitator."

Welfare work thus served a more important purpose than to quiet public criticism. It added the measure of betterment needed to win the steelworker's consent to the terms of his employment. It insured the stability of the labor system that had developed along with the industry. The reforms probably had their effect in normal times. They could not, however, counteract the shattering consequences of a world war.

[61] Gary Address, June 25, 1914, *Addresses and Statements,* II; U.S. Steel Stockholders' Meeting, April 16, 1917, p. 4.

Chapter IX

The Steelworkers in the World War

The labor system seemed in 1914 to be securely anchored. Adequate adjustments to the terms of employment existed among the steelworkers. Conditions had measurably improved during the preceding years. And the threat of organized labor was minimal. Labor stability reigned in the steel industry.

The World War profoundly altered that situation. First, the sources of labor acquiescence were disrupted. The economic conditions of war destroyed the reasons for the steelworker's silent submission; and Wilsonian propaganda gave a special appeal to trade unionism. Second, the war rejuvenated organized labor. The trade unions were strengthened by an influx of new members and, more important, by the support of the Wilson administration. For the first time, the federal government intervened to guarantee the workingman's right to organize. These two circumstances ensured the immediate success of the effort to unionize the steel mills.

A condition of peace, the old order thus collapsed under the impact of war. Steelmasters were relatively helpless while the war continued. Its sudden conclusion, however, left the industry free to battle for the restoration of its control. The issue was, in the end, resolvable only by conflict.

The labor pattern of the steel industry rested on a set of three balances: between the supply and demand for labor; between the number of immigrants becoming permanent industrial workers and the number rising into skilled, dependent jobs; and, in the steelworker's mind, between the value of his labor and the amount of his pay. All three acted to render the steelworker amenable to the conditions imposed on him. Not one of the balances could survive when war broke the two-way flow of immigrants and made national defense the object of steel manufacture.

The balance of labor supply and demand was the first to break down. Initially, the hostilities in Europe had deepened the business slump of late 1913. Employment fell sharply. At Gary, distress spread below the Wabash tracks. The U.S. Steel plant kept some men busy on repairs, contributed to relief, and suspended rent payments on company houses. The recently formed Associated Charities and the Gary city council applied their meager resources to assist the indigent. The exodus of jobless immigrants was observed approvingly by public and company officials.[1] Their sense of relief was short-lived.

The delayed effect of war became evident in early 1915. Military orders began to arrive, and employment offices reopened. But the normal rush for work did not materialize. No longer was seen the crush of job-seekers "that once crowded the mill gates of Jones and Laughlin." The war, steel men lamented, was creating "a situation altogether unusual in the labor market."[2] With immigration slowed to a trickle, there seemed no way to overcome the mounting labor shortage.

Worker unrest had normally accompanied returning prosperity. It was a sign of the temporary imbalance of the labor supply. Now the shortage was very acute, and the discontent was correspondingly extreme. "Workmen of the most docile tendencies have been making demands," John Fitch reported, noting "insignificant little rebellions verging on strikes here and there."

The situation came to a head in Youngstown. Two days after Christmas, 1915, laborers struck at the Republic tube plant for a 25 per cent increase. Spreading quickly, the strike shut down both Republic plants, and the following week the Youngstown Sheet and Tube plant in East Youngstown. On Friday afternoon, Janu-

[1] Quillen, "Gary," pp. 257–261, 266.
[2] *IA,* June 17, 1915, pp. 1357–1358; New York *Times,* October 22, 1916, VII, 8, November 5, 1916, VII, 8.

ary 7, East Youngstown laborers gathered before the bridge lead-ing to the sheet and tube plant. As they pressed forward, a nervous guard fired. Bricks flew; the shooting became general. Enraged, the mob surged through the shabby streets to set buildings aflame, destroy, and pillage. Only the arrival of National Guard units the next day restored order. Property damage reached an estimated million dollars; twenty strikers were wounded, three fatally, and many were arrested afterward.

The insensate violence outraged public opinion. The steel com-pany, however, was conciliatory. President J. A. Campbell an-nounced that the plant would remain closed for a few days, since operation "would be useless . . . while some of our workers are in the frame of mind they are in now." He had the soldiers with-drawn from the plant. And he gave assurances that he would not bring in strikebreakers. "The gates will be open for the men to work in the morning." At Republic the managers made conces-sions to committees representing newly formed unions. Both com-panies promised wage increases, and the strikes came to an end.

But the prospect was deeply unsettling. There appeared no end to the labor shortage that was behind the discontent. Conditions are "so unprecedented," the *Iron Age* observed, "as to make the ordinary manufacturer's experience of little value as a guide." Everywhere trouble threatened.[3]

The climax came in the Pittsburgh district. Westinghouse strikers from East Pittsburgh in late April took to marching from plant to plant. Steelworkers responded at many points in the district. The second parade to the Edgar Thomson Works in Braddock ended in bloodshed. Guards opened fire, killing two and infuriating the rest to violence. "Pittsburgh in a turmoil," an-nounced the *Iron Age*. "A mob of foreigners," reported a Pitts-burgh labor paper, "most of them said to be intoxicated, charged plant after plant, and many of the places were wrecked." Some mills shut down to avoid trouble. For a time, "the whole Pitts-

[3] A.F.L., *Weekly Newsletter,* January 15, February 27, 1916; *Survey,* January 22, 1916, pp. 477–480; *NLT,* January 27, 1916; New York *Times,* January 8, 9, 10, 1916; *IA,* January 13, 1916, p. 153.

burgh district was threatened with industrial paralysis." Then troops arrived, the Westinghouse strike leaders were arrested, and peace was restored. Vastly relieved, Judge Gary congratulated the Braddock workmen, who had not struck in large numbers, for their "courage, loyalty and fairness."

The underlying unrest, however, appeared unabated. "The explosive nature of the labor situation," commented the *Iron Age,* was "a factor in all forecasts."[4]

The forecasts were wrong. No further strikes of consequence occurred in 1916. After the American entry into the war, there were occasional stoppages, but only a strike of furnace workers at the Eliza plant of Jones and Laughlin in September 1917 was noteworthy. The National Industrial Conference Board report on the strike wave of the first six months of war did not even include iron and steel among the affected industries.[5]

Steel men found ways to reduce the labor shortage, and also to alleviate the consequent unrest. The immediate response was to increase wages. Having maintained rates during the depressed period, the Steel Corporation had at first opposed rises when prosperity returned. Despite evident labor discontent, the Youngstown companies followed Judge Gary's advice against advances. But, when the Youngstown strikes broke out, the Steel Corporation quickly announced a 10 per cent increase. Another raise came three months later, as Youngstown's J. A. Campbell said, "entirely unsolicited and unexpected by the men." Immediately preceding the Westinghouse troubles in Pittsburgh, the voluntary advance explained why the effect on the steel mills was "less than we feared." The steel men had learned the clear lesson, reported the New York *Times,* "that one of the surest ways to avoid discontent and strikes was to let wages mount in advance of living costs."

[4] *NLT,* May 4, 11, 18, 1916; *IA,* May 4, 1916, pp. 1104–1105; New York *Times,* May 3, 4, 1916; *Survey,* June 24, 1916, p. 334.

[5] Alexander M. Bing, *War-time Strikes and Their Adjustment* (New York, 1921), pp. 293, 295, gives the steel strike statistics: in 1916, 72, in 1917, 56; the percentage of all strikes, 1.9 in 1916, 1.2 in 1917.

The reasoning squared with Gary's view that liberality captured labor "loyalty," but not with his brief for steady wages. In any case, the extraordinary steel demand had also overwhelmed his defense of stable prices. As prices soared, the *Iron Age* observed, workmen and manufacturers shared the same attitude: "Since no such opportunity will come again, they must make the most of it." Steel companies willingly passed on some of the profits to assuage discontent and attract workers. (While wages rose 21 per cent by June 1916, steel prices doubled and tripled.)[6]

Wages advanced at regular intervals. Perhaps for the first time, steel companies were accused of excessive generosity. After yet another increase in August 1918, the Employers' Association of Pittsburgh charged the Steel Corporation with "taking the initiative to disturb all labor conditions in the country," and asked the War Labor Policies Board "to hold this gigantic corporation within reasonable bounds."[7] The steel manufacturers persistently raised wages despite the opposition even of the War Industries Board. By the war's end the hourly rate for unskilled labor in Pittsburgh and Chicago steel mills had risen from 20 to 42 cents with time-and-a-half for over eight hours.

Another rich labor supply was meanwhile being tapped. Negroes had long worked in the steel mills of the North. Frequently entering as strikebreakers, they had eventually found a permanent place in the mills. But, although they were numerous in a few Pittsburgh district plants — for instance, in the Carnegie Company's Clark mill and the Black Diamond mill — until the outbreak of the European conflict they were generally an insignificant minority.

In the spring of 1916 the Pennsylvania and Erie railroads began to pick up trainloads of Florida Negroes to fill their road gangs. Soon labor agents of the important steel companies and Mid-

---

[6] *IA*, January 13, 1916, pp. 156–157, May 4, 1916, p. 1082; U.S. Steel Stockholders' Meeting, April 9, 1915, pp. 9–10; New York *Times*, April 30, 1916.

[7] *NLT*, August 15, 1918.

western railroads were also entering the black areas of the South. In May 1916 Midvale Steel established an office in Richmond, Virginia, to route about 150 recruits each week to its four plants. The largest Pittsburgh steel mills also operated through Virginia centers. The Chicago district recruited mainly in Mississippi and Louisiana, utilizing the Illinois Central and other trunk lines running northward into Chicago. Two streams thus developed along the main north-south arteries, one feeding into the Northeast and Pennsylvania, the other into the Midwest.[8]

The Southern Negro was ripe for migration. The boll weevil, heavy floods, falling cotton prices, and crop diversification had caused distress. Low wages, poor living conditions, social, educational, and legal inequalities, and fear of mob violence had compounded the discontent. When agents appeared with offers of high wages in the North, the response was immediate. In stricken areas, whites often encouraged the Negroes to leave; but the increasing farm labor shortage quickly ended indifference. Heavy license fees and restrictions hindered agents; intimidation forced migrants to flee secretly. Once started, however, the exodus carried its own impetus. Letters, rumors, the propagandizing Chicago *Defender,* the occasional return of friends, continually stimulated the movement. Many more Negroes, probably between eight- and nine-tenths, migrated outside the organized efforts of Northern industry. Everywhere men talked of conditions up North. "You could not rest in your bed at night for Chicago," said one migrant from Hattiesburg, Mississippi. By November 1918 an estimated half million Negroes had departed for "The Land of Hope."

The migration swelled the black population of the steel towns. Housing single men posed no great problems; the companies

[8] U.S. Department of Labor, *Negro Migration, 1916–17* (Washington, 1919), pp. 27–28, 64, 86, 118–122; Emmett J. Scott, *Negro Migration During the War* (New York, 1920), pp. 55–56; Abraham Epstein, *The Negro Migrant in Pittsburgh* (Pittsburgh, 1918), pp. 24–25; Chicago Commission on Race Relations, *The Negro in Chicago* (Chicago, 1922), ch. 3; George E. Haynes, *The Negro At Work* (Washington, 1921), pp. 10–11. The following discussion is based mainly on these sources.

simply put up large barracks. Although bare, these camps generally had adequate facilities. In a few places — the Lukens plant in Coatesville, for example — they were neglected and notoriously bad. Conditions outside the camps were far worse. Migrants with families lived in one-room flats at exorbitant rents, and took in boarders. Investigators found the congestion indescribable in Pittsburgh. Segregation, the lack of construction, and already crowded conditions made housing for the Negroes deplorable everywhere. Sickness and social evils flourished. The steel companies did little. At Homestead the Carnegie Company purchased a large structure in September 1918 to serve as a community center for the colored residents; but there and elsewhere the main problem of housing the migrants went unmet.[9]

Masses of Negroes entered the steel mills. At the Gary Works their numbers rose from 189 in 1915 to 407 in 1916, 1,072 in 1917, and 1,295 in 1918. By August 1917, 4,000 were laboring at the Carnegie plants in the Pittsburgh district, 1,400 at Jones and Laughlin, and smaller numbers elsewhere. "Pittsburgh's industrial life is now partly dependent upon the Negro-labor supply," an observer commented in mid-1917.

But the colored migrants did not appear apt recruits. Labor turnover was extremely high. The employment manager at the Youngstown plant of the Carnegie Steel Company claimed to have seen 10,000 Negroes pass through the mill by September 1917. Jones and Laughlin officials later recalled that guards had kept strict watch on the Aliquippa camp to prevent the escape of men.[10] The migrants, moreover, seemed ill-suited for the heavy, pace-set labor of the steel mills. They were, employers complained, shiftless and irresponsible. The *Iron Age,* however, thought that they only needed proper handling "by a man from the South who is familiar with their habits and characteristics." Finally, company officials feared the reaction of white employees. On that account, several steel firms in Pittsburgh hesitated to hire the migrants. At

---

[9] Homestead *Messenger,* September 30, October 2, 1918.
[10] Mitchell, "The Labor Relations of Jones and Laughlin," p. 128.

Homestead a race riot was narrowly averted on Thanksgiving Day, 1917. And the opposition of whites forced one large steel company to abandon plans to house colored workmen in the neighborhood of its mill. Although eventually these difficulties were largely overcome, employers continued to consider the migrants inferior material and to relegate them to unskilled labor.

The Negro influx never fully overcame the labor shortage, aggravated as it was by the draft and greater opportunities elsewhere. Pittsburgh mill officials, an interviewer reported in the fall of 1917, were "sadly worried by their labor problem. They feel that things are going from bad to worse; that even wage increases can avail little; they hope for national conscription of labor . . . and are eager for Federal assistance." Judge Gary came out in favor of the importation of Orientals, to the accompaniment of anguished howls from organized labor. The Bethlehem Steel Company experimented with female manual laborers at its Steelton Works.[11] The situation seemed desperate indeed. Lacking the inflow of immigrants, labor remained in very short supply.

The breakdown of this first element of stability of the steel labor system undermined the second — the horizontal mobility of the unskilled immigrant workmen. Their very inability to leave the country tended to strengthen the ties to their jobs. Equally important, the apparent inadequacy of the Negroes and the continuing labor shortage reshaped the employer's attitude toward the Slavic steelworkers. He could no longer tolerate their normal rate of movement out of his mill. The methods of fostering loyalty in the upper ranks, therefore, were now directed also at the unskilled men.

Welfare work had eased the circumstances of the immigrants; but it had not, as with the skilled men, aimed at attaching them to the company. "Heretofore industrial management has been satisfied to treat the alien somewhat cavalierly," lectured an in-

[11] *Negro Migration, 1916–17,* p. 124; *IA,* January 10, 1918, p. 150, September 12, 1918, p. 670.

dustrial engineer. But the war has brought "management up with a round turn to study the alien residential and employment problem with more intelligence." [12]

The local reaction to the violent immigrant outburst at Youngstown, for instance, was notably mild. The rioters, argued the Youngstown *Vindicator,* must of course be punished. "Yet the hands of the rest of us are not clean because we have neglected to do our part by these neighbors of ours. . . . They can be made good, law-abiding citizens, or they can continue to be a magazine ready to explode under us at a moment's notice." [13] The immigrant steelworkers were suddenly very important, and, consequently, as an *Iron Age* writer observed, "never has there been a kindlier feeling among employers for aliens in our country than now."

The rechristening of Granite City's Hungary Hollow as "Lincoln Place" symbolized the changing sentiment. The Hollow — the immigrant quarter — had been isolated and shunned. "We found that this was all a mistake. The foreigners are kind-hearted, loyal and honest" when properly treated. The Commonwealth Steel Company established a Home Fellowship Department to assist the inhabitants. A room was rented for lectures and instruction; later, the entire building was leased. On March 19, 1916 the structure was christened the "Lincoln Progressive Club." Amid wild cheering, the immigrants (according to company officials) decided to rename the Hollow as well. "Many inspiring speeches" by local dignitaries inaugurated "the transformation of Lincoln Place into a dignified, respected and useful community." [14]

C. S. Robinson, general manager of the Youngstown Sheet and Tube Company, addressed the foremen in March 1917. Nothing was "more important than the welfare and contentment of the

[12] Winthrop Talbot, "Managing Alien Workers in War Time," *IA,* August 2, 1917, pp. 252–253, and "The Alien and the Industrial Worker," *IA,* August 23, 1917, pp. 430–431.

[13] Youngstown *Vindicator,* January 12, 1916.

[14] Steel Institute, *Bulletin,* April 1916, pp. 125–127.

men." He urged a "spirit of helpfulness and consideration," especially for the foreign-born workers. "These men are needed by our company. Their loyal cooperation and their progress are good things for the company." [15] The Hunky had thus risen in the estimation of the steel men.

The Youngstown firm planned housing specifically for its immigrant employees. By 1920 the steel companies of Youngstown had invested $5,000,000 in such construction. Other companies were similarly active. The American Rolling Mill Company established at Middletown, Ohio, a "Garden City Colony" designed for the special needs of the immigrants. Each bungalow contained quarters for the boarding boss's family and a dormitory room for twelve men. The other usual welfare efforts, as well as the repeated wage increases, acted also to hold the foreign-born men.

The "Americanization" movement initially had the same objective. Youngstown General Manager Robinson told his foremen that the immigrants "ought to have your help to become citizens. These men are needed by your company." The company houses were limited to "those who seek to become citizens and wish to do the right thing." Like housing, Americanization aimed at immobilizing the foreigners in the steel industry.

The citizenship campaign became widespread. The Gary Works launched a drive in September 1916 and continued it for the war duration. Over a thousand men were enrolled in evening classes in 1918. The superintendent was anxious to "Make Gary An English Speaking City." South Chicago began an Americanization campaign under the Y.M.C.A. in the fall of 1917. Although enthusiastically launched, the drive at the South Works faltered; only fifty-eight received certificates at the closing exercises. But the following year there were 1,047 applications for citizenship. The plant provided transportation during working hours to the Federal Building. And on Thursday evenings first

[15] Quoted in *AJ*, April 12, 1917, p. 1.

papers were issued at the Sullivan School amid patriotic speeches and songs.[16] Only in a few places, such as South Bethlehem, was this work neglected or delayed until late in the war.

The attempt to make a permanent employee of the immigrant had considerable success. Upward mobility, of course, continued and in fact accelerated. The openings in the upper ranks were increased by the draft and by expanded operation. Many steel plants urged attendance at evening classes in English and technical subjects as preparation for better jobs. But the opportunities for advancement were limited. The mass of immigrants remained low-paid workmen. The equilibrium between horizontal and vertical mobility thus disappeared. And with it departed that stability in the unskilled ranks which went with the knowledge that a man's job, however unsatisfactory, was acceptable because it was temporary.

America's entrance into the war, in addition to further disrupting the labor supply and immigrant mobility, broke down the third, most fundamental, basis of acquiescence: the balance, in the workingman's mind, between the value of his labor and of his remuneration. Ordinarily, this was an implicit belief. The steelworker might have felt that the value assigned to his efforts was unfairly low; but he did not doubt that he received all his job was considered worth. The war shattered that assumption of equivalence. Steel became a national necessity, and so, too, labor in the mills. The steelmaking function assumed in the workingman's mind a value much in excess of its monetary return.

Employers were eager for the steelworkers to understand their central role in the nation's struggle, for the knowledge would intensify their efforts at that time of extreme labor shortage and pressing demand for steel. It was first necessary to awaken, as U.S. Steel President Farrell told a subsidiary head, "a sense of patriotism without which we might have difficulty in carrying

[16] *Gary Works Circle,* September 1916, and following issues; *South Works Review,* July 1918, March–April 1919.

on successfully the work before us." [17] Energetic measures were taken toward that end.

Gary, Indiana, held a parade on the Saturday night of April 28, 1917. City officials led the marchers, followed by men in uniform, steelworkers with Superintendent Gleason at their head, and finally delegations from churches, lodges, unions, and foreign societies. Thousands lined Broadway. A telegram was dispatched to President Wilson: "Gary just now finished the greatest patriotic demonstration ever held in Indiana. Over 26,000 in line and all nationalities. Sentiment entirely with you." It was, said the Illinois Steel Company, "a call to arms, a challenge to Kaiserism" from the steelworkers of Gary.[18] The immediacy of the war was brought home to the mill towns.

The flag-raising ceremony, instituted everywhere, was a perfect opportunity to arouse patriotic zeal. The home office of the steel and wire subsidiary of U.S. Steel instructed its superintendents in 1918: "June 14th is Flag Day. Suggest that each plant on that day raise our flag and have some patriotic singing." Plant officials reported back highly successful rallies at which "the rank and file were very much pleased and impressed. . . . Great benefit will be derived by them from the thoughts which were given them today." [19] The Gary Works held similar "rousing" meetings, culminating with a parade through the town. "The enthusiasm," observed the plant magazine, "established beyond a doubt that our men are patriotic and loyal to the flag." On Independence Day, at occasional noon rallies, and during Liberty Bond and Red Cross campaigns, the workmen received their doses of patriotism.

Some measures were aimed specifically at foreign groups. The

[17] J. A. Farrell to W. P. Palmer, July 15, 1918, American Steel and Wire Collection.

[18] Quillen, pp. 271–272.

[19] W. P. Palmer to C. L. Miller, June 11, 1918, G. H. Peters to R. H. Ney, June 15, 1918, and other correspondence, American Steel and Wire Collection. Box 13 contains a mine of information on the wartime activities of the American Steel and Wire Company.

Homestead Works donated a steel flagpole for the new parochial school of St. Ann's Slovak Catholic Church on Fourth Avenue. Cheers of the crowd frequently interrupted the speakers at the flag-raising ceremony. "Fourth Avenue takes pride in being among the patriotic thoroughfares of Homestead," reported the local paper. St. Anthony's Polish Church, the Greek Orthodox Church, and St. Peter and Paul's Lithuanian Church likewise benefited from the generosity of the Carnegie Steel Company. Homestead held an Americanization parade on Independence Day, 1918. All the immigrant societies were represented among the 16,000 participants, some in native costume. Superintendent A. A. Corey marched in the ranks. "Perhaps nowhere in America could there be so cosmopolitan a collection of people," observed the Homestead *Messenger,* or "a more complete demonstration of unity of all these people in one great cause." The Slovaks issued a statement of loyalty. America "received us — poor, unknown and insignificant," and gave us "a freer, happier life than we had lived in our oppressed native land." That sentiment, observed everywhere, was chalked on the signs held aloft by Gary immigrant marchers: "We are not the curs that bite the hand that feeds us."[20]

The steel manufacturers saw the value of the Liberty Bond drives. "We were inspired chiefly by the desire to see our employees express their patriotism," explained James A. Campbell. "The good that will be accomplished . . . is incalculable," thought *Iron Age.* "It will make every man feel a deeper interest in the war and will bring his country nearer to him." [21] Of course, Bonds would also finance the war effort. But employers were chiefly concerned with the salutary effect on the men.

The soliciting methods were very effective. Bethlehem plants were divided into competing sections. The workmen were approached individually by teams of foremen and "progressive workmen of foreign birth." Patriotic duty was the chief appeal.

[20] Homestead *Messenger,* July 1, 3, 5, November 23, 1918; Chicago *Tribune,* August 20, 1917.

[21] *IA,* June 21, 1917, p. 1506, October 25, 1917, p. 1023.

Workmen should be convinced of the "necessity of winning the war," expounded the director of the Bethlehem drives, and of the importance of those "who are compelled to remain at home in the industries." "Every one of us, living under the banner of the U.S.A.," proclaimed the *Gary Works Circle* in six languages, must "do his part." [22]

Patriotic zeal generated considerable coerciveness. That was, indeed, implicit in individual solicitation. Superintendent Corey suggested during the Fourth Loan that each Homestead workman invest twenty-five days' pay. "This is . . . simply friendly advice in your best interest . . . that our country may live as the 'Home of the Free.'" Rejection of the "friendly advice," Carnegie workmen later charged, often meant dismissal and/or a tar-and-feathering. Some small companies adopted the slogan, "A Bond or Your Job." [23] Resentment no doubt resulted, but the fervor of the steelworkers themselves was largely the source of compulsion. Solicitors encountered little sales resistance.[24]

The Bond drives had been successful from the beginning. Invariably, plants surpassed their quotas. But the peak of enthusiasm was reached only in 1918. At Homestead, for example, Superintendent Corey started the Fourth Liberty Loan a week early to give his plant the honor of being the first to fill its quota. He charged the men:

> Seven o'clock Monday morning, September 23, is our next Zero hour. Our boys at the front . . . are confidently watching

[22] *IA,* June 14, 1917, p. 1471, October 25, 1917, p. 1023; *Gary Works Circle,* April 1918.

[23] Homestead *Messenger,* September 13, 1918; Saposs Interviews, July 27, 1920, company policeman at the Edgar Thomson Works. The Gary Works had the slogan, "A Day's Pay for the Red Cross." On payday the men were handed two checks. They were expected to contribute the smaller one as they left the plant. It was no wonder that Gary tripled its quota.

[24] A letter to the *Amalgamated Journal,* October 10, 1918, p. 29, described a stormy meeting during the Fourth Loan at a lodge in Warren, Ohio. Each man had been rated according to his pay, and most had "come across" to put the plant "over the top." But a few slackers had objected and left the meeting in disgrace. The writer fervently hoped "we will never have to witness such a sickening spectacle in our lodge room again."

for the result. By Thursday, September 26, the same hour, we should reach our objective — 100 per cent.

All Tuesday sirens signaled the fulfillment of quotas by departments. At midnight the whistles blasted the announcement of complete success. Congratulations poured in. The 12,000 steelworkers signed a telegram in reply: "The answer of the men and women of Homestead Steel Works . . . is $2,150,000 — $176 per person — 100 per cent — and bring on your fifth loan." [25]

Elsewhere, the response was equally impressive. Lackawanna, with a quota of $349,200 in the Fourth Loan, subscribed $1,200,-000. Gary stood second among American cities in per capita purchases. No figures show separately the contribution of the immigrants, but observers unanimously praised their liberality, and obviously the records could not have been achieved without them. The American Iron and Steel Institute compiled the figures after the war. The fifty-six largest companies boasted 100 per cent subscriptions; the steelworkers altogether purchased $245,296,785 of Liberty Bonds — an extraordinary figure, even taking into account possible exaggeration.

Thousands of steelworkers went to war. Here also the steel companies were markedly cooperative. The Youngstown Sheet and Tube Company, for instance, arranged for employees to enlist at the plant, and assisted men in filling out their draft questionnaires when registration began in the late spring of 1917. Despite the pressing labor shortage, managers rarely sought deferments except for irreplaceable men. Almost one-fourth of the labor force of the Gary Works served in the armed forces. According to the tabulation of the American Iron and Steel Institute, 131,504 employees of steel companies were in the war.

Again, it is impossible to set apart the immigrants; but, again, their part was clearly large, probably in proportion to their numbers. They faced, it was true, certain restrictions as enemy aliens; on the other hand, natives were more likely to be

---

[25] Homestead *Messenger,* September 13, 18, 20, 23, 24, 26, 28, 1918.

exempted for vital skills. And numbers of Slavic steelworkers enlisted in the Polish and Czecho-Slovak armies. Lists of service-men from the South Works, the Joliet Works, and Lackawanna reveal half or more Slavic and Italian names. There were many stars in the service flags of the immigrant churches and societies of Homestead. The first death from the South Works was Walter Stalmaszeck, who had enlisted. John Manjikitis was the first Homestead casualty. His father was a sheersman in the mill, and he "a typical young American." [26]

From the viewpoint of the steelmaker, wartime activities had a special purpose. They served, as an American Steel and Wire vice-president observed, "to stimulate production." [27] Patriotic involvement was translatable into greater effort in the mills. "May we who are still at home not forget the duties we have to perform," said the *Gary Works Circle* when the draft began. "Some must go. All must serve." A government speaker told the men at the Cuyahoga Works in Cleveland: "your greasy overalls . . . are as much a badge of service and honor in . . . the eyes of your country today as the uniform of the army or navy." [28] Steelworkers heard unceasingly of the vital contribution they were making to the war by doing their jobs.

There were many methods for impressing the idea on the men. Midvale Steel and Ordnance, for instance, placed this poster in all its plants:

Not Just Hats Off To The Flag But Sleeves Up For It!

The company at mass meetings asked every employee to "per-sonally pledge 100 per cent efficiency for myself by laboring at my regular duty each and every day that my department operates."

[26] *South Works Review,* June 1918; *Joliet Works Mixer,* March–April 1918; Homestead *Messenger,* July 3, 1918; D. J. Sweeney, *Buffalo and Erie County, 1914–19* (Buffalo, 1919), pp. 694–697.

[27] E. J. McCarthy to A. G. Warner, December 4, 1918, American Steel and Wire Collection.

[28] Captain J. C. Curran, Address at the Cuyahoga Works, Cleveland, October 18, 1918, American Steel and Wire Collection.

Midvale's Johnstown plant reported as a result a 10 per cent increase in production.

The American Sheet and Tin Plate Company developed an extremely effective system. The company offered a series of buttons inscribed, "100% Efficiency Man," red for thirty days without an absence, blue for sixty days, and red, white, and blue for ninety days. With the last went a "service certificate" for framing. Posters in the plants were printed in numerous languages, but the certificates came only in English so as not to be "subversive of good principles." The *Iron Age,* a close student of these plans, judged this an especially good one. Jubilant officials at Farrell reported the plant had smashed all production records. At Vandergrift patriotic workmen petitioned to run full on the Fourth of July.

The South Works held rallies for the foremen, ending on this note:

> You have heard the story of Germany at war and all that it means to America, from those who know. Your duty is now clear. Go up and down the plant and "eat 'em up." Let every foreign-born workman know what we are fighting for. Give 'em h—.

The plant magazine urged the steelworkers to "think only of the serious business on hand. . . . Work, Work, Work." Gary officials similarly harangued their employees. "You have broken many production records, there are many more to be broken. Make the sky your limit, the forced peace of the entire world your goal." Communications to the plant magazine showed the effect on the workers. "It is your patriotic duty to do all you can to increase the efficiency of your department," pronounced one open-hearth man in a typical letter.

Homestead Superintendent Corey told a cheering audience on July 2, 1918 that 179 records had fallen at the works since the start of the war. During the extreme heat of August, he had to caution against overwork. Tonnage remained normal despite the absence of one-quarter of the men during the influenza epidemic in November. The remaining workmen, an official reported, "have been working their heads off" to maintain production.[29]

The effort to involve the steelworker in the war thus experienced marvelous success. He was no longer a man who held a job worth a stipulated sum of money. Now he did more than make a living. He shouted at patriotic rallies, he bought Liberty Bonds, he went into military service. Above all, he labored to make the steel to beat the Kaiser. He was making a special contribution, and he would expect a corresponding return.

Wartime conditions heightened the sense of sacrifice. Work schedules lengthened. Seven-day labor had been largely eliminated by 1915, and the twelve-hour day somewhat restricted. Although no reliable figures exist for the next three years, it is clear that even before April 1917 the labor shortage had thrust aside these reforms. In October 1916 the Lackawanna Steel Company futilely petitioned the Industrial Commission of New York State (which state had a law forbidding seven-day labor) for permission to reinstate the seven-day week on the grounds that its competitors were doing so. After war came, the impetus for longer hours went unimpeded, indeed, supported by patriotic necessity. In 1919 the work schedule in the Pittsburgh district averaged 82 hours a week for laborers in blast furnaces, 78.5 hours in open hearths, and 70.3 hours in plate mills.[30]

Despite the efforts of steel companies, living conditions deteriorated alarmingly. The Gary *Tribune* reported in 1918 a shortage of 4,000 dwellings. "Every house and every room in Gary is crowded by human beings and there is no room for any more." Along Broadway, noisome basements were filled with beds constantly in use. In the bitter winter of 1918 the coal

---

[29] Steel Institute, *Yearbook* (1918), pp. 213–215; *IA*, May 23, 1918, p. 1339, July 11, 1918, pp. 68, 95–96; *South Works Review*, March, June 1918; *Gary Works Circle*, February, May 1918, and letters in other issues; Homestead *Messenger*, July 2, 3, November 6, 1918.

[30] Gulick, *Labor Policy of U.S. Steel*, pp. 31–39; *Survey*, September 27, 1919, pp. 891–892; New York *Times*, October 6, 1916; U.S. Bureau of Labor Statistics, *Monthly Labor Review*, October 1919, pp. 104–126.

shortage required heatless days and lightless nights. Sanitation, public utilities, and the street car system broke down under the strain.[31] Conditions were little better elsewhere. It was a hard life in the mill towns.

Finally, the wage advances proved largely illusory. Food, fuel, and rents rose rapidly during the war. There were some small methods of alleviation, for instance, a large cooperative store at the Joliet Works; but steelworkers could not avoid the main effects of a living cost rise of 70 per cent. The real wages of steelworkers, W. F. Ogburn of the National War Labor Board surmised, had advanced but 45 per cent by the end of the war. Paul H. Douglas later figured the rise of real weekly earnings in 1918 to be only 25 per cent over 1914. Even the higher figure left the income of the unskilled steelworker below the line of minimum subsistence calculated by government experts for a family of five, and the income of the semi-skilled below the level of minimum comfort.

Surely no worse off than before the war, the men in the mills now saw their situation in a new light. They accepted their hardships during the national emergency, but they had no expectation of a resumption of the old order afterward. The established sources of acquiescence had collapsed during the war years. The steelworker, particularly the immigrant, had become a new man since 1914.

The breakdown of the prewar labor pattern did not seem immediately important. Steel manufacturers, indeed, congratulated themselves on solving the difficult labor problems of wartime. The consequences awaited the arrival of peace, and also the appearance of organized labor, itself revived by the war, to give form to the expectations of the steelworkers.

[31] Quillen, pp. 278–287.

Chapter X

The Wartime Rights of Labor

Since the United States Steel attack on the Amalgamated Association in 1909, organized labor had marked the steel industry among its chief targets for unionization. The failures of 1910 and 1912–3, however, indicated little likelihood of future success. The opposition of the steel companies was unrelenting and formidable. Undiscouraged, A.F.L. leaders awaited only the propitious moment for another attempt. The opportunity, unparalleled in magnitude, came with the outbreak of the First World War.

The consequent labor shortage immediately improved the unionizing prospect. The A.F.L. responded to the first reports of unrest in the steel mills. In January 1916 organizers rushed to Youngstown to lead the strike at the Republic plants. Enthusiastically received, they were able to form 1,500 employees into craft locals and one federal union of common laborers. The company agreed to shop committees and no discrimination for union membership. When the Westinghouse trouble broke out in Pittsburgh in May 1916, Secretary Frank Morrison journeyed from Washington to investigate. He departed "in despair" after viewing the situation, too turbulent to be exploited by the A.F.L.[1] The union interest in the steel mills was, nevertheless, apparent.

Once America entered the war, employers hoped for a status quo arrangement with the A.F.L. Gompers had at the outset called a meeting of labor and management to agree that "neither employers nor employees shall endeavor to take advantage of the

[1] A.F.L., *Weekly Newsletter,* January 15, 22, February 12, 1916; *NLT,* May 18, 1916.

country's necessities to change existing standards." Management's understanding, however, was not labor's: the unions did not intend to bypass the unexampled chance for expansion.

The point was driven home to steel manufacturers in September 1917 when A.F.L. organizers successfully unionized the Pittsburgh plant of Jones and Laughlin, an antiunion bulwark since 1897. The drive was a "bona fide trade union movement of the A.F.L., and therefore a legitimate war-time activity." Although there were wage and hour demands, union recognition became the central issue. Dreading "the union as they dread the most loathesome peril," the Jones and Laughlin officials refused to budge. After a month-long strike the organizations disintegrated.[2]

Even temporary success, however, was encouraging. The labor shortage was providing "a slight opportunity for a laborer to choose," Gompers announced. "Among all this great class of labor, the teaching of trade unionism is spreading."

Meanwhile, the international unions were growing very rapidly. The United Mine Workers enrolled 50,000 miners in the summer of 1918 alone. The war, proclaimed the *Mine Workers Journal,* "has hastened the day of . . . the self-uplift of the world's workers." Only the powerful corporations were resisting effectively. Claiming three-quarters of the miners of the Colorado Fuel and Iron Company, the union was nevertheless unable to gain recognition. U.S. Steel and the independents appeared even more formidable.[3]

Other unions experienced somewhat more success in the steel industry. The Machinists, tripling in size, made important incursions into the plants of the Tennessee Coal and Iron, Midvale, and Bethlehem Steel companies. The Electrical Workers and other crafts also gained members in the mills. But for none were these achievements equal to the progress elsewhere. Strengthened and

[2] *IA,* September 20, 1917, p. 712; *NLT,* October 11, 1917; New York *Times,* September 18, 24, 1917.

[3] *United Mine Workers Journal,* May 31, 1917, pp. 4, 6, July 19, 1917, p. 5, September 1, 1918, p. 8; *AF,* January 1918, p. 48; Mine, Mill and Smelter Workers, *Proceedings* (1918), p. 31.

optimistic, these unions increasingly saw the steel industry as their chief obstacle.

Even the Amalgamated Association was rejuvenated. Lacking the resources to increase its organizing staff, the union had resorted to the use of members as temporary organizers. By May 1917 the *Iron Age* was noting "much quiet work" to unionize sheet and tin plate mills. The pace quickened sharply thereafter. In early June, 300 employees formed a strong Amalgamated lodge at the Girard, Ohio, plant of the A. M. Byers Company. This was a noteworthy victory, accomplished over bitter opposition in the largest puddling mill in the country. Enthusiasm greeted Amalgamated organizers at many plants hitherto barred to the union. In the Wheeling district, lodges appeared even at several U.S. Steel mills.

"There was never a better opportunity," said the *Amalgamated Journal*. "The power of victimization has lost its force." The chance "to organize the unorganized" was not to be missed. By the close of a year of war, thirty-five new lodges had received Amalgamated charters, the membership was up to 15,000, and the treasurer reported the union coffer filled higher than since 1891. President Williams proclaimed, "Our Association is destined to control the destinies of all men engaged in the manufacture of iron and steel products." [4]

Steel companies met the union challenge in standard fashion. Threats and discharge were vigorously employed to disrupt organizing efforts. War conditions provided additional weapons. Draft boards, when controlled by the company, could eliminate agitators. "Thus a workman exempted at the manufacturer's request becomes his slave," read a complaint to the War Labor Board from a U.S. Steel plant in Elwood, Indiana. Elsewhere, local patriots attacked union men as pro-Germans. [5] Employers were prepared, as always, to stamp out union activity.

[4] *AJ*, May 10, 1917, pp. 1–2, August 9, 1917, p. 4, April 16, 1918, pp. 1–2, 4; *IA*, May 10, 1917, p. 1128.

[5] National War Labor Board, Original Complaints, Docket 232; *AJ*, May 2, 1918, pp. 12, 14, September 5, 1918, p. 29.

Repressive methods, it was true, could not be entirely effective under the special conditions of wartime. But partial labor success did not greatly trouble the steel men; the losses could be recovered when peace came. The danger lay elsewhere. More than rising membership was renewing the confidence of the unions. Organized labor was finding in the government a powerful wartime ally.

Hitherto, the federal government had played an insignificant role in labor relations. Both employers and trade unions favored this policy of noninterference. The A.F.L. objected to any measure, even compulsory social insurance, that "takes away from the economic power . . . of wage earners." The labor struggle was a private affair.

It could not remain so in the event of war. Modern military necessity would require the administration to assume direction of industry. If that was inevitable, Gompers reasoned as a war declaration became imminent, then the A.F.L. had to maneuver itself into a position of strength. He called an urgent meeting for March 12, 1917 to formulate labor's position "in order that we may exercise a beneficent guidance rather than be forced to submit to emergency measures." The Declaration of March 12 pledged the full support of American labor on these conditions: that capital not benefit from the war; that work and wages "conform to principles of human welfare and justice"; and, most important, that organized labor be recognized as the spokesman for all workmen and be represented on all war agencies.[6]

President Wilson, for his part, was eager for cooperation. The crucial domestic question, he believed, was whether the working people would back the war effort. Organized labor had long stood in the forefront of the peace movement, and at many points only reluctantly came out in support of war. The mass of unorganized wage earners, largely Central European, was an

[6] *AF*, April 1917, pp. 277–280; Gompers to James Duncan, March 13, 1917, Gompers Papers; Grosvener B. Clarkson, *Industrial America in the World War* (Boston, 1927), pp. 281 ff.

even more doubtful element. Already sympathetic to labor and anxious to avoid compulsion, President Wilson accepted in practice the Declaration of March 12.

The administration's decision soon became evident. It turned down the numerous emergency suggestions to lower labor standards and prohibit strikes. Wilson made special efforts to woo the workers: "I am for the laboring man. Justice must be done him or there can be no justice in the country." In November 1917 the President journeyed from Washington for the first time since the entrance into war to address the A.F.L. convention at Buffalo. It was a signal honor, "a recognition of the fact that the success of the war for democracy is dependent upon faithful and constant service by the workers." [7]

The A.F.L. pressed its claim to represent all labor in the government. The Cantonment Adjustment Board, established in June 1917, marked the first direct agreement by the federal government with labor unions. Every later adjustment board had its A.F.L. man. Representation on other agencies was granted more reluctantly. "Workers demand that since they are an indispensable factor in production," Gompers thundered, "they should have a voice in determining those things which vitally affect them." In September Wilson assented. The influence of labor leaders rapidly increased. [8]

The steel manufacturers watched with growing unease as the administration became "subservient to the union labor." Gompers' "high position in the councils of the nation" was not a welcome prospect. From his official place on the Council of National Defense, Gompers was able to write to Gary to reprimand U.S. Steel for refusing to confer with Alabama employees, and to urge the Judge to accept the eight-hour day as an "industrial, economic

[7] Wilson to Gompers, August 31, 1917, *Woodrow Wilson, Life and Letters,* ed. R. S. Baker (New York, 1939), VII, 248; Wilson Address to the A.F.L. Convention, November 12, 1917, *The Public Papers of Woodrow Wilson,* eds. R. S. Baker and W. E. Dodd (New York, 1927), V, 116–124; *AF,* June 1917, p. 457, August 1917, pp. 631, 640.

[8] *AF,* August 1917, p. 642; Gompers to Robert Lansing, April 21, 1917, to Bernard Baruch, May 21, 1918, Gompers Papers.

and patriotic service." [9] This was impudence unimaginable several years earlier. And steel men found themselves obliged to deal repeatedly with union officials on the War Industries Board and other agencies.

The manufacturers were disturbed by more than the incongruity of the situation. The new importance of organized labor quickened its desire to unionize the steelworkers. Labor officials began to turn to the government for support. The Amalgamated Association, for instance, demanded that the administration free "the workers in the mills from those companies who refuse from their employees their right to become members of a labor organization." The American Federation of Labor resolved at its Buffalo convention to exert its enhanced influence in Washington to force steel companies to deal with representatives of union employees. [10]

The government was clearly sympathetic. Secretary of Labor W. B. Wilson early in the war asserted the right of workmen to join unions. The labor adjustment boards, although without instructions, consistently upheld the principle. After nearly a year of bitter controversy, the Shipping Board finally ordered the Lake Carriers' Association (made up largely of steel companies) to end its discharge book system because the purpose was "the elimination of union men," and also to submit to labor adjustment by a board including a representative of organized labor. Excepting the munitions sections, however, the steel industry proper was not under the jurisdiction of an adjustment board. For the first year of war the federal government gave little direct assistance to the efforts to unionize steel plants.

Yet the industry was deeply worried. No one, said Gary, "can tell what is going to happen with respect to the labor question, because the Government is very powerful." The administration had already amply demonstrated its wartime ability to bend the steel men to its will.

[9] Gompers to Gary, March 18, 1918, Gompers Papers.
[10] *AJ*, May 3, 1917, p. 5, November 29, 1917, p. 2; New York *Times*, November 22, 1917.

The federal government had intervened first to control prices. When the United States entered the war, the steel manufacturers promised "cheerfully [to] bear our full share of the load" by supplying steel to the government at prewar prices. They had, however, underestimated the requirements for war material; much more than the predicted 17 per cent was needed. Steel prices, already much inflated, shot skyward in anticipation of the imminent scarcity. Alarmed, the administration called for price controls. The steel companies balked, for fear that "liberty would languish," but under intense pressure they were forced to accept regulation. During the summer of 1917, a series of acrimonious meetings with the War Industries Board was held to determine price levels. Finally, on September 21, 1917, after the patience of the government had worn through, the steel men agreed to a compromise.[11]

The industry, although it bowed to regulation, fared very well. The prices proved to be very generous, and Gary himself admitted afterward that the original demands "were not justified." [12] More important, the management of the price schedules was handled, not directly from Washington, but "by the producers under Government control." The American Iron and Steel Institute administered the price agreement. Its General Committee in time assumed considerable power in the industry, setting specific prices, assisting small firms for whom the established schedules were too low, and later actually directing concerns whose production was lagging. In effect, the Institute mediated between Washington and the companies.[13]

[11] P. W. Garrett, *Government Control Over Prices* (Washington, 1920), pp. 248–250, 259–260; Bernard Baruch, *American Industry in the War* (New York, 1941), pp. 120–131; War Industries Board Minutes, September 21, 1917, U.S. Senate, Special Committee Investigating the Munitions Industry, *War Industries Board Minutes, August 1, 1917–December 19, 1918,* 74 Cong., 1st Sess., (1935), pp. 65–66, cited hereafter as War Industries Board Minutes.

[12] Steel Institute, *Yearbook* (1919), pp. 293–294; Federal Trade Commission, *Report on War-Time Profits and Costs of the Steel Industry* (Washington, 1925). No revisions were required despite considerable manufacturing cost increases later in the war.

[13] War Industries Board Minutes, August 22, 1918, pp. 444–447; Price Fixing Committee Minutes, March 20–1, 1918, U.S. Senate, Special Committee

In steel circles there was much relieved discussion of the cooperation that had developed among the producers and between the industry and the government. The war, it seemed, had accomplished the ends advocated by Gary before the antitrust suit.

Appearances, however, were misleading. In fact, the War Industries Board held the final power. And the W.I.B. acted directly to approve all construction, rearrange contracts to eliminate wasteful crosshauls, and chastise uncooperative companies. It was not long before the extent of governmental authority became starkly clear.

Dangerous shortages of steel had developed by the spring of 1918. The steel manufacturers were called together in the New York offices of U.S. Steel and sternly rebuked. "The Government will not tolerate any more the procedure of some steel companies," stated the representative of the War Industries Board. "This is a crisis, and commercialism, gentlemen, must be absolutely sidetracked." The government was assuming dictatorial powers over distribution.[14] By June, the companies were filling orders in strict accordance with priority categories; the disposal of their products was entirely out of their hands. The iron and steel trade, summed up the W.I.B. report, became "in effect a Government-controlled industry."

Adequate means were at hand to enforce government demands. The administration leveled the threat of its wartime commandeering powers against the industry as a whole, and occasionally against individual firms. The likelihood of nationalization seemed great during the uncertain months before price regulation. Government representatives went into the decisive meeting of September 21, 1917 armed with the knowledge that, if no agreement was reached, the War Industries Board "should take the steps necessary to take over the steel plants." The steel men

---

Investigating the Munitions Industry, *Minutes of the Price Fixing Committee of the War Industries Board,* 74 Cong., and 2nd Sess. (1936), pp. 52–70, cited hereafter as Price Fixing Committee Minutes.

[14] A stenographic report of the speeches at the meeting is printed in *IA,* May 9, 1918, pp. 1206–1213.

understood their precarious situation very well, and, in the considered opinion of Bernard Baruch, the W.I.B. "could not have obtained unanimous consent otherwise." [15] The steel industry never approached closer to the brink of nationalization, but the danger continued to be more or less real, especially in the dark period preceding control over distribution. "No one knows better than Mr. Farrell and I," Judge Gary told the subsidiary presidents afterward, "how easy it would have been many times for the steel business to have gone under the control and management of the United States." [16]

The steel manufacturers bowed before the necessities of war. Ringing patriotic statements attended each encroachment on their normal prerogatives; indeed, it seemed as if their enthusiasm intensified with the increase of interference and criticism. In Schwab's words, they found deep satisfaction in the knowledge that "no industry . . . has so nobly, so patriotically, so willingly and so enthusiastically done their duty by their country as the iron and steel industry of the U.S. (Applause.)" [17] Patriotism justified every sacrifice.

The steelmakers were apprehensive not so much over government direction, which would certainly pass with the armistice. The real threat rested in the accompanying ability of the administration to impose conditions — for instance, in labor — that could become permanent. Before the close of the war, steel men trembled that political meddling would smash the open-shop system of the industry. A pig iron manufacturer expressed the general fear: "They already reserve the right to say what you shall pay for ore, what you shall receive for your product — only one thing

---

[15] Garrett, pp. 248–250; War Industries Board Minutes, September 18, 1917, p. 58, September 27, 1917, pp. 68–69; U.S. War Policies Commission, *Hearings* (Washington, 1931), pp. 815–817. *IA*, May 2, 1918, p. 1150, admits that the agreement was "facilitated by the fear on the part of the iron and steel producers that failure . . . would result in drastic bureaucratic regulation, by legislative enactment."

[16] Gary Address, January 21, 1919, *Addresses and Statements,* IV.

[17] Speeches at May 31, 1918 meeting in New York, Steel Institute, *Yearbook* (1918), and at other Institute meetings and before the War Industries Board.

remains and that is the terms of labor. . . . That privilege is likely to be taken away." What troubled the industry was the uses to which organized labor might put the extraordinary powers of the government.

Considering the administration's predilections, steel men fervently hoped for inaction. "Many of the manufacturing companies do not have organized labor," said Judge Gary in March 1918, "and the government has said wisely that the question is going to be left out of the discussion and decisions during the war. We must set aside all these differences for the present." [18] The wish was clearly father of the thought. Public intervention in the labor relations of American industry was imminent

Early 1918 saw the creation of a War Labor Conference Board to establish "principles and policies which will enable the prosecution of production without stoppages of work." The Board, reporting at the end of March, asserted "the right of workers to organize in trade-unions" without interference "by the employers in any manner whatsoever." The use of coercion to force workmen to join or employers to deal with unions also was prohibited. Workers had the right to collective bargaining through shop committees. On April 9, 1918 the President transformed the Conference Board into a National War Labor Board, empowered to apply the principles to disputes in essential industries. Thus, in one motion, the steelworkers were given the right to organize and recourse to an official body, without actual legal force, but supported by the President's war powers.

Despite its principles, the War Labor Board seemed at first to be a safe solution. With employers and unions equally represented, the *Iron Age* judged, the Board would be stalemated. The National Industrial Conference Board, a reliable organization (Gompers had recently called it "the eight billion dollar combine to wipe organized labor out of existence"), appointed the five employer representatives. Both sides then chose one "public" member. The unionists picked the labor lawyer Frank P. Walsh.

[18] Price Fixing Committee Minutes, March 20–1, 1918, p. 49.

The employers' choice was William Howard Taft, who, as it turned out, firmly intended to apply the Board's principles. The expected ineffectuality consequently did not materialize.

The War Labor Board quickly made clear its willingness to take on the steel industry. In May it started proceedings in an important dispute between machinists and the Bethlehem Steel Company. The *Iron Age* noted uneasily that here was "a concerted effort of the labor unions to foster upon the industry the eight hour day and the recognition of the union." Their "wits are at work first and last to gain an advantage for organized labor." At the hearings, Bethlehem officials strenuously opposed anything "savoring of organization." "We don't employ a committee," argued a vice president, "we employ a particular individual, and naturally we are always willing to hear what he has to say and make corrections." The Board turned a deaf ear.

The award was a heavy blow, aside even from the wage increases and overtime pay. The company was ordered to institute shop committees and forbidden from interfering with union activities. True, the company did not have to recognize the unions. But shop committees and freedom from disciplinary measures, cried the *Iron Age,* "almost unfailingly . . . encourage the unionization of plants that have peacefully operated open shops for long periods."[19] One had only to survey the burgeoning organizations at Bethlehem and elsewhere.

The War Labor Board was meanwhile considering the grievances of steelworkers against the Tennessee Coal and Iron Company, Midvale Steel and Ordnance, the American Sheet and Tin Plate Company, and a number of lesser firms. A widening segment of the industry faced the imposition of shop committees and unhindered unionization. The situation appeared very threatening. The Board's activities, warned the *Iron Age,* "will encourage union leaders to seize upon the national war emergency to organize every plant heretofore maintained as a non-union or open shop." Its alarm seemed fully justified by the rising excitement and increasing activity in A.F.L. circles.

[19] *IA,* May 16, 1918, p. 1286, September 5, 1918, p. 584.

One right remained as yet undisturbed: a company's freedom to decide whether or not to deal with organized labor. The War Labor Board had, in fact, ruled that no coercion could be used to force union recognition. For the steel companies, deprived of the power to fight the unionizing of their men, this was the last line of defense for the open shop. It, too, shortly became threatened.

The creation of the War Labor Policies Board in May 1918 completed the national labor program. While the War Labor Board settled disputes, the War Labor Policies Board was designed to avoid them by standardizing wages, hours, and conditions in war industries. The W.L.P.B. followed the procedure of calling in representatives of management and labor from each industry to formulate the standards and to set up a body of adjustment and enforcement. The dangers of this practice were obvious to nonunion employers (not to speak of the unpleasant prospect of having to share the determination of the terms of employment), for the line seemed thin indeed between extended association with union officials and union recognition. And if the W.L.P.B. could rule on labor standards, why not on policy toward unions?

In early July 1918 Judge Gary received a letter from Felix Frankfurter, the head of the War Labor Policies Board, requesting the designation of a small committee from the Iron and Steel Institute. Frankfurter asked for a meeting the following week. Gary replied cautiously after a week's delay:

> We are desirous of co-operating with Governmental agencies as far as practicable. Labor problems are the most delicate of any. We have experienced little difficulty in our own labor matters in a good many years, and we dislike very much to see any agitation which is calculated to disturb our relations.

Avoiding the appointment of a committee, he suggested instead that Frankfurter visit his New York office to inform him of the area to be covered in the proposed conference. In answer, Frankfurter explained that the purpose was "to steady industrial relations," that the problems would be dealt with in a practical manner solely for the needs of the war, and that he hoped to bring labor and management together in conference. Gary was thoroughly alarmed. The open shop, in his opinion, was at stake. The situation appeared sufficiently grave to call an emergency session of steel manufacturers. The meeting took place at the Waldorf Astoria on August 28, 1918. The stenographic minutes have been preserved among Gary's collected speeches, making it possible accurately to estimate the thinking of the steel men at the point when all the forces of labor and government were converging against them.[20] There was a pervading feeling among the participants of control slipping out of their hands. Fair and liberal treatment has brought good relations with the workmen, said Gary, "but it is not easy to get along with powers in political lines who, with perhaps good intentions, sometimes interfere to the prejudice of one side or another." The trouble was, observed another manufacturer, that union partisans "are pretty powerful in governmental circles." He could "readily conceive of the Government's adopting policies in Washington" that would be "inviting disaster."

The one favoring circumstance was the common front of the steel men, developed over the years through the Gary dinners, the Iron and Steel Institute, and the unified dealings with the War Industries Board. President Eugene Grace of Bethlehem Steel, for instance, was "embarrassed today in considering our case individually before the W.L.B., as it is going to affect our associates in the general industry." When Frankfurter invited Waddill Catchings of the Sloss-Sheffield Steel and Iron Company to become a member of the W.L.P.B., possibly as a stratagem to get around Judge Gary, Catchings replied that he would first have to get the consent of Gary, and that, in any event, the industry would have to be consulted through a representative committee. The general sentiment of the meeting, as Severn P. Ker of the

---

[20] Meeting of Steel Manufacturers, August 28, 1918, *Addresses and Statements by Gary*, IV. The above letters between Frankfurter and Gary, as well as the quotations in the following discussion, come from this document. There is a brief report of the meeting in *IA*, September 5, 1918, p. 587.

Sharon Steel Hoop Company said, was that it was better to hang together than separately.

The unanimous decision was to give "full and complete power" to the General Committee of the Institute to deal with the Policies Board. The job of the Committee, said Eugene Grace, was "to see whether or not we are going to be able in any way to . . . protect the relations between labor and ourselves in our own industry."

The War Labor Policies Board endangered two areas of the labor system. It would certainly upset the established standards of the industry, including the twelve-hour day. Second, the Board would force steel men to deal with labor leaders and ultimately to make vital compromises concerning union labor. Clearly a plot was afoot, thought Ker, by the "many persons who are perhaps influential in the governmental departments at this time to organize and unionize all the iron and steel trade." These dire consequences would flow merely from entering the jurisdiction of the W.L.P.B.

The only feasible strategy, therefore, was a delaying action. The awards of the War Labor Board had been accepted by Bethlehem and other steel firms only after months of obstruction. Now the steel manufacturers decided on a "position of reserve." The General Committee, said Gary, should have "the broadest discretion . . . to act or not to act, depending upon conditions." If the War Labor Policies Board was adamant, the Committee would salvage what it could. But what the steel men dearly desired was "some arrangement whereby [labor questions] can be postponed until after the war and until after the difficulties surrounding the war have passed away."

Some lesser positions had to be abandoned. Judge Gary had stated repeatedly his opposition to the eight-hour basis. It was "sham and hypocrisy," simply a pretense to raise wages. Yet, a month after the meeting the Steel Institute reversed itself; the basic eight-hour day (that is, time-and-a-half for over eight hours) went into effect on October 1. The steel men hoped thus to fore-

stall formal negotiations with the Policies Board and, consequently, the A.F.L. They were playing desperately for time.

If the war days brought apprehension to the steel industry, they
were in equal measure days of promise for organized labor. The
War Labor Board had opened the way for the unobstructed
unionization of the steelworkers. When this was substantially accomplished, the steelmasters could without doubt be brought to
the bargaining table with the unions. Government and labor,
observed the *Electrical Workers Journal,* had formed "a partnership for the purpose of making the world fit for free men to live
in." The *American Federationist* predicted: "The two influences
converging upon the steel autocrats . . . will surely result in the
coming of a new era into the iron and steel industry of the
country." [21]

The opportunity awaited the action of organized labor. By the
summer of 1918, the time had come for the great undertaking in
the steel mills.

[21] *AF,* September 1918, p. 808; *Electrical Workers Journal* quoted in *Mine
Workers Journal,* June 20, 1918, p. 15.

Chapter XI

Organizing the Steelworkers

The immediate impulse for a steel organizing drive started in Chicago. There the local unions led by John Fitzpatrick and William Z. Foster had successfully unionized the stockyards. It was a notable victory. "If an industry so completely non-union . . . may become organized under the new conception of human rights as formulated at Washington," asked John Fitch, "what may not be possible?"[1] The Chicago unionists meant to find out.

The stockyards campaign over, Foster immediately presented a resolution to the Chicago Federation of Labor to inaugurate a national steel drive. The Amalgamated Association, to whose May convention Gompers referred the resolution, also approved it. Anxious to hasten the slow progress thus begun, Foster, under instructions as a Chicago Federation delegate, called for a conference at the A.F.L. convention in June 1918. Several promising meetings were held. "Prospects look good for a big steel campaign," Foster recorded. "The greatest optimism prevailed. Gompers and Morrison attended and gave their O.K."[2] The outcome was another conference, to be held in Chicago within a month, of responsible officials prepared to act for their unions.

The officers of fifteen internationals assembled on August 1. Presided over by Gompers, the conference formally established a National Committee for Organizing the Iron and Steel Workers with "full charge of the organizing work." Gompers was elected

---

[1] J. A. Fitch, "Labor and Politics," *Survey,* June 8, 1918, p. 288.
[2] Foster to Frank P. Walsh, July 6, 1918, Walsh Papers, New York Public Library; Gompers to Fitzpatrick, July 5, 1918, Gompers Papers.

chairman, but since he was in Europe for much of the next year, he never actually participated. John Fitzpatrick, president of the Chicago Federation of Labor, took over his post and later became the chairman. Fitzpatrick was a politically inclined trade unionist of liberal tendencies and strong humanitarian instincts. He was the dominating figure in the National Committee. Foster became secretary-treasurer. He had charge of the detail work, directed the organizers, and controlled the publicity. To a large extent Foster designed the tactics of the drive, but the decision-making power lay with Fitzpatrick and the National Committee.[3]

Essentially, the trade unionists were attempting to reconcile their fragmented structure with modern American industry. The concerted organizing effort of craft unions with jurisdiction in one industry had been tested earlier in the automobile industry and in the railroad shops of the Northwest, and had proved eminently successful in the Chicago stockyards. The National Committee recognized at the outset that it was "folly for any craft organization, however strong or skilled, to attempt to organize single handed in the iron and steel industry. To do so would be to court sure defeat."[4] The necessity for united action had become unquestioned; it was accepted almost without discussion at the Chicago meeting.

All but three of the cooperating unions agreed to a uniform initiation fee of three dollars, one of which went to the National Committee. Foster worked out an accounting system that guaranteed honesty and accuracy. A standard application was drawn up. Afterward, the recruits would be sorted out into the appropriate trades and formed into·locals affiliated in the usual manner with their internationals. The locals at each steel center would be

---

[3] National Committee Minutes, August 1–2, 1918, D. J. Saposs, "Organizing the Steel Workers," Saposs Papers, University of Wisconsin Library, pp. 3–5. This is an analysis of the minutes, mainly extended selections from them. Cited hereafter as National Committee Minutes, with page of the Saposs manuscript.

[4] National Committee Release, January 20, 1919, reprinted in *AJ*, January 30, 1919, p. 1; also, D. J. Saposs, "How the Steel Strike was Organized," *Survey*, November 8, 1919, pp. 67–69.

drawn into informal central bodies (known as Iron and Steel Workers Councils) in order to knit the local movement together, again following the plan used in the stockyards. Secretaries, answerable to the National Committee, would have full charge of the campaign at each center. Thus the National Committee formulated a sound plan to meet the circumstances of the steel industry. It was the A.F.L. response to the need for industrial unionism.

Twenty-four unions found some jurisdiction. Half of these — for instance, the Bricklayers, Coopers, and Sheet Metal Workers — could claim very few workers. The Mine Workers, Quarry Workers, and Seamen would benefit materially only if the drive extended beyond the mills. The mechanical trades ranged from 1 per cent of the steelworkers for the Boilermakers to 8 per cent for the Machinists. The blast furnace men, one-tenth of the total, went to the Mine, Mill and Smelter Workers. The Amalgamated Association claimed everyone outside any other jurisdiction, about half of all steelworkers.[5]

On the eve of the campaign, the Amalgamated was still limited to puddling, sheet, and tin plate mills. But the opportunity for expansion had awakened old ambitions. Even the unskilled and the immigrants were beginning to find a welcome. The editor of the *Journal* soon claimed "the transition of our organization from a straight out and out craft organization to a live industrial organization." Officials conceived of the A.F.L. plan simply as assistance to "the Amalgamated Association in its fight to unionize the slaves in the steel industries." They intended to profit fully from the windfall, and angrily repulsed the bid of the Hod Carriers for the laborers in the mills.[6]

[5] These calculations are based on the total numbers for which the National Committee received $1 from August 1, 1918 to January 31, 1920, broken down into the specific unions. These do not of course cover the total involved in the movement, but it is unlikely that the percentages would differ significantly.

[6] *AJ*, April 18, 1918, p. 2, May 30, 1918, pp. 4, 7, October 24, 1918; p. 4; National Committee Minutes, October 23, 29, 1918, pp. 108–109; A.F.L. Executive Council Minutes, November 11–21, 1918, pp. 50–51, May 9–19, 1919, pp. 6–8.

The organizing plan, centralized in its operation, rested on the voluntary support of the internationals. The National Committee was simply a loose federation of as many unions as decided to cooperate, within the limits of their constitutions. Decisions, although reached by majority rule, had no binding force on the member organizations. Like the A.F.L., the only disciplinary power of the National Committee was expulsion, an expedient actually used against the Stationary Engineers. Success depended on the attitude of the international unions.

Their shortsighted independence weakened the movement from the beginning. Defining their interests narrowly, the unions would neither surrender small prerogatives nor provide adequate support. The National Committee had control only of the organizers contributed by the A.F.L. and the United Mine Workers, or hired from its own funds. The others, directed from their national headquarters, often worked at cross purposes. Several jurisdictional squabbles broke out. The fight between the Electrical Workers and the Operating Engineers was particularly bitter.

The local steelworkers councils never received formal recognition. The Gary Council fruitlessly asked for clarification of its "position and powers, so that we can go ahead with the campaign here and have all the crafts pulling together." Effectiveness at the local level was thus much hindered. Finally, despite the urging of the National Committee and the Amalgamated Association, the A.F.L. turned down the suggestion of a Steel Department. The internationals jealously guarded their authority. The "strong need for a central organization, functioning nationally and locally," was never met.

Even more than disunity, meager support undermined the campaign. The cooperating unions each contributed a mere $100 to start off the work. Assessments of five cents per member brought small sums from eleven unions. By the end of 1918 the twenty-four internationals, with a combined membership of 1,500,-000, had contributed a paltry $6,322.50. The National Committee then adopted a somewhat more effective pro-rata system by which each union contributed to cover the monthly expenses. But funds were always sadly lacking. Despite Foster's pleading, the unions at the outset furnished only "a corporal's guard" of organizers. The number gradually increased until at the peak roughly a hundred organizers were working for the National Committee, plus an unknown number for the local councils. Even so, the supply of field workers was always short.

The Chicago conference had recognized that only a national drive could organize the steel industry. Simultaneous campaigns at every steel center would provide the element of surprise, avoid the danger of a partial strike, and, most important, ensure the advantage of the war situation. But slender resources made a lightning attack impossible. Reluctantly the National Committee limited itself to a start in the Chicago district.

The first efforts brought immediate success. A Gary official reported to Frank Morrison: "Overflow meetings were held in the streets — the same in South Chicago, Joliet and Indiana Harbor. . . . The campaign for organization in this district is in full blast." The early rallies enrolled hundreds, and the National Committee foresaw "an avalanche of new members." Twelve hundred were signed up in one day at Joliet, fifteen hundred in South Chicago. "It was such a tidal wave," reported an Amalgamated man of a Joliet meeting, "that the poor, misguided, penny-grabbing straw-bosses could not stem the tide and the threats went for nought and on deaf ears." The enthusiasm was contagious. "You talk about spirit," read a dispatch from Gary, "why that is all these men out here are breathing. They have been hungering for the chance to get in." By the end of September, organization was sufficiently advanced to make the Chicago steel centers a separate district and to move the headquarters to Pittsburgh.[7]

The influenza epidemic stalled the campaign for a time, but

---

[7] E. H. Nockels to Frank Morrison, September 19, 1918, Walsh Papers; National Committee Minutes, September 7, 28, 1918, pp. 9–10; *IA,* September 17, 1918, p. 671; *AJ,* September 26, 1918, pp. 1, 17, October 3, 1918, p. 24; Secretary-Treasurer's Report, Mine, Mill and Smelter Workers, *Proceedings* (1920), pp. 128–129.

preliminary surveys indicated "splendid spirit prevailing among the workers for organization." Work began in Cleveland, then spread to Johnstown, Youngstown, Wheeling, and elsewhere. Reports of climbing enrollment poured in. In Pueblo the organizing proceeded swiftly under the direction of employee leaders, with little assistance from professionals. At the close of 1918 Foster reported "good movements" in many points outside the Pittsburgh district, and Chicago thoroughly unionized. "Beyond all question the steel industry is being organized."

How can the remarkable response of the steelworkers be accounted for? Favorable war conditions clearly played a part. "If the Company wants you men to stay there," observed an Amalgamated member during the Byers dispute, "they will sign the scale and when they refuse, it shows they don't want you any longer." Jobs were plentiful; a man could afford to be independent. The attitude of the government also was encouraging. "If I am not mistaken, men are to have the right to collective bargaining," wrote an employee of the Steel Corporation. "What seems to be the matter with U.S. Steel?" Letters from Amalgamated lodges repeatedly expressed "abiding faith in" the government and confidence that the Steel Corporation would not "snap the finger of scorn at the W.L.B. and President Wilson." A Cleveland unionist summed up the prevailing feeling: "Brothers, when jobs are begging for men, and the U.S. government . . . and the A.F.L. with us, we cannot let this opportunity go by." [8] That common theme explains why steelworkers were unafraid, but not why they wanted to enroll.

William Z. Foster contended that, given their hard lot, "workers can hardly fail to respond." "All that union organizers have to do is to place before these psychologically ripe workers, with sufficient clarity and persistence, the splendid achievements of the trade union movement." [9] The speakers at the first important meeting at

---

[8] *AJ*, June 27, 1918, p. 17, July 4, 1918, p. 1, August 29, 1918, p. 23; October 3, 1918, p. 25, and other letters.

[9] William Z. Foster, *The Great Steel Strike and Its Lessons* (New York, 1920), pp. 38–39.

Youngstown made three principal points: organization would protect against longer hours and lower wages after the war; insure reinstatement of returned soldiers by reducing hours; and give helpless individuals the strength to attain their demands.[10] This appeal to the desire for improvement undoubtedly was effective.

But why should steelworkers have looked for betterment through organization? Before the war the A.F.L., using the same logic, had met with little visible success. Moreover, improvement appeared likely without unions. Capital and labor were united in the common effort, and men expected to be rewarded afterward. Rumors swept the steel mills of a promised eight-hour day.[11] Evidence of management's good intentions could be found in the repeated wage increases, the solicitude for workmen's welfare, and the establishment of the basic eight-hour day on October 1, 1918 — before the organizing drive reached the steelworkers outside the Chicago district. Neither the acute labor shortage nor the standard union arguments fully explain the impact of the organizing campaign.

Trade unionism attracted the steelworkers because it seemed relevant to their war experience. The administration had recognized at the outset the imperative necessity of gaining popular support. The Committee on Public Information created the extensive machinery to persuade the people of the righteousness of the American cause. Nowhere, not even in the mill towns, could men escape the war propaganda.

Chief among the arguments was that the Allies were fighting to make the world safe for democracy. Organized labor found this view particularly congenial, for it justified the painful A.F.L. repudiation of pacifism. A war for democracy was, necessarily, a people's war. Workingmen "would refuse their consent," said Gompers, "if they were not convinced that the war would further the cause of democracy." The American Alliance for Labor and Democracy, created by Gompers in the summer of 1917 to combat the pacifistic People's Council, became the unofficial C.P.I. agency

[10] *AJ*, December 26, 1918, p. 26.
[11] Saposs Interviews, Joe Mann, July 23, 1920, Homestead.

for the labor audience. The Alliance insisted "that the overshadow-
ing issue is the preservation of democracy. . . . On this prime
issue we take our stand." [12] For other propagandizing organs, democracy was an important theme; for the Alliance, it became the
only theme.

The implications speedily dawned on labor leaders. Unionism
clothed itself in the exalted ideals of the war. "If the world is to
be made safe for democracy," reasoned the *American Federationist*
in May 1917, there must be "economic democracy with political
democracy." The connection was instantly made. Industrial democracy, meaning unions and collective bargaining, became the
clarion call of organized labor. John R. Commons, for instance,
wrote a pamphlet for the American Alliance on *Why Workingmen Support the War.*

> This is an American workingman's war, conducted for Ameri-
> can workingmen, by American workingmen. Never before has
> democracy for wage-earners made so great progress. . . . If this
> continues, American labor will come out of this war with the
> universal eight-hour day, and with as much power to fix its
> own wages by its own representatives as employers have.

More than 300,000 copies were printed. Likewise, Frank P. Walsh's
widely circulated Labor Day Message emphasized, "Political
Democracy is a delusion unless builded upon and guaranteed by a
free and virile Industrial Democracy." [13]

Letters to the *Amalgamated Journal* showed the effect on the
rank and file. "If a man thinks he is intelligent enough to have a
voice in government," reflected a Cleveland unionist, "then he
ought to be man enough to stand up and assert his right to a
voice in the adjustment of his hours of labor, wages, and working
conditions." Having successfully established a lodge at Washington, Pennsylvania, the local unionists considered themselves "victorious in our first fight for democracy over here." A new member

---

[12] Gompers, in *AF,* May 1917, p. 357; American Alliance for Labor and
Democracy, *Our War Aims Clearly Stated* (September 6, 1917).

[13] *AJ,* August 29, 1918, p. 1.

from Elwood, Indiana, asked, "How are you going to feel when the boys come home from France and ask you what you have been doing for industrial democracy, while we have been fighting for world democracy?" Unionization became a duty.

It is impossible to gauge the penetration of such thinking in the nonunion steel mills. Certainly, the managers did nothing to encourage it. The plant magazines at Gary, Joliet, and South Chicago contain not a single reference to industrial democracy, nor indeed anything that might turn minds in that direction. Labor Day 1918, the high point in the dissemination of union propaganda, was ignored in Homestead and given over to sports — not speeches — at Gary. Even the meaning of political democracy was distorted. Judge Gary defined democracy to Gary steelworkers as "a whole people unified, with equal law for rich and poor, equal opportunities for all men." [14] The subject was shunned in the mills. Yet, given the newspapers, the Four-Minute speakers, and the posters, millworkers could hardly have thought otherwise than that they were slaving to make the world safe for democracy.

Possibly, the implications began to occur to steelworkers, either spontaneously or from what they had read or heard. In any event, the organizing campaign — for "the further spread of industrial democracy in America," the A.F.L. had said — immediately drove the point home. A Cleveland man recorded his impression of the speeches at a mass meeting: "now is our time to build an industrial army to be able to demand full democracy that the suffering and dying are fighting for on the battlefields at this moment." We must "get behind this campaign for industrial democracy," concluded another writer's description of a rally at Niles, Ohio. [15]

The drive took on a strong patriotic flavor. Started in the midst of the Fourth Loan and final battle of the war, speakers made it seem equally necessary to join the union as to oversubscribe the bond quota and keep up steel production. Significantly, most of the new Amalgamated lodges took names like Democracy, Liberty

[14] Quillen, "Gary," pp. 275–276.
[15] *AJ*, October 10, 1918, p. 23, September 19, 1918, p. 7; also, Report of organizer Pat Trant, *AJ*, January 9, 1919, pp. 1–2.

and Old Glory. Men who "won't try to get collective bargaining from the steel trust are not even first-class Americans," proclaimed one Indiana unionist. The organizing campaign thus made its appeal not only on sound trade union principles, but also on powerful patriotic and ideological grounds.

The democratic argument had its strongest effect on the immigrants. The English-speaking steelworkers had an alternative, probably more compelling, reason for supporting the war: the defense of America from foreign attack. The immigrant, a foreigner himself, could not very well share the chauvinism of the natives. Of necessity, he accepted the idealistic explanation of his sacrifices. The democratic theme made trade unionism comprehensible to him. We must "tell them what democracy means," stated an Amalgamated organizer, "that they are not free men even if their sons did fight on the fields of France to crush the Kaiser rule." [16] Organization promised the war ideals in an immediate way.

The evidence in organizers' reports and observers' comments indicates that the great initial response came from the immigrant steelworkers. They were the first to crowd the mass meetings and sign up for membership. The benefit lists of the Amalgamated Association show a sharp increase in the number of Slavic names, distributed mainly in new lodges whose officers were also immigrants. The foreign segment was for the first time being effectively tapped by the A.F.L.

The National Committee took into account the ethnic composition of the mills. Its bulletins came out in several languages; twenty-five of its organizers spoke the tongues of the immigrant steelworkers; and the rest were coached to talk slowly, clearly, and simply. Frequently held in immigrant society halls, the meetings invariably included speakers in the dominant languages of the communities. [17] The immigrants flocked into the organization.

In comparison, the natives were, according to all reports, an unenthusiastic lot. "The average American should be ashamed of himself for his lack of interest," complained the Amalgamated

[16] *AJ*, December 12, 1918, p. 28.
[17] Foster, pp. 202–205. Meetings described in *AJ, passim.*

organizer stationed at Gary. A Wheeling writer attacked the skilled men:

> The poorest foreign laborer . . . wants to get organized and you don't. . . . Remember this Mr. Smart non-union American that we are coming to your tin and sheet mills and take your foreign speaking men and put them into the Amalgamated Association and then they will make you come clean. They will show you what Americanism really is, one who stands up for his rights.

Many letters complained that the skilled men were ambitious, fearful for their jobs, and discouraged by earlier defeats.[18]

Natives did join the movement in large numbers, not in the rush of the first rallies, but after the organizations in their mills had been partly perfected. Delegations of fellow craft workers proved a very effective technique for organizing skilled men, particularly in the case of the rod and wire men in Cleveland. Had this plan been pursued more energetically, Foster thought, it would have, together with the "bottom upward" movement of the mass meetings, made the campaign irresistible. There were also places with comparatively fewer immigrants, for instance the Minnequa Works in Pueblo, where the campaign was instantly successful.

Negro steelworkers were everywhere impervious to the arguments for organization, with the notable exceptions of Cleveland and Wheeling. Those who had entered the Northern mills earlier had been rebuffed or badly used by unions. And the mass of new colored workmen were in much the same situation as the unskilled immigrants before the war. They lacked understanding of trade unionism, suspected the white workers, and were concerned far more with immediate prospects than with distant reform. Their leaders, moreover, generally opposed the unions. The mechanical trades unions in the National Committee, for their part, continued even during the campaign to exclude Negroes. Despite strenuous

[18] *AJ*, February 16, 1919, p. 23, January 16, 1919, pp. 14, 23, September 5, 1918, p. 18, October 3, 1918, p. 3.

efforts by steel organizers, the black workmen, Foster acknowledged, "lined up with the bosses." [19]

The organizing campaign had, nevertheless, gone far in its
opening months. It presented a challenge unmatched in the history
of the industry.

The steelmakers were in a painful predicament. To permit the
unionizing work to continue unobstructed was obviously dangerous. But so, too, was opposition, for, under the existing wartime
conditions, that would certainly cause labor trouble and invite the
intervention of the government. The president of the Buffalo
Union Furnace Company, speaking at the Waldorf meeting of
August 28, 1918, had it "very direct" that the plan was to start a
strike at one of the lesser companies. "Then the W.L.P.B. will
insist that it be adjusted, and will call on the patriotism of that
company to consent to union labor during the war only. You all
know what that would mean" — the unionization of the entire
industry. And, if the manufacturers objected, "it is a question of
whether or not the labor organizations of the country have not
power enough to have the U.S. Government take over the iron
and steel industries." Clearly, the pretext of a strike was to be
avoided at all costs.

A holding operation was the only choice, as it had been in dealing with the governmental agencies. Steel men began to consider
innocent methods of retarding, even temporarily, the swift growth
of organization. That was one of the determinants, union men
charged, in the decision to institute the basic eight-hour day on
October 1, 1918.

It was possible also to find a virtue in the necessity of establishing collective bargaining under War Labor Board principles. Even
employers came to see the logic of industrial democracy. Having
fought "the war for democracy in government," *Iron Age* observed,
"it would be strange if the people of the United States came out
of the war without any concessions to the growing demand for

[19] Foster, pp. 209–212; *The Negro in Chicago,* pp. 420–429; S. D. Spero and
A. L. Harris, *The Black Worker* (New York, 1931), pp. 260 ff.

more democracy in industry." Shop committees could prove to be an effective answer to the union threat. That would "depend upon the success of the produers of steel in winning their workmen to industrial democracy as represented by the new plan," that is, avoiding "the domination of a body outside the employees." [20]

Steel men already had an example of employee representation. John D. Rockefeller, Jr. had introduced the plan three years earlier at the Colorado Fuel and Iron Company in the aftermath of the bloody coal strike of 1914. The experiment had been carefully, if skeptically, observed, and by mid-1918 there appeared little doubt of its success in settling grievances and alleviating discontent.

On September 22, 1918 the Midvale and Lukens Steel companies voluntarily accepted employee representation. Midvale workmen were requested to elect committeemen to meet with management to adopt "a plan of representation by the employees which shall be thoroughly democratic and entirely free from interference by the companies." The *Iron Age* enthusiastically believed that the move "should break down to a degree the military system, too commonly prevalent in industry, that puts a premium on a superintendent's or foreman's ability to drive his men." The steel manufacturers "now have the gage thrown down to them for a real test of their willingness to make their industry a safe place for democracy." [21]

Shortly afterward, Bethlehem Steel announced not only its compliance with the W.L.B. order at South Bethlehem but its intention to introduce employee representation at its other plants. The next few months, the war now over, saw the adoption of shop committees at the Youngstown Sheet and Tube, Inland Steel, Wisconsin Steel, and Standard Steel Car companies. Varying in details, all the plans set up machinery for the election of workers' committees or councils to deal with management on grievances and, in some cases, general questions of hours and wages.[22]

[20] *IA*, March 7, 1918, p. 634, October 3, 1918, p. 846, April 11, 1918, p. 957.

[21] *IA*, September 26, 1918, pp. 763, 764.

[22] See, for example, the Bethlehem plan of April 1919 in N.W.L.B., Docket 22, Exhibit D; and analysis of Colorado Fuel and Iron plan in Selekman, *Employes' Representation*, ch. 3.

Union spokesmen had at first welcomed employee representation. The A.F.L. had urged workmen not to wait for the War Labor Board to establish committees. These would be the first stage of organization, link up with the unions, and then operate as the bargaining vehicle until recognition was won.[23] At Bethlehem and elsewhere union men easily gained control of the shop committees. Although specifically acknowledging the right to join unions, however, most steel companies clearly considered representation a means to discourage unionism. Bethlehem, for instance, requested the withdrawal of W.L.B. examiners as soon as the war ended, discharged some of the leading union delegates, and attempted to hold a new election. On the other hand, the management of the Pueblo Works scrupulously avoided discharging active unionists, despite the complaints of lesser officials. Nevertheless, shop committees were shortly labeled as antiunion devices in labor circles.

Employee representation was not designed to strengthen the bargaining position of workmen, but rather to provide, as the Wisconsin Steel Company announced, "a definite and durable basis of mutual understanding and confidence," or, as Inland Steel stated, "effective communication and means of contact . . . and to insure justice, maintain tranquility, and promote the general welfare." C. S. Robinson explained how the Youngstown Sheet and Tube Company had reached its decision. For a long time the company had supported welfare work and profit-sharing without creating good will among the workmen. Three years before it had expanded its welfare program to include a department to handle grievances. Then, seeing the success elsewhere of shop committees, it had taken the further step. But, Robinson emphasized, "the powers necessary to an enlightened management are not abridged."[24] The object of "industrial democracy," like welfare work, was to create contented workers.

[23] *AF*, July 1918, p. 581, September 1918, pp. 807–810. See also the interesting "propositions" to settle the Bethlehem dispute suggested by John Fitzpatrick in letter to Frank Walsh, August 30, 1918, Walsh Papers.

[24] C. S. Robinson, "The League of Labor and Capital," *IA*, March 13, 1919, pp. 683–684, also, March 27, 1919, p. 832, January 9, 1919, pp. 122–123.

The Steel Corporation rejected employee representation. The War Labor Board had ordered, and had actually held elections for, shop committees in several of its sheet and tin mills, but there the matter died.[25] Although acknowledging the right of representation "in principle," Judge Gary doubted the efficacy of shop committees (to create contentment, that is) and perhaps saw dangers in them. But chiefly, his commitment to welfare work caused the rejection.

"There is only one way of combatting and overcoming the wave of unrest" he lectured the subsidiary presidents.

> Satisfy your men if you can that your treatment is fair and reasonable and generous. Make the Steel Corporation a good place for them to work and live. Don't let the families go hungry or cold; give them playgrounds and parks and schools and churches, pure water to drink, every opportunity to keep clean. . . .

But retain "the control and management of your affairs, keeping the whole thing in your own hands." Using the same welfare argument, Gary persuaded the steel manufacturers not to reduce wages in the slump immediately following the war. "Let us retain their confidence and loyal support by our action. They will meet us half way if they are permitted to exercise their own judgment and spirit of fairness."[26] If welfare worked, what need for dangerous democratic experiment? Both, nevertheless, aimed at the same end of allaying labor unrest.

Little more could be done against the organizing drive during the war period except by indirection. The Gary *Tribune* ran a front page editorial likening the organizers to German invaders and asking, "Is Gary to become the Belgium of America?" Illinois

[25] N.W.L.B., Docket 232, Findings and Original Complaint. Judge Gary himself wrongly testified that U.S. Steel had never dealt with the N.W.L.B. U.S. Senate, Committee on Labor, *Investigation of Steel Strike,* 66 Cong., 1st Sess. (1919), I, 206.

[26] Gary Address to Subsidiary Presidents, January 21, 1919, and Meeting of Steel Manufacturers, December 9, 1918, pp. 8–10, *Addresses and Statements,* IV.

Steel Company plants held mass meetings to head off organization. All men were asked to sign a "Pledge of Patriotism."

I recognize that the enemy propaganda throughout the country is spread abroad to create discord among workmen, and I am opposed to any action that would tend to disturb the good relations that have for years existed between the Joliet Works Management and ourselves.

As a matter of patriotism and assistance to our boys in the trenches, I pledge my loyalty to our country and to the company for which I work.[27]

Plant magazines hinted darkly of "Pro-German Agitators," and urged readers to be loyal, dependable workers. "A Knocker Never Wins," said the *Gary Works Circle,* "A Winner Never Knocks." The *Joliet Works Mixer* stated that "Loyalty to enemies of the industry . . . is of necessity disloyalty to that industry, just as in time of war, he who is friendly to the enemy is a traitor." Consistently, the effort was to link unionism to disloyalty.[28]

But, not fair and liberal treatment, nor employee representation, nor patriotic argument, seemed to stem the unionizing drive. Organization went on apace.

Then the war came to its sudden end. The War Industries Board and the War Labor Policies Board were immediately disbanded. The War Labor Board continued in order to dispose of pending cases; only 107 of 724 had been settled by the end of November 1918. But the Board now lacked the necessary coercive powers. In the exceptional case of Bethlehem, it was able to force partial compliance by publicizing the facts and accusing the company of bad faith. Generally, the postwar decisions went no further than to order the establishment of committees to settle grievances.

[27] Meeting on October 9 described in *AJ,* October 24, 1918, p. 12, and pledge reprinted on p. 25; *South Works Review,* October 1918.
[28] See, for example, the poster which appeared during the efforts to organize the McClintic-Marshall Company in Rankin, reproduced in *Survey,* January 4, 1919, p. 454.

The W.L.B. dragged on into the summer of 1919, but it had long since lost any importance. The time had come, the *Iron Age* observed with satisfaction, for workingmen to get over "the idea that they have a special power or influence with the government."

Time had favored the steel manufacturers. Afterward, Foster thought of what might have been. His plan for a simultaneous drive would have organized the entire industry at a time when steel production was imperative and an industry-wide strike out of the question. "The steel manufacturers would have been compelled to yield. . . . The trade unions would have been re-established in the steel industry." [29] As it was, the war was over and the industry only weakly organized. Their vulnerability had hardened the determination of the steel men and perfected their united front. They came out of the war thoroughly alarmed and prepared to fight the spread of unionism.

From the day of the armistice every circumstance — the implacable hostility of the employers, the objectives of organized labor, the heightened expectations of the workmen, and the weak neutrality of the administration — converged to make a great conflict inevitable.

[29] Foster, p. 22.

Chapter XII

The Great Strike

Armistice Day celebrations had hardly subsided when employer resistance came into the open. Organizers starting the drive in the Pittsburgh district found their way blocked. The mayor of McKeesport refused permits for meetings. No halls could be rented in Homestead, Braddock, and Monessen. When a Rankin landlord resisted pressure, the Board of Health closed the building. At Aliquippa and other towns a "hive of Pinkerton yellow back detectives" stopped union men at the railroad stations. Pittsburgh authorities allowed meetings, but, as elsewhere, prohibited the distribution of advertising literature. Western Pennsylvania was the heart of the industry. "Drastic action must be taken," the National Committee determined, "or no hope of success could be expected in this campaign." [1]

"Political methods" were the first resort. A committee of three presented the union case at a McKeesport Council meeting. Gompers sent an indignant letter, Pennsylvania Governor W. C. Sproul promised to exert his influence, and Secretary of Labor Wilson started an investigation. Meanwhile, the National Committee whipped up union sentiment. "Despite its indispensable services to the government in the great war, the A.F.L. is treated as an outlaw," read a description of conditions along the Monongahela River. "Every trade union hall in America should ring with protest." A special convention met at the Pittsburgh Labor Temple in February 1919 to condemn the infringements on free speech and

[1] National Committee Minutes, November 25, 1918, pp. 14-15.

assembly as "un-American, illegal and fatal to peace and progress."[2]

But a "conspiracy of silence" blanketed the protests. The results of the Labor Department investigation were never disclosed; nor did the other efforts come to anything. At the end of winter the Pittsburgh district remained tightly closed to the unions. Yet the free speech campaign, Foster thought, had served to keep alive workmen's interest and to focus attention on the situation. The actual organizing work proceeded in the other steel centers. The strategy was to surround the Monongahela Valley with unionized mills, and then, at peak strength, force the capitulation of the main stronghold.

Away from Pittsburgh, resistance varied. The Colorado Fuel and Iron Company offered no opposition at all. The manager of a Waukegan plant, learning of an organizing rally, rented the largest hall in town for the same night, engaged all the music available, and advertised an evening's free entertainment. Elsewhere, hostility was more virulent. Company officials frequently blocked the entrances to meeting halls. "Brothers, don't let the spotter with the wild west boots frighten you," wrote a Coatesville man, "don't let him stand in your way." Undercover agents circulated in the mills. "The Spy! Oh Lord deliver us," exclaimed a unionist from Franklin, Pennsylvania. "We were on the lookout. At last . . . we have the goods on him. Any suggestion that anyone can make in any way of a punishment without violating the law please hand it to us, as we will apply it with a will." Detective agencies like Corporations Auxiliary and the Sherman Service were supplying hundreds of "representatives" to the steel companies.[3]

In late winter mass dismissals began at Johnstown. When warn-

[2] National Committee Minutes, November 25, 1918, p. 15, February 15, 1919, p. 19; *AJ*, February 27, 1919, pp. 1, 6, December 5, 1918, pp. 1, 3; E. Nockels to Walsh, November 27, 1918, Walsh Papers.

[3] P. E. Borden, J. E. Cross, and L. V. Mitchell, "Brief History of the Pueblo Strike," *AJ*, March 11, 1920, p. 1; *AJ*, January 16, 1919, p. 2, November 28, 1918, p. 4; *New Majority*, April 19, 1919; Interchurch World Movement, *Public Opinion and the Steel Strike*, ch. 1.

ings failed, the Cambria managers embarked on a "policy of frightfulness," apparently selecting for discharge employees with large families and mortgaged homes. Organizer T. J. Conboy wrote in alarm that "to stand idle long will mean to allow our forces to be cut to pieces bit by bit." Johnstown was an extreme case, but the practice became increasingly common elsewhere.[4]

These tactics did not contain the campaign. By the spring of 1919 the National Committee counted close to 100,000 recruits in nearly every steel center outside the Pittsburgh district. The time had come to move into Allegheny County.

A "Flying Squadron" under B. L. Beaghen, head of the Pittsburgh Bricklayers' Union, was formed for the dangerous work of opening the mill towns. They faced arrest, abusive officials, and sizable fines; Beaghen himself was jailed eight times. But direct action was effective. A meeting was announced to take place in the streets of Monessen, forty miles from Pittsburgh on the Monongahela River. On the date set, April 1, thousands of miners from the surrounding coal country marched in with uniformed ex-service men at their head. The burgess was forced to acquiesce; the right to hold meetings was established. Several miles down river in Donora the struggle was won when the miners began to boycott the town.

The important steel towns closer to Pittsburgh succumbed next. Thousands turned out to hear the speakers at the first illegal meeting in McKeesport on May 18, 1919. Despite his public warnings, Mayor G. H. Lysle dared not intervene, and street meetings were held regularly in McKeesport thereafter. Rankin, Clairton, Homestead, and Braddock were similarly taken. The Pittsburgh district was being in slow stages opened to the organizers during the spring and summer of 1919.

Meanwhile, discontent was mounting. Peace had brought to the steelworkers a terrible sense of betrayal. Wherever they turned, they found the wartime promises shattered. A Reading, Pennsylvania, workman recalled the past enthusiasm. "That was war, that

[4] National Committee Minutes, March 1, 8, 1919, pp. 20–22.

was glorious, but the war is over now, and it is not so glorious." "The justice of the demand for a fairer share has been established," asserted a union member from Canton, Ohio. "It is not going to be given up now that the war has ended. . . . A few millions of wage earners have been fighting for . . . democracy not only in government, but in industry."[5]

The War Labor Board was bitterly disappointing. Its inability "to force any manufacturer to abide by its findings," observed the *Amalgamated Journal,* has shaken "the faith of the toilers of our nation." After months of delay, the W.L.B. had directed the men of a Granite City lodge to negotiate for themselves — "which they would have been glad to do seven months ago had they not been forced to do otherwise. The boys have become disheartened, as they worked faithfully, thinking that the board was sincere." "Where is all the patriotism that the board had last spring?" asked another writer. Frank P. Walsh was right when he urged the ending of the W.L.B. because "it cannot be anything but a disappointing mirage to working people of the country."[6]

Employee representation deepened the disillusionment. Even at the Pueblo Works, where the committees gained the straight eight-hour day, the Rockefeller plan was "needless to say . . . always considered a joke by most union men." In the meetings, employees told an investigator, they simply took what management was willing to give. Bernard J. May, for six months committee chairman at South Bethlehem, testified that "we could not get anything that would go into the men's envelopes." Finally, he quit to avoid being marked "as a man who had sold out to the Bethlehem Steel Company."[7]

[5] *AJ,* January 30, 1919, p. 18, February 6, 1919, p. 30. The steelworkers' statements in the following discussion, unless otherwise indicated in the notes, come from their letters to the *Amalgamated Journal,* and will not be specifically cited.

[6] Walsh to V. A. Olander, December 4, 1918, Walsh Papers.

[7] *Strike Investigation,* II, 1030 ff.; Saposs Interviews, J. W. Hendricks and Mr. McCanlogue; N.W.L.B., Docket 22, in re Special Features of Bethlehem Steel Plan, April 11, 1919.

The Midvale Steel and Ordnance Company revealed how inept could be the handling of shop representatives. After the elimination of the union members, the committees met at the company's expense in August 1919 at Atlantic City. There they resolved that the demand "for a shorter day's work and an increased wage in order to meet the present high cost of living is uneconomic and unwise and should not be encouraged." At Johnstown, consequently, the wavering men crowded into the unions. Despite the company's threats, the steelworkers stayed out on Labor Day to parade under such banners as "We are for the shorter day and more pay" and "The Collective Bargaining Association must go." [8] Wherever the shop committees existed, the unions thrived.

The steelworkers had concrete grievances. Unemployment spread in the months after the armistice. The labor force at the five Bethlehem plants, for example, shrank from 28,000 on November 11, 1918 to 11,000 in March 1919. A Lancaster man wrote angrily: "I tell you the employers are showing their patriotism now, you know how they used to preach to us to be patriotic, keep on working to your full limit. . . . They were patriotic . . . for the dollars alone. Since the fighting there is nothing would please them more than to turn us all out on the streets and compel us to beg from door to door." The thought rankled even after the return of full operation in the spring of 1919.

Hours were a graver issue. Except at Pueblo and on the Pacific coast, the expected reform had not materialized. Notwithstanding Judge Gary's denials, hours in the spring of 1919 differed little from those a decade earlier. Invariably, interviewed workmen asserted that "the hours were too long. . . . I had no pleasure with my children, working twenty-four hours and then I would sleep all day and go right back to work." They could forego more money, the women said, if only their husbands could have shorter hours and still bring home the same pay. The Pueblo steelworkers

---

[8] Atlantic City report, reprinted in *Strike Investigation,* I, 474, also see 409–410; *IA,* August 28, 1919, p. 590; "Suicide of a Company Union," *AJ,* September 18, 1919, p. 8.

demanded the eight-hour day despite the cost; with a 10 per cent increase, the unskilled men earned two dollars less for eight hours than they had for twelve hours. Yet investigators found unanimous enthusiasm for the change. Even the Homestead superintendent, admitting the injustice, during the strike went around the mill promising to do his best for the men. "Eight hours and the union" was the battle cry of the steelworkers.[9]

The antiunion efforts of the steel companies were the final blow. "This is the U.S. and we ought to have the right to belong to the union," exclaimed a Hungarian workman in Clairton to investigating Senators. A Parkersburg, West Virginia, unionist bitterly assailed the repressions in the Pennsylvania mill towns, "all this in spite of the fact that we have strained every muscle to keep up production and render a service to our government in winning the war." The discharges at Johnstown drove the steelworkers to the verge of a strike, and only the pleas of Frank Morrison and other leaders restrained them.[10] But, as the spring of 1919 passed, from everywhere came reports of rising discontent, impatience for action, and threatening strikes.

The National Committee decided on a general conference "to give the men who have waited so long something tangible to look forward to." The aim was to "pacify the restless spirits." Five hundred eighty-three representatives of the local unions met at the Pittsburgh Labor Temple on May 25, a Sunday, since most were workmen. They came armed with specific instructions. The union officials quickly disabused them of their expectations; only the internationals had the power to call strikes. The conference did air the steelworkers' grievances and pass a resolution directing the National Committee "to enter into negotiations with the various

[9] *Strike Investigation*, II, 495, and in the testimonies of many other strikers; Walker, *Steel*, pp. 62–80; Selekman, *Employes' Representation*, pp. 84–86; Saposs Interviews, Joe Mann, July 22, 1920, Homestead.

[10] National Committee Minutes, March 8, 1919, p. 22. *AJ*, March 27, 1919, p. 20, describes the meeting.

steel companies." Failing that, the conference urged preparations for a national strike. The pleas of experienced unionists for moderation could not stem the rising discontent.[11]

The Pittsburgh conference in effect backfired. Disappointed by the lack of concrete action, many men dropped out or withheld their dues. Others continued to demand walkouts. The meeting served notice on the National Committee that it could not await the perfection of the organizations before approaching the steel companies.

The following week the National Committee appointed a subcommittee to start preliminary negotiations with the industry. After conferring with officials of the twenty-four unions, Gompers wrote on June 20 to Gary requesting an interview for the subcommittee. The anxiously awaited response never came.[12] Foster warned the National Committee on July 11, "Some action must be taken that will secure relief. All over . . . men are in a state of great unrest. In Johnstown, Youngstown, Chicago, Wheeling and elsewhere, great strikes are threatening." The danger of allowing control to slip away balanced the risk of a strike without adequate preparation. The National Committee voted at last to recommend a strike vote, subject to reconsideration at the next meeting.

On July 20 the ground was reëxamined in four hours of soul-searching debate. By then the breaking point was approaching. Foster read a wire from the Johnstown Workers' Council: "Unless the National Committee authorizes a national strike vote to be taken this week we will be compelled to go on strike here alone." All agreed that it would be far better to continue the drive until at least 60 per cent were organized. (Roughly 100,000 — perhaps 20 per cent — were reported to be unionized at that point.) "But the

[11] National Committee Minutes, April 5, 1919, pp. 25–27; Conference Minutes, May 25, 1919, in National Committee Minutes, pp. 28–41.

[12] Shortly before the Pittsburgh conference, the Amalgamated Association had independently attempted to enter negotiations with the Steel Corporation. Gary claimed afterward that he had not replied to Gompers' letter because his earlier response to Tighe had been construed to mean he was "in communication" with the union and had encouraged men to join.

steel barons are not going to let us choose our fighting time and place. They are practically compelling us upon disruption of our organization to make a move." The strike ballot resolution was upheld, only the Amalgamated Association and the United Mine Workers voting in opposition. The National Committee also adopted twelve general demands as a basis for negotiation.[13]

The balloting consumed a month. Partly, strict trade union procedure required this lengthy period; each union held its own vote. More important, the work was not rushed because the voting process greatly strengthened the organizations, invigorating and rapidly increasing their ranks. The bulk of the furnace workers' locals in the Pittsburgh district, for example, was chartered in this period. According to the National Committee, sentiment was almost unanimous—98 per cent—in favor of a strike. The date was to be set in ten days unless negotiations were begun.

Thus armed, the conference subcommittee appeared at Judge Gary's offices on August 26, 1919. He was in, but sent word that he preferred to deal with the committee by letter. Gary reiterated in writing the open-shop policy against meeting with union representatives. The committee did not approach any other steel companies, assuming that Judge Gary spoke for the entire industry, as he did.

Still reluctant to meet the issue, the National Committee turned to President Wilson. Visiting him on August 28 with Gompers at their head, they assured the President that a conference was their only demand. They asked him to arrange a meeting with the Steel Corporation. President Wilson, Gompers reported to the Executive Council, "stated that the time had passed when any man should refuse to meet representatives of his employees and

[13] National Committee Minutes, July 20, 1919, pp. 45–48. The demands were: 1. Right of collective bargaining; 2. Reinstatement of discharged men with pay for lost time; 3. Eight-hour day; 4. One day's rest in seven; 5. Abolition of twenty-four-hour shift; 6. Increase of wages to guarantee American living standard; 7. Standard scales of wages; 8. Double rates for overtime over forty-eight hours, holidays, and Sundays; 9. Check-off system of collecting union dues; 10. Principles of seniority; 11. Abolition of company unions; 12. Abolition of physical examination of applicants for jobs.

that he would do what he could to comply with the request." [14] Bernard Baruch was commissioned to approach Judge Gary.

The union men departed with raised hopes. But a week passed without word. The National Committee, in desperation, sent a telegram on September 4 to the President, who was then on his ill-fated western tour advocating the League of Nations. The attacks on the unions "have brought about a situation such that it is exceedingly difficult to withhold or restrain the men. . . . We cannot now affirm how much longer we will be able to exert that influence." The meeting of union presidents on September 9 heard Tumulty's reply that the President was discouraged but continuing his efforts. When a second telegram the next day substantially repeated the first, the vote was unanimous for a national strike on September 22. The strike order was wired to the steel centers and the union officials scattered to their posts.

On the next morning, September 11, Gompers received an apparent reprieve. A third telegram had arrived from Tumulty with a request from the President for postponement until after the Industrial Conference in Washington on October 7, 1919. A week before, Gompers had warned that the situation was "incomparably the most important facing organized labor." Confidential information told him that open-shop interests had decided to have U.S. Steel make the decisive fight against trade unionism. Forwarding the presidential request to the twenty-four unions, Gompers urged compliance if at all possible "without injury to the workers and their cause." Seven internationals telegraphed their representatives to vote for deferment. Union circles generally endorsed Gompers' view.

But decisions had by then passed out of official hands. Fitzpatrick wired Gompers "that any vague, indefinite postponement would mean absolute demoralization and utter ruin for our movement. . . . Our only hope is the strike." A Pittsburgh meeting on September 17–18 provided the final proof. Telegrams from men in the field claimed that deferment would be "suicidal." A Youngs-

[14] A.F.L. Executive Council Minutes, August 28–30, 1919, p. 12, also pp. 2, 22.

town organizer wired, "We cannot be expected to meet the enraged workers who will consider us traitors if the strike is postponed." Some districts had voted to go out on September 22 irrespective of the decision of the National Committee. The unions had no choice but to stand by the strike date. Only the Machinists, Boilermakers, and Plumbers voted negatively, and they agreed to abide by the wish of the majority.[15]

Gompers pleaded against the strike to the last. Fitzpatrick came to see him on September 19. "I stated instance upon instance," Gompers told the Executive Council later that day, "of enthusiasm and impetuosity of unorganized [men] in driving their movements to destruction . . . all to no purpose. The unorganized, the newly organized recruits, were to be even against the best judgment of the experienced men."[16] Pressure from below had cast the deciding ballot.

The strategy of the steel companies assumed the allegiance of the steelworkers. "We do not think you are authorized to represent the sentiment of a majority of the employees," Gary had written to the union committee seeking a conference. They would not strike, Gary said, because they "have received . . . better treatment . . . than they could expect through the efforts of labor unions." Reassuring reports came from steel centers — for instance, this one from Youngstown — that "the majority are contented, and prefer to remain at their jobs. . . . Professional, imported agitators have been able to make little headway in fomenting discord among them." What support the unions had came from the expendable unskilled workers. As the strike day approached, company officials distributed "I Am Loyal" buttons, circulated foreign language pamphlets, and took polls to determine the sentiment in the mills.

[15] Fitzpatrick to Gompers, September 12, 1919, also, Fitzpatrick to W. H. Johnston, September 17, 1919, Gompers Papers; National Committee Minutes, September 17, 1919, pp. 54-60.

[16] A.F.L. Executive Council Minutes, September 19, 1919, in Gompers Papers.

Youngstown, Lackawanna, Gary, and other centers confidently predicted a response from no more than 10 or 15 per cent of the steelworkers.[17] An effective national strike did not seem possible.

But the steel men underestimated the discontent in the mills. They missed, moreover, the symbolic importance of Judge Gary's refusal to confer. He "sets himself up as a czar," said John Fitzpatrick. "When Judge Gary has refused to meet our chosen representatives," asked a Cleveland man, "what other course is there left to them but that last resort, strike?"[18] Gary had helped to revivify the Wilsonian ideology. The steelworkers slipped back naturally to wartime terminology as September 22 approached. "We are all on the firing line once more and we are going over the top as we did in 1918 over there," wrote a workman from Steubenville, Ohio. "For we are determined to lick the steel barons and Kaisers of this country as we were to lick the German Kaiser." Once more, the steelworkers were fighters against "autocracy."

Finally, company officials made the elementary mistake of judging union sentiment on the basis of membership. Foster had said: "In iron and steel where men work together in big bunches, we can get everybody to strike even though we have only ten per cent — the most important and leading ten per cent — with us."[19] The proof would be in the response on September 22. It was, as Presi-

[17] *IA*, July 24, 1919, p. 253a, August 21, 1919, pp. 514–515, August 28, 1919, pp. 585–587; *NLT*, August 7, 21, 1919; Pittsburgh *Gazette-Times*, September 21, 1919.

[18] United Mine Workers, *Proceedings* (1919), p. 509; *AJ*, September 11, 1919, p. 21, also, other letters and Tighe's strike message, October 2, 1919, p. 1. Even *Iron Age* acknowledged the importance of this feeling. When one reporter was told of Gary's "arbitrary" attitude, he tried to explain that, although Gary would not deal with unions, he was glad to see individual workers. "But I doubt whether my explanation was convincing, for the reason that there has been so much talk about the arbitrary attitude of Judge Gary that it is going to be difficult to remove the erroneous impression which has been lodged in the minds of even reasonable men." *IA*, September 18, 1919, p. 786.

[19] Williams, *What's on the Worker's Mind*, pp. 173–174; also, D. J. Saposs, "How the Steel Strike was Organized," *Survey*, November 8, 1919, pp. 67–69.

dent J. F. Welborn of the Colorado Fuel and Iron Company told the local union committees: "All the men on the outside on Monday will be yours and all those on the inside will be mine."[20]

September 22 gave a clear answer. The steel mills were almost entirely shut down in the Pueblo, Chicago, Wheeling, Johnstown, Cleveland, Lackawanna, and Youngstown districts. In many places the response, as the Gary *Post* observed of its city, "was a surprise to both" sides. The walkout was mixed in the Pittsburgh district, ranging from complete in Monessen and Donora, middling in the Carnegie towns of Homestead and Braddock, to ineffectual in Duquesne and Jones and Laughlin's Pittsburgh plant. The strike was weak in the East and South. The Bethlehem plants, which were outside the National Committee's jurisdiction, did not close on Strike Monday. There the management had made concessions and the union leaders hoped for an acceptable compromise. But the men, seeing the strike elsewhere, demanded immediate union recognition and, on the company's refusal, struck with partial effectiveness on September 29.

Altogether, the National Committee claimed 365,500 out on September 30. The steel companies disputed specific figures, especially in the Pittsburgh district, but never offered their estimate of the total number of strikers. The *Iron Age,* however, put pig iron production on October 1 at 50,100 tons. The national furnace capacity per day was 93,360 tons. Considering that operating mills were straining to break records and that the many merchant furnaces were largely unaffected, the undoubtedly conservative *Iron Age* figure indicates the astonishing dimensions of the strike for union.[21]

The steelworkers faced the most formidable and determined opposition. The steel manufacturers, reported *Iron Age,* felt "relief, if not . . . satisfaction, that organized labor has actually determined to fight out the issue of the closed shop." "If it came to a question of wage demands alone," the steel companies "might

<hr>

[20] "Pueblo Strike," *AJ*, March 11, 1920, p. 1.

[21] *IA,* September 25, 1919, pp. 881 ff., Emergency Market Bulletin, October 2, 9, 1919.

meet the union officials in a conciliatory spirit." But the main issue was "whether an outside union . . . shall be allowed to dictate to the employer how he shall operate his plant." Here no compromise was possible.

According to Arundel Cotter, the independents had feared that Judge Gary would bow to the outside pressure for a conference. The entire industry united behind him after he showed his firmness. In the midst of the strike, 1,600 steel men gathered to demonstrate their unanimity at the annual meeting of the Iron and Steel Institute. The resolution praising Gary's leadership, the minutes read, was "carried amidst great applause and cheers, the assembled gentlemen rising." It was, said Cotter, "an unequivocal admission of his right to supreme command." Under Gary, the resources of the steel industry were applied remorselessly to the struggle.[22]

The battle lines were drawn tight between a third of a million steelworkers and a powerful phalanx of American business.

The strike was fought out on two fronts — in the steel towns and before the country. Initially, the steel companies were at a disadvantage in the contest for public opinion. They had to justify the refusal, even at the President's request, to meet with the unions. Judge Gary advanced the standard open-shop thesis that to "negotiate with the labor unions . . . would indicate the closing of our shops against nonunion labor." The steel companies were defending the right of every man to "engage in any line of employment that he selects, and under such terms as he and the employer may agree upon . . . depending on his own merit and disposition." The workmen were treated in accord with "the highest standards of propriety and justice." [23]

But to a country anxious for social and economic harmony, this did not outweigh the consequences of a nationwide steel strike.

[22] Arundel Cotter, *United States Steel: A Corporation with a Soul* (New York, 1921), pp. 5, 257; Meeting, October 24, 1919, Steel Institute, *Yearbook* (1919), p. 333.

[23] *Manufacturers' Record,* September 19, 1919, quoted in *Strike Investigation,* I, 97–98.

Union leaders disclaimed any intention to enforce a closed shop: "There is only one question, and that is the question of a conference." The sharp examination by the Senate Committee on Labor and Education, moreover, uncovered baser instincts under Gary's open-shop moralism.[24] The Springfield *Republican,* among others, believed that he showed "beyond dispute his opposition to unionism both in principle and practice." Some agreed with the *Wall Street Journal* that "Judge Gary is fighting the battle of the American Constitution," but the weight of conservative, as well as liberal, opinion rejected the open-shop contention. Not even the unions' refusal to heed President Wilson's request for postponement rubbed off the onus on the industry.[25]

Fortunately for the steel companies, another issue swiftly obscured the more mundane matters of trade unionism. In its issue of September 18 the *Iron Age* published a full-page editorial on "The Real Question at Pittsburgh." A few days earlier, George Smart, one of its editors investigating the situation in the steel center, had "discovered evidence connecting at least the leading spirit of the strike agitation with extreme Syndicalism and other forms of revolutionary propaganda."

William Z. Foster's radical past had been no secret; the Pittsburgh *Labor World* had carried on an abusive campaign against him months earlier. Now his I.W.W. career was injected as a main issue into the strike. He had written in 1911 in a revolutionary pamphlet, *Syndicalism,* that capitalism was "the most brazen gigantic robbery ever perpetrated since the world began."

---

[24] See Gary's testimony in *Strike Investigation,* I. Senator D. I. Walsh asked if Gary would deal with the union only for those belonging. Gary feared that this would jeopardize the majority. Suppose the majority preferred the union? Gary insisted this was not the case. He hedged, at one point saying that he might deal with a union that specified that it would make agreements for only its members, but finally stated that he would deal with no union no matter what percentage belonged to it. In effect, he had to acknowledge, he was opposed to unionism.

[25] Quotations in *Literary Digest,* October 4, 1919, pp. 9–13, October 18, 1919, pp. 12–14; J. A. Fitch, "The Closed Shop," *Survey,* November 8, 1919, pp. 53–58.

The syndicalist is as "unscrupulous" in his choice of weapons to fight his every-day battles as for his final struggle with capitalism. He allows no considerations of "legality," religion, patriotism, "honor," "duty," etc., to stand in the way of his adoption of effective tactics. . . . With him the end justifies the means.

This, and much more of the same, was read into the record in Congress, and printed in newspapers across the country, often as the principal news of the strike. Foster was branded a man unfit for "the name of an American citizen and the protection of that flag." The press widely agreed that he had forced the strike "for the purpose of revolutionizing industry." [26]

But no one could question the loyalty and conservatism of the A.F.L. That difficulty was overcome by the claim that the radicals had engineered a *coup d'état*. Gompers' opposition to the strike was well known. The New York *Tribune* gave a popular version:

When Mr. Gompers returned from Europe he was confronted with accomplishment. When Foster urged that the moment to strike had arrived, Mr. Gompers and the other conservative leaders associated with him were obliged either to agree or step aside or stand the combined attack of the radical factions of the A.F.L., thus endangering their control of the organization.

As one loyal steelworker said, "Somebody got in and scuttled the A.F.L."

Gompers of course repudiated these charges. Foster had outgrown his youthful radicalism, the old man claimed. "He was a man of ability . . . and I encouraged him. . . . I was willing to welcome an erring brother into the ranks of constructive labor." Foster himself disclaimed any destructive intent before the Senate investigating committee. Actually, he was obviously equivocal on his personal opinions. In his autobiography, Gompers claimed to have by then lost confidence in his protégé's sincerity. Long after

[26] William Z. Foster and Earl C. Ford, *Syndicalism* (n.p., 1911); Interchurch World Movement, *Public Opinion and the Steel Strike*, pp. 302 ff.; *Strike Investigation*, I, 220, 318, 392–393, II, 509; *Literary Digest*, October 11, 1919, pp. 12–13; Pittsburgh *Gazette-Times*, September 20, 24, 1919.

he had become a Communist, Foster himself recorded that he had been a "borer from within." No doubt he had hoped, as he had openly stated in his 1920 account of the strike, that the success of conservative trade unionism would ultimately end the wage system. Even if his aims were more radical, however, Foster did not have control of the National Committee. The strike was just what its supporters claimed it to be: an effort by labor unions under conservative leadership to win recognition. The campaign had followed strictly trade union procedure, and there was hardly a word open to radical interpretation.[27]

The question of Foster's motives is in any event academic. The important fact is that he was considered a radical bent on overturning the standing order. The *Iron Age* observed with satisfaction that its exposé of "the strike leadership has had a telling effect upon public sentiment." The Senate investigating committee concluded that "some radical men not in harmony with the conservative elements of the A.F.L. are attempting to use the strike as a means of elevating themselves to power within the ranks of organized labor." The National Committee itself privately admitted, "the men in active charge of the strike have been thoroughly discredited." [28]

The ethnic composition of the strike lent credence to the belief in its revolutionary character. Reports emphasized that the mass of strikers were immigrants. The issue, according to the New York

[27] *Strike Investigation,* I, 111–119, 178–179, 386–429; Gompers, *Seventy Years,* II, 514–518; William Z. Foster, *From Bryan to Stalin* (New York, 1937), p. 133. Foster had left the I.W.W. arguing that dual unionism was fruitless; the radicals should work within the conservative unions to gain their ends. For an incisive analysis of this, see D. J. Saposs, *Left Wing Unionism* (New York, 1926). Saposs, who knew Foster at that time, has suggested that Foster's reticence before the Senate Committee was because he already saw that his future lay with the Communists. On the one hand, he did not want to antagonize them; on the other, he did not want to injure the strike. D. J. Saposs, Interview with author, March 22, 1955. See also, Theodore Draper, *The Roots of American Communism* (New York, 1957), pp. 313–314.

[28] *Senate Report 289,* 68 Cong., 1st Sess. (1919), pp. 13–14; National Committee Minutes, December 1, 1919, pp. 90–91.

Tribune, was "Americanism vs. Alienism." The Slavic steelwork-ers, noted the New York *Times,* were "steeped in the doctrines of the class struggle and social overthrow, ignorant and easily mis-led." And, the Philadelphia *Inquirer* added, they were "penetrated with the Bolshevik idea." [29] Sharing the underlying bias, many labor leaders could only answer weakly, as Gompers did, that the steel companies, having imported the aliens, were reaping what they had sown.

Reports from strike centers fed the fears of revolution. RIOT-ING SPREADS IN STRIKE, MANY SHOT — TWO DEAD, screamed characteristic headlines early in the strike. The climax came during the reportedly bloody riots at Gary. That the strike was in fact notably peaceful was irrelevant for the effect on public opinion.[30] The raids on known nests of radicals in Gary netted much Bolshevik literature. Here was proof, stated the Portland *Oregonian,* of "an attempted revolution, not a strike." It signified to the Boston *Evening Transcript* "the extraordinary hold which 'Red' principles have upon the foreign born populations in the steel districts." Colonel Mapes's later admission that there was no connection between the Gary radicals and the strikers did little to erase the popular image of the strike as a dangerous Bolshevik plot.

Privately, steel manufacturers tended to discount talk of revolu-tion. But, in fact, the assumptions of the welfare labor policy made that analysis, stripped of its ideological overtones, the only satis-factory explanation of the strike. Gary's central idea was that "wise, just, considerate treatment . . . toward others will result in reciprocity and cooperation." The steelworkers did not respond properly because the war had "abnormalized" their minds. Then

---

[29] Quoted in *Literary Digest,* October 11, 1919, pp. 11–12.

[30] Robert K. Murray, *Red Scare* (Minneapolis, 1955), pp. 144–149. The *Iron Age,* October 2, 1919, p. A, noted the absence of violence. Afterward, George Smart commented, "It is agreed by all who are familiar with the strike that it was remarkably free from violence, due largely to prohibition." *IA,* August 12, 1920, p. 391. It is significant that Murray concluded that the strike was bloody. His sources included only the public press, from which no other conclusion could have been drawn.

unscrupulous agitators precipitated the strike "by threats, intimidations, and promises of various kinds which appeal to the natural cupidity of uneducated workmen." Unhinged minds, not legitimate grievances, caused the "temporary disorder," or, for the public, Bolshevik strike.

Yet the spectacle of a steel strike of such dimensions — even without any revolutionary end — appeared in itself to threaten the established order. Even friends of the strike held this view in the early stages. The *Nation,* for instance, thought it "no mere squabble over wages and hours and collective bargaining and the open shop. . . . The real question is, Who shall control our steel industry?" [31] The more radical press hailed the strike as OPEN CLASS WAR.

Conservative editors and Senators were understandably frightened. Following hard upon the Seattle general strike, the May bombings, and the Boston police strike, it inevitably appeared in the red glare of the Bolshevik Revolution. "Its motive is political," said the New York *Tribune,* "its leaders have mobilized industrial alienism for a disruptive purpose; and its purpose is un-American." The misfortune of the steel strike was its coincidence with the crest of the Red Scare.

The popular view of the strike had two fateful consequences. First, it excluded government intervention. That eventuality had been half expected by both union and steel interests. Gompers' eagerness to comply with Wilson's request for postponement rested largely on his hope for presidential action. Once the strike began, the leaders turned their attention to the President's Industrial Conference scheduled to begin October 7 in Washington. The National Committee urged the labor representatives at the Conference to "use their best efforts to bring about a settlement of the steel strike . . . at the earliest practical date." [32] That, clearly, would require pressure from the administration.

Prevailing public sentiment, together with Wilson's collapse on

[31] "The Revolution — 1919," *Nation,* October 4, 1919, p. 452.

[32] Foster to Gompers, October 7, 1919, in A.F.L. Executive Council Minutes, October 5–22, 1919, p. 15.

September 26, ended the possibility of any form of aid from Washington. Tumulty and Baruch advised neutrality to avoid political embarrassment to the government. Secretary of Labor Wilson hastily rebuffed a suggestion of the National Committee to reëstablish the War Labor Board for the strike. Leading figures of the administration, in fact, openly supported the employers, and the activities of the Justice Department materially damaged the strikers' cause. "We did not expect much consideration from any government agency," Fitzpatrick said bitterly later in the strike, "for the reason that the steel trust has dominated the government." [33] Public support, the vital ingredient in the wartime successes, was totally absent in 1919.

The second result of national hysteria was to give the steel manufacturers complete freedom of action in the strike. The efforts at mediation, for instance, first in the Industrial Conference and later by the Interchurch World Movement, were easily brushed aside. Immediately after leaving the Judge's offices, Bishop Francis J. McConnell dictated his impressions of the interview in which he had urged mediation.

> Mr. Gary insisted that the point of issue was not now unionism as such, but whether the American Government should be supported and American institutions be upheld. . . . The whole movement of the steel strike was a movement of red radicals. . . . The only outcome of the victory for unionism would be Sovietism in the U.S. "and the forceable distribution of property." [34]

The identical reasoning could justify every tactic against the strikers. Concerning the settlement of the strike, Judge Gary had an easy answer: "See to it that in no place are the laws violated [and] the employees, who are the ones interested, will settle this question for themselves." [35] His irony, no doubt unintended, was monumental.

[33] *New Majority*, November 1, 1919.
[34] *Public Opinion and the Strike*, p. 336; National Committee Minutes, December 13, 1919, p. 93.
[35] *Strike Investigation*, I, 217.

The outcome of the strike, both sides recognized, would turn on the Pittsburgh district. The steel companies meant to break the strike there at all costs. Feverish preparations preceded September 22. Sheriff W. S. Haddock deputized 5,000 employees of the Steel Corporation "upon whom they can depend to remain at work . . . to protect themselves and others who refuse to strike." The towns likewise pressed into service veterans and tradesmen. State constabulary were stationed at commanding points throughout the district. Armed, newly uniformed men guarded the mills, and, so union officials claimed, machine guns covered the entrances. "It is as though preparations were made for actual war," observed the New York *World*.

The hard-won fruits of the free speech fight were immediately canceled. Two days before the strike Sheriff Haddock in a remarkable proclamation prohibited outdoor meetings anywhere in Allegheny County. On Sunday afternoon state troopers rode down a peaceful gathering in Clairton, wielding their clubs and arresting many for "inciting to riot." Glassport, adjoining McKeesport, witnessed a repetition on Monday. Both meetings had received local approval. Some towns, including Braddock and Homestead, permitted closely regulated indoor meetings for a time. In Pittsburgh the Labor Temple and a small North Side hall were approved for gatherings, but both were inconveniently distant from the strike zone. Elsewhere, town officials prohibited indoor meetings, in some instances even for the business sessions of union locals. McKeesport police forbade the congregation of more than six strikers in their own headquarters.[36] The steelworkers of western Pennsylvania were effectively isolated.

They were, in addition, thoroughly intimidated. The Pennsylvania constabulary — known to the strikers as "Cossacks" — set the pace in most localities. They clubbed men and women off the streets, dragged strikers from their homes, abused and jailed them

---

[36] *Public Opinion and the Strike*, pp. 183–185, 201, and *passim*, ch. 3; S. A. Shaw, "Closed Towns," *Survey*, November 8, 1919, pp. 59–62; Pittsburgh *Gazette-Times*, September 21, 1919; *AJ*, October 9, 1919, p. 8, November 27, 1919, p. 6.

on flimsy charges. Deputized guards of the companies did the brutal work at Newcastle. Here one hundred strikers were arrested during the first week for "carrying concealed weapons, disorderly conduct, and suspicion." Bail was fixed at from $1,000 to $1,500 except for a number held on suspicion. These, vowed the police chief, would be incarcerated for the strike duration, even if he "had to build a new jail to house them." At Monessen men were merely terrorized, but where mills were partially operating, large numbers were hauled into jail and fined. Usually, a promise to return to work sufficed to free a man. Hundreds of sworn statements testified to the effectiveness of the state troopers, deputies, and local functionaries.[37]

The strike leaders were dismayed. "Unless this course can be checked very shortly and these indispensable rights re-established," Foster warned Gompers in early October, "the favorable outcome of the strike will be greatly endangered." The efforts of the A.F.L., however, were unavailing.[38] The suppression of civil rights continued until the end of the struggle.

The strike was never fully broken in the Pittsburgh district. But the strategy of terrorism succeeded well enough, for western Pennsylvania continued to turn out steel. Taken together with the East and South (in both areas October production exceeded August), the total output was sufficient to enable the manufacturers to wait out the strike elsewhere. After a month the *Iron Age* estimated the national production at 60 per cent of normal. At that level, the strike was doomed.[39] But it would not be an easy job to wear down the enthusiasm of men (as one Elwood, Indiana, striker wrote) "standing shoulder to shoulder, fighting for a share of the profits of reconstruction and pulling down the

[37] H. M. Vorse, "Civil Liberties in the Steel Strike," *Nation*, November 15, 1919, pp. 833–835; *Strike Investigation*, various testimonies; *Public Opinion and the Strike*, ch. 3; Foster, *Steel Strike*, ch. 8; *AJ*, October 2, 1919, p. 1, October 9, 1919, pp. 8, 9, October 16, 1919, p. 9.

[38] Foster to Gompers, October 7, 1919, in A.F.L. Executive Council Minutes, October 5–22, 1919, p. 15, and pp. 16, 75, on A.F.L. efforts.

[39] *IA*, October 23, 1919, p. A. *IA*, December 4, 1919, p. 1146, gives production by districts and months from August to December 1919.

cloud of democracy that it might sail through the ranks of labor." [40] The industry bent itself to the task.

Repression was not common outside the Pittsburgh district. Steelworkers met, paraded, and picketed without interference or assault. Mayor Davis of Cleveland actually prohibited the importation of strikebreakers. As the strike dragged on, however, local impatience mounted. At Johnstown a mob of respectable citizens headed by the secretary of the Y.M.C.A. forced the departure of Foster and the local organizers in early November. Soon after, petitions began to circulate in Youngstown against the strike leaders; the mayor prohibited meetings, "the object of which is the discussion of matters pertaining to prolonging the strike"; and numbers of union men were arrested.[41] But, outside the Pittsburgh district interference did not materially alter the course of the strike.

Gary, Indiana, was the important exception. After two calm weeks, rioting broke out, provoked, according to strike leaders, by special police and strikebreakers. The fighting was never serious. "Believe nothing," an organizer reported. "A few thrown from a street car was the sum trouble. . . . All quiet as usual despite reports." The situation, however, seemed desperate to the mayor. At his request, a division of Army regulars under General Leonard Wood arrived on October 6, and Gary assumed the appearance of an occupied city. Martial law was declared, outdoor meetings prohibited, strike leaders and pickets arrested and put to work splitting wood and sweeping streets across from the city hall. Union men charged that mill officials used the soldiers to frighten immigrant strikers back to work. In any case, military restrictions strangled the strike, and by early November the Gary ranks were breaking. State militia, leaving Gary on the arrival of the federal troops, accomplished the same results in nearby

[40] *AJ*, October 2, 1919, p. 18.
[41] Youngstown *Vindicator*, November 24, 1919; *New Majority*, November 22, 1919; *IA*, November 27, 1919, p. 1093; *AJ*, November 27, 1919, p. 6.

Indiana Harbor.[42] The collapse of these strongpoints was a critical defeat for the unions.

Nothing mattered more than the morale of the steelworkers, lacking as they did trade union discipline and strike benefits. When they would fear the strike lost, it would indeed be lost. The steel companies enjoyed crucial advantages here. Their claims dominated the strike coverage of the local press. MORE MEN RETURNING TO MILLS, announced the Pittsburgh *Gazette-Times* on September 24. The more sanguine *Leader* on the same day ran a banner headline: PITTSBURGH MILLS RUNNING FULL. Throughout the early weeks full-page multi-language advertisements in the Pittsburgh papers proclaimed, THE STRIKE HAS FAILED; GO BACK TO WORK. The coverage in Cleveland, however, was fair, especially in the *Plain Dealer*.[43]

The news situation was uniformly bad in the mill towns. In mid-October, at the height of the strike, the Joliet *News Herald* claimed that the struggle was over everywhere but in the Chicago district. Joliet was simply acting the goat in the strike and would lose its mills as a result. The Donora *Evening Herald* carried a full page advertisement comparing the bleak Christmas ahead with the September promises of the strike leaders.

Now who is going to buy your Christmas Dinner?

. . . .

Have these leaders redeemed any of their promises?
Have any of them come true? Have you been paid benefits?
Has your family been clothed and fed?

[42] Quillen, "Gary," pp. 356–370; *AJ*, October 9, 1919, p. 9; G. Taylor, "At Gary," *Survey*, November 8, 1919, pp. 65–66. For A.F.L. efforts to persuade the government to withdraw the troops from Gary, see Executive Council Minutes, November 9–12, 1919, pp. 13–14.

[43] There are numerous clippings from the Cleveland press on the strike in Scrapbook, Vol. 18, American Steel and Wire Collection.

The page ended: "Go Back To Work Monday, Make Your Family Happy."[44]

Only inadequate means were at hand to combat "this defeatism." The National Committee bulletins told strikers, "Pay no attention to the lying statements in the press. . . . Now is the time to win our great victory. We cannot lose if we will but stick together." Many letters in the *Amalgamated Journal* warned readers to ignore false claims of the opening of local mills. At Wheeling the trade unions urged their members to cancel their newspaper subscriptions. At some points — in Youngstown, Cleveland, and Chicago — the reports of the National Committee found space in at least part of the press; elsewhere, the strikers were, as one Johnstown man complained, "up against it for news." Prohibited from meeting together and without a single dependable public or labor newspaper, the strikers of western Pennsylvania lived in ignorance of the actual course of the strike.

There were other ways to demoralize the steelworkers. Committees of loyal men sent out by company supporters brought back to the strikers of Wheeling and Steubenville false reports of almost normal production elsewhere. The army of undercover agents spread its quiet story of defeat. Nothing weakened the resolve of weary strikers more, the steel companies well knew, than the sight of smoke rising from the mills and the sound of whistles announcing the change of the shift. It was worth the expense and waste to make a start with strikebreakers.[45]

In late October numbers of Negroes began appearing in steel centers. They swiftly became an alarming threat to the strike. Chicago leaders reported that it hurt the "morale of the white men to see blacks crowding into the mills to take their jobs." Mexicans were shipped into Pueblo and Chicago. According to National Committee estimates, 3,500 Negroes were brought into

[44] Donora *Evening Herald,* December 6, 1919, clipping, *ibid.*

[45] Of course, steelworkers often were not taken in by appearances. They knew the difficulties of running with inexperienced men. In many cases, the number of cars entering and departing was used as a gauge of successful operation. In Johnstown the plant whistle was known derisively as "The Call of the Last Hope."

Homestead, 2,000 into Buffalo, and 5,000 into Youngstown; altogether, the industry received between 30,000 and 40,000. In despair, the National Committee requested Gompers to call together Negro leaders for a conference, but nothing came of it. "Niggers did it," company officials were heard to remark of the strike failure afterward.[46]

Strikers consoled themselves that the inexperienced Negroes did more harm than good in the mills. Skilled steelworkers were another story. Many workmen, union and nonunion, took jobs for the strike duration in other districts to avoid the dreaded reputation of "scab." A Sparrows Point striker complained of the difficulty of getting back jobs "which them rats from Weirton and McKeesport have stolen from us." The practice was especially damaging in the Youngstown district.[47]

The varied attacks on morale had their effect. After the sixth week confidence began to wane perceptibly.

The twenty-four cooperating unions contributed their share to defeat. Their representatives appeared before the Executive Council of the A.F.L. on October 6 to request aid. Amalgamated President M. F. Tighe asserted that "if the strike was lost by lack of support on the part of the Federation as a whole, it would reflect against the Federation." Gompers thereupon asked how much the Amalgamated planned to contribute to the strike fund. Tighe, evidently taken aback, replied that he was unprepared to say, that only 5,000 members were at work. A poll of the other union representatives revealed similar reluctance. In the end, the twenty-four unions agreed to put up $100,000 on the same pro-rata basis used to cover the expenses of the National Committee.

[46] National Committee Minutes, November 24, 1919, pp. 133–136; J. F. Blackwell to Gompers, October 31, 1919, Gompers Papers; *New Majority,* July 3, 1920, reprints National Committee Report on Negroes; *Negro in Chicago,* pp. 364, 394, 428–430; Paul S. Taylor, *Mexican Labor in the United States: Chicago and the Calumet Region* (Berkeley, California, 1932), pp. 117–118, 182.

[47] *AJ,* December 11, 1919, p. 10, January 15, 1920, p. 16; Foster, *Steel Strike,* p. 176; National Committee Minutes, November 24, 1919, p. 131.

And the Federation issued a call for contributions from the rest of organized labor.[48]

The bulk of the $418,000 eventually raised for the commissary fund came as a result of the A.F.L. appeal, very little from the treasuries of the involved unions, although some of these provided benefits for their own members. The Amalgamated Clothing Workers, not an A.F.L. affiliate, alone donated $100,000.[49] Outside contributions, plus the dues of the steelworkers, made the strike practically self-supporting. The Amalgamated Association, in fact, emerged with a handsome profit. The heavy investment of both money and men needed to carry the strike was never forthcoming.

Most of the cooperating unions felt the strike insufficiently important to their interests to warrant sacrifices. Exactly opposite logic led the Amalgamated Association to the same conclusion. "The Amalgamated Association was the basic organization of the iron and steel industry," President Tighe explained afterward. "Its very life depended on maintaining that position; if it lost that it had no other to fall back on."[50] Therefore, it had to proceed with utmost caution. Its counsels were unfailingly fainthearted. Nowhere were Tighe's "determined efforts to protect our organization" more damaging than in the contracts controversy.

On September 22, many Amalgamated mills were shut down. The skilled men were clearly violating the contract. Even worse, so were the new union members. The agreements contained a clause covering men who came into the Association during the contract year — and that meant all the unskilled and semiskilled workers. The union could present a scale for them, but if the companies rejected it, as they invariably did, the recruits could not strike until the expiration of the contract. That is, the men were ruled by an agreement to which they had not been parties. Under increasing pressure, the Amalgamated Association

[48] A.F.L. Executive Council Minutes, October 5–22, 1919, pp. 8–11, 15–16, 77.

[49] Secretary's Report, A.F.L. Executive Council Minutes, December 11–18, 1919, p. 4; Foster, *Steel Strike,* pp. 220–222, 228–236.

[50] *NLT,* May 20, 1920.

in early November ordered all its members in the contract mills back to work, whether covered by scales or not. The agreements would be honored "at whatever cost."

The result was disastrous. Within the National Committee angry friction was generated. Its officers, said Tighe afterward, were "mere carpet baggers . . . determined to do as they pleased irrespective of what the consequences might be to our organization in the final outcome." In the field, the order's effect was even worse. Rebellious lodges lost their charters; obedient ones faced the jeers of the strikers. The district official at Youngstown, J. E. McCadden, labeled as deserters all union men who returned to work. The local representatives of the National Committee everywhere fought the order. An Amalgamated organizer reported "a great deal of dissatisfaction" over the policy among the members, and a widespread desire to "disregard their pledge to this organization." The *Iron Age* believed that the clause governing new members "broke the strike in every plant in the [Youngstown] district with which the Amalgamated had a contract." [51]

Internal squabbling broke into the open at other points. H. S. Comerford of the Steam and Operating Engineers, bitter over the jurisdictional dispute with the Electrical Workers, stated publicly that the officials of the National Committee had lost the sympathy of organized labor. The National Committee appealed on December 15 to the A.F.L., but the Executive Council voted to defer action.[52] Enough suspicion and uncertainty had developed by then to immobilize the union leadership.

Organized labor failed the steelworkers. The fault was in part structural. Voluntary, concerted effort by autonomous internationals proved a weak substitute for industrial unionism in the

[51] *Strike Investigation*, II, 632–661, reprints an Amalgamated contract; *IA*, February 5, 1920, p. 415; *AJ*, November 20, 1919, pp. 1, 16, December 18, 1919, p. 1; National Committee Minutes, November 13, 1919, p. 104.

[52] Foster to Frank Morrison, December 15, 1919, in A.F.L. Executive Council Minutes, December 11–18, 1919, p. 9. On the unsuccessful efforts to persuade the Brotherhood of Railway Trainmen to call a strike on the switching lines of the steel mills in the Pittsburgh district, see Foster, *Steel Strike*, pp. 163–165; National Committee Minutes, September 24, 1919, pp. 119–120.

steel industry. The conflicts of authority and interest might have been overcome with imagination and courage. These qualities, however, the labor leaders did not possess in sufficient abundance.

The course of the struggle followed the economic and ethnic geography of the steel towns. As always, the commercial interests aligned themselves with the steel companies. In some places the strength of the unions won the strikers sizable local support until the waning weeks. But the businessmen ordinarily were, as the historians of the Pueblo strike wrote, "of course . . . against us from start to finish." The respectable elements were, in theory, "entirely disinterested" in disputes between labor and management. They usually supported the company unobtrusively, in the name of law and order, or local prosperity. But this was no ordinary strike.

In Indiana, for instance, those "who are for Gary from the ground up" revived the Loyal American League of the war days to protect the city from the "Red Menace." "There is such a thing as Americanism," the League announced in the Gary *Tribune,* "and it is involved, it seems, in this strike." The American "is not going to desert it for the imported theories represented by Mr. Foster and Mr. Fitzpatrick . . . revolution by paralysis of industry." The League was "determined that talk of the 'power' of these agitators shall cease — even if it is necessary to demonstrate how weak they are." The arrival of Army units relieved them of that patriotic duty.[53]

This excited view justified violence, Citizens' Protective Leagues, restrictions on civil liberties, and refusal of credit to strikers. Right was clearly on management's side.

The conservative elements thereby also had the means to draw the English-speaking steelworkers away from the strike, "Workingmen — defend your rights against being coerced by *radical agitators* . . . into making trouble for yourself, your family and the community," urged a pamphlet of the McKeesport Chamber

[53] Gary *Tribune,* September 15, 19, 29, 1919; Quillen, pp. 348–350.

of Commerce. The President of the Allegheny Valley Chamber of Commerce appealed to the men "to remain at work as loyal Americans." Simultaneously, a wedge was driven between the native and immigrant steelworkers. In one steel town, a circular announced:

WAKE UP AMERICANS!!

Italian Laborers, organized under the American Federation of Labor are going to strike Monday and are threatening workmen who want to continue working.

These foreigners have been told by labor agitators that if they would join the union they would get Americans' jobs.

The *Gary Works Circle* printed Edgar Guest's poem, "Dan M'Gann Declares Himself." Dan tells a "foreign man" working at the next bench, "I stand for America. I'm done with your fads, and your wild-eyed lads. Don't flourish your rag o' red. . . . I'm boostin' for Uncle Sam." The local press was filled with talk of the radical and alien character of the strike. In the mill towns, as elsewhere, the issue was "Americanism vs. Bolshevism." [54]

The propaganda was not wasted. One striker urged members to attend a forthcoming meeting at Catasauqua, Pennsylvania, "and see if Mr. Foster is as bad as the paper says." A local official in Steubenville, Ohio, confessed to Gompers: "the men as a whole say they will not follow Foster but will follow the leader of the A.F.L., Gompers." A New Kensington, Pennsylvania, workman wrote contemptuously: "Have you heard it — that great piece of rotten trickery that the employer is using? No man can be a loyal American unless he is a scab." Reporting a company notice calling Americans back to work, a Mingo Junction man asked, "Does this mean that only men of foreign birth are loyal union men . . . and the Americans are . . . willing to be classed as

---

[54] *Gary Works Circle*, August–September, 1919; Pittsburgh *Gazette-Times*, September 20, 21, 23, 1919; *IA*, September 4, 1919, p. 641; *NLT*, October 2, 1919; *AJ*, September 18, 1919, p. 8; Foster, *Steel Strike*, p. 199.

strikebreakers when the U.S. Steel Corporation hands them a little 'bull' about being loyal Americans?" [55] That, it seemed, was very largely the case.

Observers on both sides agreed that few "Americans" had struck in the Monongahela Valley. Then and afterward skilled Pittsburgh steelworkers told investigators that they had neither been approached nor knew the reasons for the strike. They considered it a "Hunky" affair. Elsewhere, the weaknesses of the skilled ranks appeared later. Cleveland officials reported the beginning of desertions in early November, "and strange to say these have been among the American workers." Several weeks later, the National Committee found the Johnstown skilled men "showing anything but a good union spirit, they being the first to develop a weakness." [56] In Cleveland, Pueblo, and Bethlehem, however, the higher paid men were notably strong strikers.

Urged on by tradesmen and company officials, a nucleus in most mill towns formed "Back To Work" movements. At Pueblo, for instance, such an organization began in October. By mid-November the patternmakers, bricklayers, and a few rod mill men were at work. The rest of the rod men defected after a time, followed by the "select organization" of roll turners, who handed in their Amalgamated charter. Less than 100 men returned before the official end of the strike, but they were all skilled. The pattern was repeated with greater effect on the strike in other mills.

In contrast, the National Committee noted, the immigrant workmen "are proving to have wonderful powers of resistance." A striker from Berwick, Pennsylvania, wrote in admiration: "We certainly must hand it to the foreign element. They certainly stick to their obligations. If the American brothers would

[55] C. Hinkle to Gompers, December 4, 1919, Gompers Papers; *AJ*, October 2, 1919, p. 4, October 16, 1919, p. 26, November 20, 1919, p. 25.

[56] Saposs Interviews, *passim; Strike Investigation*, I, 286, 359, II, 481–482, 516; *AJ*, November 13, 1919, p. 8; National Committee Minutes, November 24, 1919, p. 132. See also Fitzpatrick's reports in Chicago Federation of Labor Minutes, November 16, December 7, 1919, *New Majority*, November 22, December 13, 1919.

have struck like the foreign brothers we would have won this fight long ago." The peasant sense of community held the immigrants together. And the war experience gave them a cause. A Polish striker expressed the common feeling at a Pittsburgh meeting.

> For why this war? For why we buy Liberty Bonds? For mills? No, for freedom and America — for everybody. No more [work like] horse and wagon. For eight-hour day.[57]

After several months of field investigation during the strike, David Saposs concluded that only those expecting to return to Europe remained at work. Not even the disapproval of their leaders — the benefit society officials, the editors, and most of the priests — could sway the immigrants.[58]

The war years, on the other hand, had made the English-speaking men susceptible to antiradical, nativist appeals. They felt, moreover, closer kinship to the respectable elements than to the immigrants. Many strikers who returned to work, said one bitter unionist, "called themselves good loyal Americans." They had, in addition, strong practical reasons. Many feared to jeopardize well-paying jobs and the good opinions of the bosses. A Joliet striker thought some returned because they had habitually spent all their earnings to keep up with their neighbors. When the strike came, they quickly ran out of money and preferred breaking the strike to lowering their living standard.[59] In any event, the skilled steelworkers were the soft flank in the strikers' ranks.

[57] National Committee Minutes, November 24, 1919, p. 132; *AJ*, December 15, 1919, p. 14, also, October 16, 1919, p. 1, giving National Committee Report, October 9, 1919; Foster, *Steel Strike*, pp. 200–205; *Survey*, November 8, 1919, p. 91.

[58] D. J. Saposs, "The Mind of the Immigrant Communities," *Public Opinion and the Strike*, pp. 235–239.

[59] *AJ*, January 15, 1920, p. 29, December 18, 1919, p. 6; J. Dunbar, letter to the editor, Pittsburgh *Gazette-Times*, September 20, 1919; and testimony of loyal workers in *Strike Investigation*.

Company repression, weakening morale, strikebreakers, union hesitancy, patriotic propaganda, all had their effect on the steelworkers. Meanwhile, winter was approaching and savings were dwindling. The strike began to falter significantly in the sixth week. The Chicago district collapsed first. By November 21 the mills had 75 per cent of their work force in Gary, 85 per cent in Indiana Harbor, and 80 per cent in South Chicago. Johnstown, Youngstown, and Wheeling weakened next. The National Committee, meeting on December 13, estimated that 109,300 men were still out. Over the protests of the Amalgamated Association, the Committee voted to continue the strike. It was, scoffed the *Iron Age,* "the last gasp of a dying cause."

The springs of resistance slowly unwound. Soon the strike remained effective only in Pueblo, Lackawanna, Joliet, and scattered mills in the Pittsburgh and Cleveland districts. On January 8, 1920 the National Committee announced that the steel companies had by "arbitrary and ruthless misuse of power" crushed the steelworkers. The great steel strike was ended.

Chapter XIII

Restoration

The strike left in its wake hatred and dislocation. The steelworkers suffered the humiliations of defeat. At Pueblo they were required to take physical examinations, receive the recommendation of the "Austrian" priest, and sign a pink card pledging "to cooperate in maintaining the laws and agreements relating to my service and the laws of my state and country." The Vandergrift superintendent, like most managers, refused to arrange for the return to work through the strikers' committee. The men would have to apply individually. "We who worked on the sheet floor might have to remove ashes from the furnace pits or work out in the pickling department," worried one union man.[1] Frequently no work was available for active strikers.

Some steelworkers remained defiant. A number did not try to claim former jobs. A Sharon, Pennsylvania, correspondent reported that most of his lodge brothers were working in union mills, as track repairmen, or in the coal mines. "I judge that there will be very few of us going back in the near future." The resulting shortage of experienced men hindered operations considerably for a time.

During the weeks following the strike, men sensed "a great feeling of discontent existing among the workers." At isolated points, the strike dragged on for a short time. Pueblo leaders had to plead for several hours to persuade the men to obey the order ending the strike. Elsewhere, the organizations remained intact,

[1] *AJ*, January 15, 1920, p. 3. The steelworkers' statements in the following discussion come from their letters in the *Amalgamated Journal*, unless otherwise stated in the footnotes, and will not be individually cited.

and men spoke of the next round. Many strikers returned, as a Sharon workman said, with "the satisfaction of an honorable part and bright contemplation of facing the future with erect head."

But more entered the mills suspicious and fearful. "Mill notes are scarce to get," wrote a correspondent from Lebanon, Pennsylvania. "Most of the men that are working at the plants are afraid to talk." David Saposs and a team of interviewers, working through the summer of 1920, found an uneasy calm in the mill towns. The strength of the companies, steelworkers repeatedly told them, was too great. Said a heater in the U.S. Steel tin mill in McKeesport, for instance: "It is useless to strike or fight the big corporations. They have the constabulary, the courts, the state government and the city government on their side." Hopelessness bred apathy.[2]

For their part, the steel companies, having rooted out the agitators, were eager to restore good feelings. "The tube department is a nice place to work since the strike," a Benwood, West Virginia, workman wrote. "The men are getting treated a little better now." Similar reports came from elsewhere. When eastern mills announced a 10 per cent increase for February 1, 1920, the Pueblo management agreed to send three workmen along with the company official to ascertain the detailed rates. For the first time, the employee representation plan seemed to have some effect.[3]

In addition to the pay raise, the spring of 1920 saw a flurry of welfare efforts. Carnegie, Bethlehem, Youngstown, and Inland Steel companies announced expanded home building programs. The American Bridge Company, among others, formed cooperative clubs to counter the high living costs. Some firms bought big lots of food to sell at wholesale prices to their employees. Bethlehem set up a new savings plan. Government securities were sold at cost to employees, who paid in weekly installments while the interest was accruing to them. Youngstown Sheet and Tube and

[2] Saposs Interviews, on N. Soho St., McKeesport, July 19, 1920, and other interviews, and report of Bertha T. Saposs.

[3] Selekman, *Employes' Representation*, pp. 90-93.

other Mahoning Valley companies introduced stock purchase plans for the first time.

Finally, business conditions contributed a calming influence. A sharp decline hit the steel industry. By February 1921 unemployment was widespread, and continued so for the rest of the year. As always, hard times had a sobering effect (which employers were quick to mark). When prosperity returned in 1922, the steelworkers had come around to the frame of mind of 1914. The steel industry was again at peace.

The sources of labor stability had broken down in the World War. Now the rebuilding processes began. The restoration was remarkably complete. The twenties witnessed a total reconstruction of the prewar labor situation.

The central problem was to start another free-flow supply of unskilled labor. At first, the regular European immigration seemed an easy solution. The movement of Slavic peasants into the industry was just approaching its earlier level, however, when the Johnson Act went into effect in 1921. Depressed conditions for a time obscured the consequences. But at the return of prosperity, quota restrictions pinched off the customary rush of immigrants. By the summer of 1922, with the mills not yet nearing full operation, the scarcity of common labor was acute. Steel men immediately set up a cry.

Unfortunately, they had been instrumental in convincing the country of the undesirability of the Eastern European. Their embarrassment led to strange arguments. "Steel wants and must have the foreigner," reasoned one writer. "Steel is ready and willing to deal with the strike question among the foreigners. Then why not . . . let steel have its labor and at the same time hold steel responsible for . . . its imported product?" [4] Most steelmakers argued more sensibly for a "selective" policy, "sufficiently flexible to supply industry." It was, however, soon clear that Con-

[4] George Walter, "Why Foreigners are Needed in Steel Plants," *IA,* August 9, 1923, pp. 331–332, also, for example, *IA,* January 11, 1923, pp. 163–164.

gress was more concerned with safeguarding American "racial" purity than with the needs of industry. The steel companies were forced to seek their unskilled labor elsewhere.

Southern Negroes had constituted the chief source during the war, and their numbers continued to mount afterward. The census of 1920 showed that they made up 11.4 per cent of the steel labor force in Illinois, 14.2 per cent in Indiana, and 10.9 per cent in Pennsylvania. Their importance grew further after the 1921 depression. The Negro supply did not entirely please the steel men. The president of Inland Steel thought "it would be better for the industry and the country at large if the mills could continue to recruit their forces from [Europe]. The negroes should remain in the South."[5] The migrants were commonly considered inferior workmen. By careful selection, it was possible to cull an efficient force from the mass available on Chicago's State Street. But that course left a still pressing shortage.

Between April 6 and May 30, 1923, nearly a thousand Mexicans arrived at South Bethlehem, Pennsylvania. Trainloads proceeded also to Bethlehem plants at Lackawanna and elsewhere. The Mexicans were recruited through employment agencies in San Antonio, Texas, sent northward in special trains at a cost to be repaid out of future wages, and fed and lodged in company houses at $1.10 a day.[6] The importation of Mexicans in this manner became widespread in the steel industry.

After the initial contingent, the movement usually continued without further company effort and without the need to provide housing. In the Chicago district, where some Mexicans had been employed since the war, their number jumped sharply in 1923. By 1925, they constituted 11.7 per cent of the steel working force in the district. According to the census, the percentage of Negroes in the steel mills did not increase between 1920 and 1930. At three

[5] *IA,* August 9, 1923, p. 333. According to the National Committee, most of the Negro strikebreakers were discharged within a few months. *New Majority,* July 3, 1920.

[6] Paul S. Taylor, *Mexican Labor in the U.S.: Bethlehem, Pennsylvania* (Berkeley, California, 1931), pp. 2 ff.; *IA,* August 2, 1923, p. 285; *Literary Digest,* June 2, 1923, pp. 103–104.

major mills for which statistics are available, the relative percentages of Mexicans and Negroes in the labor force in 1924 — 12.1 and 14.3 — were reversed in 1928 — 14.2 and 11.1.[7] Between the two groups, the industry had developed an adequate unskilled labor supply.

The Mexican and prewar Slavic immigrations were strikingly alike. The peons were mainly young men, single or with wives left at home, and intent on earning money and returning to Mexico. As in the case of the earlier immigrants, their living conditions were makeshift, crowded, and unhealthy. By 1930 permanent Mexican communities were taking root in the mill towns. Increasingly, the womenfolk followed and established humble homes. At the Gary and South works, 19.1 per cent of the Mexican employees by 1928 had advanced into the semiskilled, 1.8 per cent into the skilled ranks. A similar process was occurring among the Negroes: in 1928, 16.2 per cent were semiskilled workers, and 4.7 per cent were skilled.

Meanwhile, the Eastern Europeans were occupying the lesser positions once held by the "English-speaking" workmen. As they rose, the numbers of Slavs in the mills shrank. At one time 58 per cent of Jones and Laughlin labor force, the immigrants comprised only 31 per cent in 1930. There were 30 per cent fewer Eastern Europeans in the Illinois Steel Company mills in 1928 than in 1912. Now largely the immediate bosses of the Negroes and Mexicans, the immigrants disdained their inferiors much as the natives had once disliked them.[8]

The bad feeling generated by the Red Scare abated only gradually. In Gary, the Ku Klux Klan flourished. But the respectable solidity of the immigrant communities in time put to rest unreasoning fear. The children were passing through the schools and into businesses and higher jobs in the mills. Each year the number of homeowners increased, the businesses prospered, and the churches and societies became more substantial. The immigrants

[7] Taylor, *Mexican Labor in Chicago,* pp. 36–37, 46.
[8] See, for example, Taylor, *Mexican Labor in Chicago,* pp. 109–115, and *Mexican Labor in Bethlehem,* pp. 15, 21.

were assuming a middling social and economic position in the steel towns.[9]

Labor mobility was thus perpetuated. There was a free flow in and out of the industry at the unskilled level, and a simultaneous movement upward into the dependent, better-paid jobs for those electing to become permanent industrial workers.

The renewal of the prewar labor pattern relieved the industry of the necessity, despite the experience of 1919, for a reappraisal of its labor policies. So long as mobility existed at the lower levels and dependence among the skilled men, a measure of benevolence would suffice to ensure stability. Welfare work, as it had developed by 1914, remained the cornerstone of the industry's labor program. No new departure emerged in the twenties.

Employee representation, the one added feature, continued to have its adherents. A few steel men were still affected by the wartime fervor. Speaking at an engineers' convention in November 1920, W. B. Dickson of Midvale Steel warned of "a grave menace to our American ideals in the highly civilized, autocratic control . . . in our great industries." He pointed to the "benevolent autocracy" of United States Steel. It practiced "industrial feudalism . . . with a high degree of comfort and safety for the worker, I grant you, but none the less, feudalism." Turning to Samuel Gompers, whom he unexpectedly had found sitting with him on the platform, Dickson added, "lest my position should be misunderstood, I desire to make it clear that in the recent steel strike the course taken by the Steel Corporation had my hearty approval."[10] The limits of idealism were well-marked.

Most proponents of the shop committee, however, were concerned only with its usefulness. The objective was to create good will, said an Armco Steel official, not to take "responsibility for the execution of plans and policies away from . . . management." President J. F. Welborn of the Colorado Fuel and Iron Company, admitting that the plan had not prevented his men

[9] See, for example, Quillen, "Gary," pp. 423 ff.
[10] *IA*, November 11, 1920, pp. 1252–1253.

from striking, insisted that it had eased tensions both before and after the strike. His company was now improving the committees by expanding the role of the representatives and the foremen. Bethlehem Steel found employee representation an effective means of retaining "the helpful cooperation of the employees." "When the crisis came and a reduction in wages was necessary," explained Schwab, "they met it without a ripple of discontent." [11] Despite its ineffectuality in 1919, the representation plan remained popular in the twenties.

Judge Gary was not persuaded. The Steel Corporation found more beneficial its own policy of allowing every employee "access to the office of the foreman or to any other superior, even to the highest." (Gary did not specify the frequency of workers' applications to his office on Broadway.) Most of the schemes, Gary pointed out, had been adopted under stress as a lesser evil than unionization. In principle, "any plan which seeks to deprive the investor of the control of his property and business is inimical to the fundamental ideas of our country and to the public welfare." It followed, therefore, that "the only proper way to give an employee a connection with the management of the affairs of the Corporation is through a stockholding interest." The stock purchase plan became a sop to opinion in favor of industrial democracy.[12]

Until his death in 1927, his influence undiminished, Judge Gary held to his welfare labor views: "You must be unselfish, reasonable, fair, sincere, and honest. You should, without interruption, give evidence of a disposition to conciliate and cooperate." [13] Yet, for all the publicity and reiteration, the Gary philosophy never became more than a veneer on the hard calculus of steelmaking. It was noteworthy, for example, that the depres-

[11] *IA*, January 29, 1920, pp. 351–352, November 10, 1921, p. 1207, June 14, 1923, pp. 1689–1697; Selekman, ch. 10; J. A. Fitch, "Rockefeller Plan," *Survey*, March 15, 1925, pp. 742–744; *They Told Barron*, pp. 82–83.
[12] "Principles and Policies of U.S. Steel," Stockholders' Meeting, April 18, 1921, pp. 20–22.
[13] Steel Institute, *Yearbook* (1920), p. 18.

sions of 1913–14 and 1921 noticeably diminished the popularity of expensive welfare programs among steel manufacturers.

Again, Gary's policy of wage maintenance did not survive the sharp postwar depression. The Eastern companies slashed their rates 20 per cent immediately, followed by the other independents in February 1921. The Steel Corporation resisted until May. Having yielded then, U.S. Steel made further cuts without hesitation, although always after the independents. Extra pay for over eight hours was abolished in late July; on August 31 the hourly rate of common labor was further lowered from 37 to 30 cents. The reductions were uncommonly severe. While steel wages dropped 50.2 per cent, rates in the automobile industry slipped only 7.2 per cent and 17.6 per cent in railroad car building. As for Judge Gary, he was observing philosophically that, although he still wanted "to be fair and reasonable," wages depended, like the cost of any commodity, on "the willingness of the man to work at a certain price." [14] Meanwhile dividends continued without interruption.

The fundamental unconcern for the workingman's interests was clearest in the excessive schedule. According to a Labor Department report, the twelve-hour day was roughly as prevalent in 1920 as in 1910. A seven-day week was still worked by one-quarter of the men in blast furnace, Bessemer, and open-hearth departments. U.S. Steel and a number of independents had, it was true, again abolished this practice. Even so, there were frequent infractions, and, of course, many men could — and did — work overtime without being on a formal seven-day schedule. As before the war, the goad to progress would have to come from outside the industry.

The memory of editors and public figures had proved short indeed in 1919. Few had recalled, in condemning the strike as a radical outburst, their earlier agitation for improved labor condi-

[14] Stockholders' Meeting, April 16, 1923, p. 7. Labor Department figures showed for steel an average hourly rate of 30.1 cents in 1913, 74.5 in 1920, 51.3 in 1922. *Monthly Labor Review,* May 1927, pp. 164–165.

tions. Judge Gary was able to observe comfortably on May 28, 1920, "The majority of the people of this country are tired of petty animosities. . . . They are disgusted with muckraking." Two months later to the day, the Commission of Inquiry of the Interchurch World Movement, a recently formed organization of American Protestant churches, released to the press the results of its investigation of the steel strike.

The report caused an immediate sensation, refuting as it did the popular view of the strike with an impressive array of facts. The grievances that preceded the strike were detailed, the causes for its failure analyzed, and extensive recommendations advanced. The report, judged the New York *World,* received more press attention than any similar investigation in fifty years. The Commission itself estimated that 2,000 columns were devoted to it in most of the newspapers and periodicals across the country. An analysis of hundreds of newspaper clippings showed a heavily favorable reaction.

The response to the Interchurch report was channeled into one mighty chorus of denunciation of the long hours of labor. The revelations on strikebreaking methods did not make a lasting impression, even after the Commission of Inquiry released its later report covering these matters in shocking detail. And the Wilson administration rebuffed suggestions for an investigation of civil liberties in western Pennsylvania and for a special federal agency to establish a "conference" relationship in the industry. But the information on the twelve-hour day, deepened in the following months by further investigations of engineers and economists and by comparisons with the eight-hour day in European steel industries, had a great impact. Concerning its work schedule, the American industry thereafter had no rest.

A minority of trade, financial, and public papers (including the New York *Times*) followed the well-publicized response of the *Iron Age* that the religious leaders of the Interchurch Movement, personally well-meaning men, had been duped by the "socialistically inclined employees of the commission [who] were very closely connected with Foster, if indeed he did not direct their movements." That might account for the sympathetic treatment of the strikers, but the exposure of long working hours could not thus be explained away. That section, as observed among many others the New York *Tribune,* was such as to require the Steel Corporation either to "refute the charges or change its policies." [15]

The industry perforce was silent; it had no effective defense. Judge Gary escaped to Europe within a few days without a word. Late in the year, the Steel Corporation distributed as a kind of indirect reply many thousands of copies of a pamphlet by a New England clergyman, E. Victor Bigelow, who objected to the Interchurch report chiefly because it assumed "the hobo's doctrine" of "reducing 'hours of labor to the lowest practicable point.'" "How could it ever be advocated by a confessed follower of the ceaseless Toiler of Galilee?" the Reverend Bigelow asked.[16] His piety, however, did little to quiet misgivings over the twelve-hour day.

Under continuing pressure, Judge Gary finally moved to appoint a committee of subsidiary presidents. In May 1921 he reported as the outcome an "expectation of making the elimination of the twelve hour day during the coming year." Many companies went on three shifts during the depressed months to spread the work. But the very intensity of the depression distracted attention from long hours, and the sharp wage cuts made the income for one-third less hours seem impossibly low. Judge Gary's intention to end the twelve-hour day quietly expired in the later stages of the depression. When prosperity returned, accompanied

[15] *IA,* July 29, 1920, pp. 272–273, September 9, 1920, pp. 664, 687–688; New York *Times,* July 31, August 22, 1920; New York *Tribune,* July 29, 1920; *Literary Digest,* August 7, 1920, pp. 26–36, September 4, 1920, pp. 40–41. The *Report on the Steel Strike of 1919* has evident deficiencies, particularly in its discussion of wages and hours. See Marshall Olds, *Analysis of the Interchurch World Movement Report on the Steel Strike* (New York, 1923), which is a defense of the industry. Used carefully, however, the *Report* and the later volume, *Public Opinion and the Steel Strike,* provide a wealth of information on the strike.

[16] E. V. Bigelow, *Mistakes of Interchurch Steel Report* (November 22, 1920).

by a growing labor shortage, the long day seemed as firmly entrenched as ever.

Then, in late May 1922 President Harding asked forty-one leading steel men to dinner. Gary for the benefit of the uninvited afterward described the "very simple, homelike and frank" meeting. The President had noted "a well-defined sentiment against the twelve-hour day. He knew it would be difficult to make this important change except by concerted action of all the industry. . . . He did not intend to insist unduly, but if he could be helpful in bringing about the abolition of the twelve-hour day, it would be very pleasing to him." The steel men could do no less than promise to consider this request, coming as it did from the august heights and unanimously applauded as it was in the press.[17] At the Steel Institute meeting a few days afterward an investigating committee was appointed.

The committee lengthened its deliberations over an entire year. Finally, Judge Gary read its report at the May 1923 meeting of the Steel Institute. Obviously tense, he tired after an hour devoted largely to reflections on his recent trip to the Holy Land. Schwab, who was sitting in the first row, had to finish his speech. The committee doubted that the twelve-hour day injured the steelworkers, was opposed by them, or kept them from their families any more than did the diversions of men with shorter work days. The change, moreover, would increase costs 15 per cent and require 60,000 unobtainable men. The decision was not final, Gary's speech emphasized, but for the present reform was deferred. The Steel Institute accepted the report without discussion.

Not so the rest of the country. A wrathful storm broke on the heads of the steel men. The industry had hardly a defender outside the trade and financial journals. Men who had "assumed that the appointment of an investigating committee a year ago meant that the industry was going to yield" took the rejection as an outright betrayal. The New York *World* reflected the general feeling in its Rollin Kirby cartoon depicting obviously exhausted men

<hr />

[17] *IA*, June 1, 1922, pp. 1491–1492; *Literary Digest*, June 3, 1922, pp. 14–15.

leaving a U.S. Steel mill, and, underneath, Gary's remark: "The workmen prefer the longer hours." The Federal Council of Churches, the National Catholic Welfare Council, and the Central Council of American Rabbis jointly condemned the "unworthy and untenable" report and demanded "that this morally indefensible regime of the twelve-hour day must come to an end." [18]

When Harding wrote to Gary on June 18 of his disappointment, the Judge capitulated. He immediately called a meeting of the directors of the Steel Institute. On June 27 the President, then on his fatal western trip, received a pledge of the industry to end the twelve-hour day as soon as men became available. The Institute was acting, Gary wrote, because of "a strong sentiment throughout the country . . . and especially because it is in accordance with your own expressed views." [19] His accomplishment must have brightened the last shadowy days of the President's life.

Events moved swiftly. July was taken up by intensive conferences of operating officials. The difficulties seemed to loom even larger on closer inspection. But, on August 2 the Steel Institute directors met in New York City, and afterward Gary announced that "substantially the entire industry" would "now begin the total elimination of the twelve-hour day." The following week, Steel Corporation mills in the Pittsburgh and Chicago districts started the shift to eight hours, followed by the independents. The difficulties largely turned out to have been overmagnified or to have unexpected solutions. Before the end of 1923 the great reform was completed — to no one's regret.[20]

[18] Digests of press opinion in *Literary Digest,* June 9, 1923, pp. 7–9, and June 30, 1923, pp. 33–34; *Current Opinion,* LXXV (July 1923), 16–18; *American Federationist,* July 1923, pp. 556–558.

[19] *Twelve Hour Day* (pamphlet) reprints letters and Gary's press interview, July 6, 1923; *IA,* July 12, 1923, pp. 71–73, 92–93. Gary, it appears, remained unbending until Harding's intervention. In his Remarks to Subsidiary Presidents, June 13, 1923, only a few days before, he was still holding to his position.

[20] A 25 per cent hourly increase, although still involving sizable income reductions, proved acceptable to steelworkers. Many benefited from promotions to jobs created by the change, others were able to go on ten-hour work

Public opinion and Warren G. Harding, not the good intentions of Judge Gary and the steel magnates, had secured the eight-hour day for the steelworkers.

However it had come about, Judge Gary expected the enlightened use of labor ("treated . . . better than the employees of any large industrial concern . . . in any country or in any period") to produce contentment in the mills. "Our men as a rule," he stated, "would always be perfectly satisfied, except for the uncalled for and unjustified interference of outsiders." There was the rub, for even the happiest steelworkers, through ignorance or intimidation, were susceptible to unscrupulous labor agitators. In addition, "the contemplated progress of trade unions, if successful, would be to secure the control of the shops, then of the general management of business, then of capital, and finally of government." [21] It was necessary, therefore, to insulate the steelworkers from the contagion of organized labor.

If antiunionism had hardened earlier, in the twenties it became implacable and merciless. The industry was not content to rest on the defensive. Erectors employing union labor, for instance, found it impossible to buy structural steel since the great strike. U.S. and Bethlehem Steel would supply only members of the National Erectors' Association and other open-shop structural associations. By the end of 1920, the structural steel union was virtually starving out of existence in the Eastern cities.[22] And the aggressive growth of the open-shop movement of course had the support of the steel companies.

For its part, organized labor gave little cause for alarm. The National Committee had ended the steel strike defiantly, promis-

---

— both possibilities overlooked earlier. The increased cost was roughly 5 per cent, not the 15 per cent forecast by Gary. Fewer men were needed than had been expected, and they were readily available.

[21] U.S. Steel Stockholders' Meeting, April 18, 1921, and April 16, 1923; Steel Institute, *Yearbook* (1920), p. 19.

[22] N.Y. Joint Legislative Committee on Housing, *Intermediate Report* (Albany, 1922), pp. 128 ff.

ing "a vigorous campaign of education and reorganization" that would "not cease until industrial justice has been achieved in the steel industry." But dissension swiftly dispelled the sense of moral victory and rendered impossible decisive action.

The leadership of the Amalgamated Association was bitterly angry over its mistreatment in the National Committee. After passage of the motion to end the strike, Tighe had moved to disband the Committee. To continue, he told Gompers, would be "nothing more than a waste of time and the money remaining." Its motion of disbandment failing, the union on February 4, 1920 withdrew from the National Committee. Gompers' repeated conciliatory efforts were ignored. Finally, Assistant President D. J. Davis appeared before the A.F.L. Executive Council in June. He stated afterward, "We are through with this Committee for all time, unless its officials get out." The Association would consider joining a new organization, if it held "51 per cent of the stock." John Fitzpatrick and officials of five of the internationals discussed the matter before the Executive Council. The campaign could not continue without the Amalgamated, they concluded, nor could they accept Tighe's terms. The National Committee, therefore, had little choice but to disband.[23]

Although the A.F.L. convention in June 1920 had instructed the Executive Council to continue organizing efforts, the summer passed without incident. A Washington conference in late September decided to postpone action until after the national election. By the time an organization of fourteen unions was formed with Amalgamated President Tighe at its head the depression had set in. There was occasional talk of an "educational campaign" in the next year, and possibly a little halfhearted work, but no results of any consequence.

Foster, who had quit the National Committee at the end of the steel strike, was meanwhile casting a shadow on the achievements of 1918–19. Returned from a visit to Russia, he openly

[23] M. F. Tighe to Gompers, February 23, 1920, in A.F.L. Executive Council Minutes, February 24–March 3, 1920, p. 77; Minutes, June 5–26, 1920, pp. 6–9; *NLT*, May 20, July 8, 1920; *New Majority*, July 10, 1920.

praised the Communist system, launched a movement to "amalgamate" all the unions of each industry, and, worst of all, made "boring from within" a real threat to the conservative labor leadership. Gompers publicly repudiated him. The venerable Federation President admitted that "a lot of men in the labor movement, and that I for a time had been deceived by his declarations of loyalty to the labor movement." Gompers acknowledged that the steel strike "was premature and that it was badly conducted." The strike seemed, as the industry had charged (and as *Iron Age* now complacently noted), a disguised radical maneuver. Instead of a proud example, the great strike became the ignominious past of any organizing campaign.[24]

Backed by sixteen unions and the $70,000 remaining in the treasury of the defunct National Committee, a modest drive started in the early summer of 1923 in the Chicago, Cleveland, and Bethlehem districts. The first weeks were devoted to education in preparation for mass meetings in the fall. Circulars in several languages assured the steelworkers that no strike was contemplated. The drive was a dismal failure, coming as it did at the same moment as the eight-hour day. William Hannon, a Machinists' official in charge at Chicago, reported in October: "The campaign as conducted at present is not meeting with the sensational success we experienced in 1918–19. . . . Indifference . . . is not confined to the unorganized steel mill workers. Little interest has been manifested by officers and representatives of the several international organizations." That marked the end of serious intentions on the steel industry for the rest of the decade; the A.F.L. was having difficulties enough preserving its established boundaries.[25]

As for the Amalgamated Association, its wartime gains quickly evaporated in the hostile air of the twenties. The *Iron Age*'s

[24] *AF*, March 1923, pp. 315–317, November 1923, pp. 935–936; *IA*, May 11, 1922, p. 1296; D. J. Saposs, "What Lies Back of Foster," *Nation*, January 17, 1923, pp. 67–69.

[25] *IA*, July 12, 1923, p. 109, October 18, 1923, p. 1030; *AJ*, April 10, 1924, p. 2; Lorwin, *A.F. of L.*, p. 219.

praise of the Association as "An Honorable Labor Union" which honored its contracts did not long deter employers. In June 1921 the Wheeling Steel Corporation refused to renew its union contract. A bitter lockout ensued, effective for nearly a year and lasting officially for three years. That was only the most important of the Amalgamated losses to the open-shop proponents.

A quiet technological revolution was meanwhile proceeding. After four years of experimentation, the American Rolling Mill Company perfected in 1924 its widestrip continuous sheet mill, rendering obsolete the manual skills on which rested the power of the Amalgamated Association. The consequences were seen in 1929 when a disagreement arose between the union and the company. Rather than obey the strike order, the lodges returned their charters, thus ending an amicable union relation of thirty years.[26] In 1929 the Amalgamated Association was reduced to a membership of 8,605, little more than in 1914, and, apparently, a dark future. Organized labor posed no threat in the postwar decade.

Every essential of the prewar labor situation was thus reproduced in the twenties. Mobility among the unskilled, dependence in the upper ranks, the repressive power of the steel companies — all served to reinforce the acquiescence of the steelworkers. Welfare work continued to play its role, supplemented by employee representation and, more important, by the institution of the eight-hour day in 1923. The permanence of the nonunion labor system of the steel industry seemed assured.

The successors of Judge Gary might look forward to an indefinite future whose profitable course would be dictated solely by the owners — or rather, the managers — of the industry. They could not foresee the great depression that would disrupt every element of their labor program and lead to the industrial unionism of today.

[26] Christy Borth, *True Steel* (Indianapolis, 1941), pp. 253–256, 281.

BIBLIOGRAPHY
INDEX

Bibliography

Manuscript Sources

American Steel and Wire Company Collection, Baker Library, Harvard University.

Andrew Carnegie Papers, Library of Congress.

Samuel Gompers Papers, A.F.L.-C.I.O. Headquarters, Washington, D.C.

David J. Saposs, "Organizing the Steel Workers," analysis of the Minutes of the National Committee for Organizing Iron and Steel Workers, mainly long selections. In Saposs Papers, University of Wisconsin Library.

—— Personal Interviews with Steel Workers during the Summer of 1920, Saposs Papers, University of Wisconsin Library.

Frank P. Walsh Papers, New York Public Library.

(The George W. Perkins Papers were not available to me. They were, however, utilized by J. A. Garraty in "The United States Steel Corporation Versus Labor: The Early Years," *Labor History,* I (Winter 1960), 3–38. This article, which appeared after the completion of this manuscript, confirms my views on the Steel Corporation.)

Trade Publications

American Institute of Mining Engineers, *Transactions,* 1902, 1905, 1909.

American Iron and Steel Association, *Statistical Report,* 1882, 1890, 1900, 1904.

American Iron and Steel Institute, *Monthly Bulletin,* 1913–1921.

—— *Yearbook,* 1912–1924.

American Rolling Mill Company, *The First Twenty Years.* Middletown, Ohio, 1922.

—— George M. Verity, *Papers by the President.* Middletown, Ohio, 1922.

British Iron and Steel Institute, *The Iron and Steel Institute in America in 1890.* London, n.d.

British Iron Trade Association, *American Industrial Conditions and Competition*, ed. J. Stephen Jeans. London, 1902.

Engineering and Mining Journal, 1892, 1893, 1898, 1903, 1904.

Inland Steel Company, *Fifty Years, 1893–1943*. Chicago, 1943.

Iron Age, 1882, 1887, 1893, 1902–1929.

Iron and Steel Trade Journal, 1900.

Iron Trade Review, 1893, 1903, 1914.

Reading Iron Company, *Wrought Iron Pipe vs. Steel Pipe*. 12th ed., n.p., 1908.

——— George Schumann, *Iron and Steel*. N.p., 1908.

United States Steel Corporation, *Addresses and Statements by Elbert H. Gary*, compiled by the Business History Society. 8 vols., November 1927.

——— Committee of Safety, *Bulletin*, 1911–1914.

——— Stockholders' Meetings, 1914–1924.

——— Illinois Steel Company, *Gary Works Circle*, 1916–1919.

——— Illinois Steel Company, *Joliet Works Mixer*, 1914–1920.

——— Illinois Steel Company, *South Works Review*, 1916–1920.

Youngstown Sheet and Tube Company, *Fifty Years in Steel*. Youngstown, 1950.

Labor Publications

Amalgamated Association of Iron, Steel and Tin Workers, *Amalgamated Journal*, 1909–1929.

——— *Proceedings*, 1893, 1895, 1901–1910.

American Federation of Labor, *American Federationist*, 1897–1925.

——— *Proceedings*, 1893, 1900–1925.

——— *Weekly Newsletter*, 1911–1924.

Chicago *Daily Socialist*, 1906, 1909, 1910.

Cleveland *Citizen*, 1909, 1910.

International Association of Machinists, *Machinists' Journal*, 1909.

——— *Proceedings*, 1918–1920.

International Union of Mine, Mill and Smelter Workers, *Proceedings*, 1918, 1920.

Lancaster (Pennsylvania) *Labor Leader*, 1909–1910.

National Labor Tribune (Pittsburgh), 1885–1901, 1909–1921.

New Majority (Chicago), 1919, 1920.

United Mine Workers of America, *Mine Workers' Journal*, 1917–1919.

—— *Proceedings,* 1911, 1918–1920.
Youngstown *Labor News,* 1901.

Newspapers and Periodicals

Chicago *Tribune,* 1906, 1917, 1918.
Christian Science Monitor, 1910.
Commercial and Financial Chronicle, 1880–1900.
Current Opinion, 1920–1923.
Harper's Weekly, 1903, 1907, 1910–1914.
Homestead (Pennsylvania) *Messenger,* 1918.
Independent, 1901, 1909–1914.
Literary Digest, 1901–1927.
Nation, 1901, 1909–1914, 1919–1924.
New Republic, 1919–1925.
New York *Herald,* 1910.
New York *Times,* 1915–1924.
New York *Tribune,* 1901, 1910, 1920.
Outlook, 1901, 1903, 1909–1914, 1920–1924.
Pittsburgh *Dispatch,* 1901.
Pittsburgh *Gazette-Times,* 1919.
Review of Reviews, 1903, 1910–1914.
Scientific American, 1909.
Survey (Charities and the Commons until 1909), 1908–1925.

Government Publications

Chicago Commission on Race Relations, *The Negro in Chicago.*
    Chicago, 1922.
Illinois Bureau of Labor Statistics, *Annual Report,* 1882, 1886.
New York Joint Legislative Committee on Housing, *Intermediate Report.* Albany, 1922.
Ohio Bureau of Labor Statistics, *Annual Report,* 1882, 1900.
U.S. Bureau of Census, *Eleventh Census* (1890), IV, V.
—— *Twelfth Census* (1900), X.
—— *Thirteenth Census* (1910), VIII.
—— *Census of Manufacturers* (1914), II.
U.S. Bureau of Labor, *Report on Conditions of Employment in the Iron and Steel Industry.* 4 vols., Washington, 1911–1913.

—— *Report on the Strike at the Bethlehem Works*. Washington, 1910.

U.S. Bureau of Labor Statistics, *Bulletin* (No. 168), April 1915.

—— *Monthly Labor Review*, 1915–1927.

U.S. Commissioner of Corporations, *Report on the Steel Industry*. 3 vols., Washington, 1911–1913.

U.S. Commissioner of Labor, *Annual Report*, 1886, 1890, 1900, 1904.

—— *Regulation and Restriction of Output*. Washington, 1904.

U.S. Committee on Public Information, *The Activities of the Committee on Public Information*. Washington, January 17, 1918.

—— *Four Minute Men Bulletin*, Nos. 14, 31, 37.

U.S. Committee on Industrial Relations, *Final Report and Testimony*. Washington, 1916. XI.

U.S. Department of Labor, *Negro Migration, 1916–1917*. Washington, 1919.

—— *Wartime Policies of Wages, Hours, and Other Labor Standards, 1917–1918* (mimeographed). May 1942.

U.S. Federal Trade Commission, *Report on War-Time Profits and Costs of the Steel Industry*. Washington, 1925.

U.S. House of Representatives, Committee on the Investigation of the United States Steel Corporation, *Hearings*. 8 vols. 62 Cong., 2nd Sess., 1911–1912.

—— Committee on the Judiciary, *Investigation of Homestead Troubles*. Report 2447. 52 Cong., 2nd Sess., 1892–1893.

—— Committee on Ways and Means, *Tariff Hearings*. 53 Cong., 1st Sess., 1893.

—— *Tariff Hearings*. 60 Cong., 2nd Sess., 1908–1909, II.

—— *Tariff Hearings*. 62 Cong., 3rd Sess., 1913.

U.S. Immigration Commission, *Reports: Immigrants in Industries, Iron and Steel Manufacturing*. Washington, 1911. VIII, IX.

U.S. Industrial Commission, *Reports*. Washington, 1899–1901. I, VII, XIII.

U.S. National War Labor Board, Dockets, 1918–1919.

U.S. Senate, Committee on the Employment of Armed Bodies of Men for Private Purposes, *Report 1280*. 52 Cong., 2nd Sess., 1892–93.

—— Committee on Labor and Education, *Investigation of Strike in the Steel Industry*. 2 vols. 66 Cong., 1st Sess., 1919.

—— Special Committee Investigating the Munitions Industry,

Minutes of the Price Fixing Committee of the War Industries Board. 74 Cong., 2nd Sess., 1936.

―――― *Minutes of the War Industries Board, August 1, 1917–December 19, 1918.* 74 Cong., 1st Sess., 1935.

U.S. War Policies Commission, *Hearings.* 3 vols., Washington, 1931.

Books, Pamphlets, and Dissertations

Adamic, Louis, *Dynamite, The Story of Class Violence in America.* New York, 1934.

American Alliance for Labor and Democracy, *Our War Aims Clearly Stated.* September 6, 1917.

Balch, E. G., *Our Slavic Fellow Citizens.* New York, 1910.

Baruch, Bernard, *American Industry in the War.* New York, 1941.

―――― *My Own Story.* New York, 1957.

Bell, Thomas, *Out of this Furnace.* Boston, 1941.

Bent, Quincy, *Seventy-Five Years of Steel.* Princeton, 1939.

Berglund, Abraham, *The United States Steel Corporation.* New York, 1907.

Berthoff, R. T., *British Immigrants in Industrial America.* Cambridge, Mass., 1953.

Beuttenmueller, Doris R. H., "The Granite City Steel Company," Unpublished Ph.D. thesis, St. Louis University, 1952.

Bigelow, E. V., *Mistakes of the Interchurch Steel Report.* November 22, 1920.

Bing, Alexander M., *War-time Strikes and their Adjustment.* New York, 1921.

Boisko, W. S., "A Sociological Study of the Steel Strikes of 1919 and 1952." Unpublished Master's thesis, University of Pittsburgh, 1953.

Borth, Christy, *True Steel.* Indianapolis, 1941.

Bridge, J. H., *The Inside History of the Carnegie Steel Company.* New York, 1903.

Burgoyne, Arthur G., *Homestead, A Complete History of the Struggle of July, 1892.* Pittsburgh, 1893.

Butler, Joseph G., *Recollections of Men and Events.* New York, 1927.

Byington, Margaret F., *Homestead: The Households of a Mill Town.* Vol. IV of *Pittsburgh Survey,* ed. Paul U. Kellog. 6 vols., New York, 1909–1914.

Carnegie, Andrew, *Autobiography.* Boston, 1924.

———— *Miscellaneous Writings.* 2 vols., New York, 1933.

Casson, H. N., *The Romance of Steel.* New York, 1907.

Clarkson, Grosvener B., *Industrial America in the World War: The Strategy behind the Lines.* Boston, 1927.

Commons, John R., *Why Workingmen Support the War.* (American Alliance for Labor and Democracy pamphlet.)

Corey, Lewis, *The House of Morgan.* New York, 1930.

Cotter, Arundel, *The Gary I Knew.* Boston, 1928.

———— *The Story of Bethlehem Steel.* New York, 1916.

———— *United States Steel: A Corporation with a Soul.* New York, 1921.

Creel, George, *How We Advertised America.* New York, 1920.

Daugherty, C. R. et al., *The Economics of the Iron and Steel Industry.* 2 vols., New York, 1937.

Davis, Horace B., *Labor and Steel.* New York, 1933.

Davis, Jerome, *The Russian Immigrant.* New York, 1922.

Douglas, Paul H., *Real Wages in the United States, 1890–1926.* Boston, 1930.

Draper, Theodore, *The Roots of American Communism.* New York, 1957.

Dunbar, Donald E., *The Tin-Plate Industry.* Boston, 1915.

Eastman, Crystal, *Work-Accidents and the Law.* Vol. II of *Pittsburgh Survey.*

Epstein, Abraham, *The Negro Migrant in Pittsburgh.* Pittsburgh, 1918.

Evans, Henry O., *Iron Pioneer: Henry W. Oliver.* New York, 1942.

Fitch, John A., *The Steel Workers.* Vol. III of *Pittsburgh Survey.*

Foster, William Z., *From Bryan to Stalin.* New York, 1937.

———— *The Great Steel Strike and Its Lessons.* New York, 1920.

———— *Misleaders of Labor.* New York, 1927.

———— and Earl C. Ford, *Syndicalism.* N.p., 1911.

Fritz, John, *Autobiography.* Boston, 1912.

Gamio, M., *Mexican Immigration to the United States.* Chicago, 1930.

———— *The Mexican Immigrant: His Life Story.* Chicago, 1931.

Garrett, P. W., *Government Control over Prices.* Washington, 1920.

Gilmore, A. F., *Fellowship: The Biography of a Man and a Business.* Boston, 1929.

Girdler, Tom M., *Bootstraps.* New York, 1943.

Gompers, Samuel, *Seventy Years of Life and Labor.* 2 vols., New York, 1925.

Green, Marguerite, *The National Civic Federation and the American Labor Movement*. Washington, 1956.

Grosse, R. N., "The Determinants of the Size of Iron and Steel Firms in the U.S., 1820–80." Unpublished Ph.D. thesis, Harvard, 1948.

Gulick, C. A., *Labor Policy of the United States Steel Corporation*. New York, 1924.

Handlin, Oscar, *The Uprooted*. Boston, 1951.

Harvey, George, *Henry Clay Frick: The Man*. New York, 1928.

Haynes, George E., *The Negro at Work During the World War and During Reconstruction*. Washington, 1921.

Hendrick, B. J., *The Life of Andrew Carnegie*. 2 vols., New York, 1932.

Hogg, J. B., "The Homestead Strike of 1892." Unpublished Ph.D. thesis, University of Chicago, 1943.

Hourwich, I. A., *Immigration and Labor*. New York, 1912.

Interchurch World Movement, Commission of Inquiry, *Report on the Steel Strike of 1919*. New York, 1920.

———— *Public Opinion and the Steel Strike*. New York, 1921.

Kent, Raymond P., "The Development of Industrial Unionism in the American Iron and Steel Industry." Unpublished Ph.D. thesis, University of Pittsburgh, 1938.

Lengyel, Emil, *Americans from Hungary*. Philadelphia, 1948.

Lorwin, L. L., *American Federation of Labor*. Washington, 1933.

May, E. C., *Principio to Wheeling*. New York, 1945.

McCallum, E. D., *The Iron and Steel Industry in the United States*. London, 1931.

Mitchell, A. W., "The Industrial Backgrounds and Community Problems of a Large Steel Plant. Aliquippa Works." Unpublished Master's thesis, University of Pittsburgh, 1932.

———— "The Labor Relations of a Large Steel Company in the Pittsburgh District. Jones and Laughlin." Unpublished Ph.D. thesis, University of Pittsburgh, 1939.

Mock, J. R. and C. Larson, *Words That Won the War*. Princeton, 1939.

Morris, James O., *Conflict within the AFL*. Ithaca, New York, 1958.

Murray, R. K., *Red Scare*. Minneapolis, 1955.

National Industrial Conference Board, *Strikes in Wartime, April 6–October 6, 1917*. March 1918.

Northrup, H. R., *Organized Labor and the Negro*. New York, 1944.

Olds, Marshall, *Analysis of the Interchurch World Movement Report on the Steel Strike*. New York, 1923.

Park, R. E., *Old World Traits Transplanted*. New York, 1921.

Perlman, Selig and Philip Taft, *History of Labor in the U.S., 1896–1932*. Vol. IV of J. R. Commons et al., *History of Labor in the U.S.* 4 vols., New York, 1918–1935.

The Pittsburgh District: Civic Frontage. Vol. V. of *Pittsburgh Survey*.

Popplewell, Frank, *Some Modern Conditions and Recent Developments in Iron and Steel Production in America*. Manchester, England, 1906.

Pound, A. and S. T. Moore, eds., *They Told Barron*. New York, 1930.

Proceedings of the First Industrial Conference, 1919. Washington, 1920.

Quillen, Isaac J., "Industrial City. A History of Gary, Indiana, to 1929." Unpublished Ph.D. thesis, Yale, 1942.

Reitell, Charles, *Machinery and its Benefits to Labor in the Iron and Steel Industry*. Menasha, Wisconsin, 1917.

Robinson, Jesse S., *The Amalgamated Association of Iron, Steel and Tin Workers*. Baltimore, 1920.

Saposs, David J., *Left Wing Unionism*. New York, 1926.

Schroeder, Gertrude G., *The Growth of Major Steel Companies, 1900–1950*. Baltimore, 1953.

Schwab, Charles M., *Andrew Carnegie, His Methods with His Men*. Pittsburgh, November 25, 1919.

Scott, Emmett J., *Negro Migration during the War*. New York, 1920.

Scott, Estelle H., *Occupational Changes among Negroes in Chicago*. Chicago, 1939.

Selekman, Ben M., *Employes' Representation in Steel Works*. New York, 1924.

Smith, J. R., *The Story of Iron and Steel*. New York, 1913.

Spero, S. D. and A. L. Harris, *The Black Worker*. New York, 1931.

Steiner, E. A., *The Immigrant Tide*. 2nd ed., New York, 1909.

—— *On the Trail of the Immigrant*. 3rd ed., New York, 1906.

Sweeney, D. J., *Buffalo and Erie County, 1914–19*. Buffalo, 1919.

Taft, Philip, *The A.F. of L. in the Time of Gompers*. New York, 1957.

Tarbell, Ida M., *All in the Day's Work*. New York, 1939.

—— *Elbert H. Gary*. New York, 1925.

Taylor, Paul S., *Mexican Labor in the U.S.: Bethlehem, Pennsylvania*. Berkeley, California, 1931.

—— *Mexican Labor in the U.S.: Chicago and the Calumet Region.* Berkeley, California, 1932.

Thomas, W. L. and F. Znaniecki, *The Polish Peasant in Europe and America.* 2 vols., New York, 1927.

The Twelve Hour Day in Industry. N.p., 1923.

United States v. United States Steel Corporation, 223 F. 55 (1912). *Testimony.* 30 vols.

—— *Defendants' Exhibits.* 9 vols.

—— *Government Exhibits.* 14 vols.

Vanderblue, H. B. and W. L. Crum, *The Iron Industry in Prosperity and Depression.* Chicago, 1927.

Vorse, H. M., *Men and Steel.* New York, 1920.

Wages-Earning Pittsburgh. Vol. VI of *Pittsburgh Survey.*

Walker, Charles R., *Steel: The Diary of a Furnace Worker.* Boston, 1922.

—— *Steeltown.* New York, 1950.

Warshow, R. I., *Bet-A-Million Gates.* New York, 1932.

Williams, Whiting, *What's on the Worker's Mind.* New York, 1920.

Willoughby, W. F., *Government Organization in War-Time and After.* New York, 1919.

Wilson, Woodrow, *The Life and Letters of Woodrow Wilson,* ed. R. S. Baker. VII, New York, 1939.

—— *The Public Papers of Woodrow Wilson,* eds. R. S. Baker and W. E. Dodd. V, New York, 1927.

Winkler, John K., *Incredible Carnegie.* New York, 1931.

Wood, Charles W., *The Great Change.* New York, 1918.

Yellen, S., *American Labor Struggles.* New York, 1936.

Articles

Bemis, E. W., "The Homestead Strike," *Journal of Political Economy,* II (June 1894), 369–396.

Bull, R. A., "Eight Hours vs. Twelve Hours Shifts," *Engineering Magazine,* XXXIV (January 1913), 559–561.

Copley, F. B., "A Great Corporation Investigates Itself," *American Magazine,* LXXIV (October 1912), 643–654.

Daniels, F. H., "Wire Rod Rolling Mills and Their Development," American Society of Mechanical Engineers, *Transactions,* XIV (1893), 583–618.

Drury, H. B., "Three Shift System," *Independent Management*, January 1, 1921, 63–67.

Fitch, John A., "Labor in the Steel Industry," American Academy of Political and Social Science, *The Annals*, XXXIX (March 1909), 307–315.

———— "Old Age At Forty," *American Magazine*, LXXI (March 1911), 655–664.

Fritz, John, "The Progress of the Manufacture of Iron and Steel," American Society of Mechanical Engineers, *Transactions*, XVIII (1897), 39–69.

Glocker, T. W., "Amalgamation of Related Trades in Unions," *American Economic Review*, V (September 1915), 554–575.

Hoagland, H. E., "Trade Unionism in the Iron Industry: A Decadent Organization," *Quarterly Journal of Economics*, XXXI (August 1917), 674–689.

Hunt, R. W., "The Evolution of American Rolling Mills," American Society of Mechanical Engineers, *Transactions*, XIII (1892), 45–69.

"Industrial Competition and Combination," American Academy of Political and Social Science, *The Annals*, XLII (July 1912).

King, Willis L., "Recollections and Conclusions from a Long Business Life," *Western Pennsylvania Historical Magazine*, XXIII (December 1940), 223–242.

Marchbin, A. A., "Hungarian Activities in Western Pennsylvania," *Western Pennsylvania Historical Magazine*, XXIII (September 1940), 163–174.

Meyer, B. H., "Fraternal Beneficiary Societies in the U.S.," *American Journal of Sociology*, VI (March 1901), 646–661.

Morgan, C. H., "Some Landmarks in the History of the Rolling Mill," American Society of Mechanical Engineers, *Transactions*, XXII (1901), 31–64.

Wloszecewski, S., "The Polish 'Sociological Group' in America," *American Slavic Review*, IV (August 1945), 142–157.

Wright, C. D., "Amalgamated Association of Iron and Steel Workers," *Quarterly Journal of Economics*, VII (July 1893), 400–432.

Yoder, D., "Economic Changes and Industrial Unrest in the United States," *Journal of Political Economy*, XLVIII (April 1940), 222–237.

Index